Ford Cortina
50
The complete history

Ford
Cortina
50
The complete history

Russell Hayes

Haynes Publishing

First published in January 2012

A catalogue record for this book is available from the British Library

ISBN 978 1 84425 988 5

Library of Congress control no. 2011935256

Published by Haynes Publishing, Sparkford, Yeovil, Somerset BA22 7JJ, UK
Tel: 01963 442030 Fax: 01963 440001
Int. tel: +44 1963 442030 Int. fax: +44 1963 440001
E-mail: sales@haynes.co.uk
Website: www.haynes.co.uk

Haynes North America Inc.
861 Lawrence Drive, Newbury Park,
California 91320, USA

Design and page layout by Rod Teasdale

Printed in the USA by Odcombe Press LP,
1299 Bridgestone Parkway, La Vergne, TN 37086

Cover and title page picture credits:
Main front cover: John Colley/Magic Car Pics
Front cover inset, rear cover and page 2: Ford of Britain

Contents

Bibliography

The author is happy to acknowledge his debt to the authors below, especially David Burgess-Wise, Graham Robson and Jonathan Wood.

Baldwin, Nick. Georgano, Nick. Clausager, Anders. Wood, Jonathan: *Britain's Motor Industry, the First Hundred Years* (Foulis, 1995).

Bellu, Serge: *De Simca à Renault: 40 ans de design, sur les pas de Patrick Le Quément* (ETAI, 2010).

Burgess-Wise, David: *The Complete Catalogue of Ford Cars in Britain* (Bay View Books, 1991).

— — *Ford at Dagenham, The Rise and Fall of Detroit in Europe* (Breedon Books, 2007).

Chapman, Giles: *My Dad's Cortina* (Haynes, 2009).

Clarke, R.M. (editor): *Brooklands Books Cortina 1600E & GT 1967–1970 Road Test Compilation* (Brooklands Books).

— — *Lotus Cortina Brooklands Road Test Portfolio* (Brooklands Books).

Crombac, Gerard 'Jabby': *Colin Chapman: The Man and His Cars, the Authorised Biography* (Haynes, 2001).

Daniels, Jeff: *British Leyland, the Truth about the Cars* (Osprey, 1980).

Gauld, Graham: *Gentleman Jack, the Official Biography of Jack Sears* (Veloce, 2008).

Iacocca, Lee, with William Novak: *Iacocca, an Autobiography* (Bantam, 1986).

Munro, Bill: *Carbodies – The Complete Story* (Crowood, 1998).

Pressnell, Jon: *Mini – The Definitive History* (Haynes, 2009).

Rawbone, Martin: *Ford in Britain – A History of the Company and its Cars* (Haynes, 2001).

Read, Robin: *Colin Chapman's Lotus, the Early Years, the Elite and the Origins of the Elan* (Haynes, 1989).

Robson, Graham: *Ford Escort RS* (Osprey, 1981).

— — *The Sporting Fords Vol 1: Cortinas* (Motor Racing Publications, 1989).

— — *Cortina –The Story of Ford's Best-seller* (Veloce, 2007).

Roland, Martin-Paul: *Ford Taunus 1948–1982 Schrader Motor-Chronik* (Schrader Verlag, 2002).

Walton, Jeremy: *Capri – the Development & Competition History of Ford's European GT Car* (Foulis, 1985).

Wood, Jonathan: *Ford Cortina Mk1* (Osprey, 1984).

Where indicated, 1974 interview material with Sir Terence Beckett was taken from an interview conducted by Ivor Morgan at Ford of Britain in June 1974.

Some detail of the Corsair Monza endurance run can be found in *Classic Ford* magazine, January 2009.

Information for the Cortina turbo project (Chapter 7) can be found in a paper presented to the Institution of Mechanical Engineers, Automobile Division, London 19 February 1974. Vol 188 5/74 (http://www.imeche.org).

Material used for research on the Ford Cardinal development, Ford's front-drive programme and Corsair and Mk1 Cortina styling decisions (1962–64) from the Benson Ford Research Center, Dearborn, is as follows:

(i) *Product and Program Planning Series; Cardinal Car Program subseries and Segment 1 economy car planning, Accession 1942, International Division Purchasing Office records 1947–1962 (Bulk 1960–1961), Benson Ford Research Center, The Henry Ford Museum.*

(ii) *(Aveley) meeting minutes, Styling review 1962–1964, box 13 Accession 1790, Ford Motor Company Ltd collections, Benson Ford Research Center, The Henry Ford Museum.*

(iii) *The Jack D. Collins records subseries, Accession 1931, Research and Engineering Center (Ford Motor Company) Engineering Division (Ford Motor Company) records series. Ford Motor Company Engineering records collection, Benson Ford Research Center, The Henry Ford Museum.*

(iv) *Roy Brown: 6-28-84 #1974. Automotive design histories; oral interviews, Box 2.*

Acknowledgements

Many people have enthusiastically contributed to this book, even though I was asking some to recall events fifty or more years ago. It's a long list!

I would especially like to thank Sir Terence Beckett and Dennis Roberts for providing me with clear and relevant insight and research material, Patrick Le Quément for several hours of phone calls and Harry Calton for perspective and much random fact-checking. Many thanks also to Geoff Howard for sound perspective and technical detail.

Thanks also to the following ex-Ford people (in alphabetical order): John Bacchus, Bill Barnett, Ron Bradshaw, Peter Cambridge (who sadly passed away in 2010), David Garrett, Ian Goddard, Roy Haynes, John Hitchman, Eric Jackson, Mick Jones, Tom Karen, Peter Kennedy, Rod Mansfield, Howard Panton, Charles Thompson, Ernie Unger.

At Ford of Britain, Dave Hill in the photographic archive provided friendly and efficient service and John Nevill in the press office answered many fiddly questions and allowed me easy access to old records.

America: Marguerite Moran at the Ford Motor Company Archives, Dearborn, and Linda Skolarus and her colleagues at the Benson Ford Research Center, The Henry Ford Museum, Dearborn. Also in the US, Don Gwynne, Bob Winkelmann and Bob Woolner for Lotus Cortina info.

Argentina: Alejandro Luis Angrigiani, www.clubtaunus.com.ar.

Australia: Garry Saunderson and Greg Wallace for images of their cars and background information.

Germany: Beate Falke at the Ford of Germany press office, and former Ford of Germany engineer Matthias Horne.

South Africa: Mike Armstrong, Basil Green and Koos Swanepoel.

Thanks also to: Mike Costin, Steve Cropley, Peter Eldridge, www.icfm.com, and Eric Foléa for research materials, Rob Ford for suggestions and contacts, Paul Havill for his support and German translation, kit car expert Steve Hole, Gail Huckle for Crayford-related material, Graeme Hurst of *Classic & Sportscar* for South African connections, Ray Hutton, Alexandra Mattholie, Mark Kempson, David McMullan, Rikki Nock from the Lotus Cortina Register, www.lotuscortina.net), Henry Pearman and Paul Brace from Historic Classics, www.historicclassics.com, Barry Priestman of the Crayford Convertible Car Club, Roger Raisey, technical adviser of the MkI Cortina Owners Club, www.mk1cortina.com, Tom Robinson, Terry Sanger, Rob Sargent, www.urensavagev6cortinamk2.co.uk, Anthony Walsh, Jeremy Walton, Nick and Rona Walton, Ford Cortina MkII & 1600E Owners Club, www.mk2cortina-1600e.co.uk, Sir John Whitmore, Alan Yentob.

Finally I am grateful to all those who contributed to the Cortina family album (page 8): Alan Bush, Doug Crighton, Graham Darby, Julie Fletcher, Andrew Hollingdale, Paul Maycock, Roger Raisey, Julie Rissbrook, Rosa Van der Meersch.

Unless otherwise stated, all photographs are courtesy Ford of Britain.

Preface

I hope readers will find this book enjoyable and revealing – the Cortina story is a good yarn. It might not have been a technical trailblazer, but the Cortina's effects on the motor industry, motor sport and Ford itself were far-reaching. It even became a standard measurement of British export success in the 1960s.

Setting out to give a complete history has been daunting, but I trust all of the significant aspects of the car are presented here, along with some new information. Nonetheless, I have carried out a little pruning for the sake of space and clarity. There is not an exhaustive list of motor sport achievements, and those campaigns mentioned are of necessity mostly British-backed, although some run by other territories are included.

It can sometimes appear a random combination of initials, but the way the Cortina was split into multiple trim levels was crucial to its success and influenced the rest of the industry. This book mentions most UK Cortina engine sizes and trim specifications, but I chose not to dwell on variants for other markets with only cosmetic differences, preferring the most heavily modified cars. The German Ford Taunus also features, as it was an important parallel development which eventually converged with the MkIV Cortina.

Ford of Britain's export department would also concoct small runs of very specific engine/trim combinations of all Ford cars to suit individual markets. MkIII Cortinas, for example, had to be narrowed for Japan, while to fit maximum-length regulations in Bermuda the Corsair had a foot lopped off its boot by the local dealer.

Although nowadays car weights and measures are given in metric units, I have used imperial measurements of pounds and hundredweights and feet and inches throughout, because that is how they were expressed at the time.

One pound (lb) of weight equals 0.4536kg. One hundredweight (cwt) equals 112lb or 50.8kg. So, in its first, lightest production form the kerb weight (unladen but with fuel for 50 miles) of the standard 1962 1200 Cortina two-door saloon was 15.5cwt, or 787.4kg. That was very light. To give some context, a 2011 English-market Ford Focus 1.6 – of course containing a lot more amenities and safety equipment – weighs 1,270kg and is 4.3m long. A MkI Cortina (and the one thing that didn't vary from generation to generation of Cortina was the length) was considered generous at 14ft or 4.26m in length.

Brake horsepower is expressed as the net, rather than the larger gross figure, as used by magazines at the time.

As to names, I join the majority who say Lotus-Cortina but it was always Cortina-Lotus to Ford. Where its Lotus/Ford engine is concerned I have used the words twin-cam and where it is a model name Twin Cam. Also of course Ford never used the terms MkI and MkII etc. These tags have been applied retrospectively, as have names for engines.

Russell Hayes, London, 2011

Chapter 1:
Pre-Cortina

Ford of America became part of the British motor manufacturing scene in 1907, when the first licence was granted to distribute the Model T, shipped part-assembled or 'knocked down'. Production of a British version began at Trafford Park near Manchester in October 1911, the same year that the Ford Motor Company (England) Ltd was formed. Adopting a small-scale version of the parent company's revolutionary moving assembly track in Detroit, output reached 20 units a day by 1913. In contrast Morris was taking a week to produce the same number of cars. Commercial vehicles were also added and tractors became a crucial part of the business (especially in wartime), these ultimately being manufactured at a plant in Cork, Southern Ireland. Undercutting most of its rivals on price, Ford had the capacity to produce 8,300 cars by 1914, double that of native manufacturers, although that lead was soon to be eroded as mass production spread.

After the First World War, the appeal of the no-frills Model T eventually began to wane on both sides of the Atlantic, and to cater for the expansion in the passenger-car market Ford of America determined that its English operation would be the ideal springboard into Europe with new models. Hence it started to look south for new factory space with easy access to shipping, finding what it required in 1924 at Dagenham, then a patch of marshland east of London but crucially on the banks of the Thames. A 300-acre site was purchased, and at the same time London County Council began building rented housing so 25,000 families could leave the city's slums.

Modelled on Ford's Rouge River plant in Detroit, the Dagenham works shared many of its features, such as foundations built on thousands of piles driven into the marshland. At a cost of £5m, it was a paragon of modern motor manufacturing, a fully integrated plant with raw materials arriving at its own dock and processed through its own blast furnace (from 1934) and foundry, power coming from its own power station (the much-photographed riverside building topped by a Ford logo). American body-building firm the Briggs Manufacturing Company joined Ford on the Dagenham estate; both their fortunes would be inextricably linked through the following decades, as would those of the other smaller firms which joined the Ford village.

The first vehicle down the track at Dagenham in October 1931 was actually a Model AA truck. Although Dagenham was to become the largest automobile manufacturing facility in Europe, production in fact got off to a faltering start. The

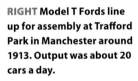

RIGHT Model T Fords line up for assembly at Trafford Park in Manchester around 1913. Output was about 20 cars a day.

ABOVE An early view of the vast Dagenham estate. The impressive Ford sign on the 'power house' was added in 1936 and said to be the largest neon sign in Europe.

successor to the Model T, the 1928–32 Model A, fell flat on the English market, not only because of the Depression but because with an engine of over three litres it was hampered by an English horsepower tax based on engine capacity – or more exactly upon the bore of the engine. The Model B followed, still with limited success, joined by very small numbers of V8 saloons, which again found few takers.

The Ford Motor Company Ltd (thus renamed in 1928), which eventually became known as Ford of Britain, was headed by the respected Sir Percival Perry and general manager Rowland Smith. But Perry's aversion to small cars – or rather, small profits – left the company without a competitive small car while others such as the Austin Seven enjoyed a runaway success. Finally Perry despatched Rowland Smith to Detroit with a set of specifications and a request for a new small car (at a cost to the company of $210,000). Smith and the Detroit team worked flat-out to produce a car in just ten months and the smart-looking eight-horsepower Model Y proved an instant success.

Interestingly, it was shown to the public before its official launch and the feedback from this very early customer clinic resulted in a number of changes before sale.

The £100 Ford

An important milestone was reached in 1935, when by a process of ruthless cost-cutting and pared-down dealer profits, the Model Y was reduced in price to £100. As the Model Y Popular, it thus became Britain's cheapest genuine four-seat saloon. Model Ys were assembled across Europe and in Australia (briefly) and South Africa. Despite a 1937 restyle, the essential design of this upright 'sit up and beg' little car lasted through to 1959 little changed under the skin, becoming along the way the Anglia and finally again taking the Popular name.

In spite of its early domestic commercial stumbles, Dagenham was always a strategic outpost for export. Henry Ford and Percival Perry created the '1928 Plan' which gave Ford Ltd 51 per cent ownership of all of Ford's European

It can be yours –

THE £100 FORD SALOON

LEFT Ford of Britain confounded rivals when it reduced the price of the Model Y to £100 in 1935. Derivatives of the 'Y' lasted until 1959.

subsidiaries, with Dagenham designated the centre of Ford's European operations until the end of the Second World War, controlling (or attempting to control) sales and manufacture in Belgium, Denmark, Egypt, Finland, France, Germany, Greece, Ireland, the Netherlands, Norway, Poland, Portugal, Romania, Spain and Sweden.

Although the British government initially required little of Dagenham to support the war effort (viewing it still as largely a foreign company), its facilities and expertise were pressed into active service from 1940, producing a wide variety of supplies, from chemicals to engines, and a highly successful four-wheel-drive truck. Tractor production was vastly increased, with Dagenham-built Fordsons playing a key role in the 'Dig for Victory' campaign to boost domestic food production.

A significant contract was to redesign the hand-built Rolls-Royce Merlin aero engine for mass production at a dedicated factory in Manchester. This had far-reaching consequences for Ford, recalled Sir Terence Beckett, when interviewed by the author in 2010. "Rolls-Royce was a bit astonished that

Ford would be producing Rolls-Royce engines. And Ford for its part – although they'd got the highest regard for these Rolls-Royce engineers – didn't think they'd got much of a clue in producing things in volume. So, there was a very important interaction between the two. A very fertile one, and incidentally it continued for ten years after I joined the company. We had frequent visits from Rolls-Royce people to us, and our people to Rolls-Royce."

Aside from the human cost to its workforce and their families, by the end of the conflict around 200 bombs had fallen on the Dagenham plant, which had built more than 180,000 military trucks. In Manchester, meanwhile, Ford had built around 30,000 of the 150,000 Merlin engines produced in Britain and America.

Increasing autonomy

Wartime had also formed the company's next generation of leaders. Rowland Smith was knighted in recognition of his war work and one Patrick Hennessy – later to be a crucial backer

ABOVE **Sir Patrick Hennessy, pictured here on retirement in 1963, masterminded much of Ford of Britain's post-war success, not least the Cortina. 'Sir Pat' remained as chairman until 1968.**

War and was beset by management in-fighting. Although Edsel's son Henry Ford II became vice-president in 1943, to all intents and purposes the firm continued to be run by ex-prizefighter Harry Bennett, who had been brought in by Ford senior to subdue the unions. He appeared to be on the verge of taking complete control until Edsel's widow forced the old man to install her son as president. The dynamic Henry ousted Bennett in September 1945 (for the benefit of the press Bennett was said to be amicably staying on as 'adviser'), and replaced him with former FBI man John Bugas – who himself would become a player in the Cortina story. The founder of Ford died two years later.

New Fords for England and the World

Car production at Dagenham resumed almost seamlessly, with 31,974 vehicles built in 1946. Production facilities were expanded with the purchase of wheel and brake supplier Kelsey-Hayes the following year and in 1949 of a smaller factory in Buckinghamshire for commercial vehicles. Sites throughout Essex continued to be taken up as outposts of Dagenham.

Now the mightiest car plant in Europe, with a capacity of 200,000 units, Dagenham produced vehicles for Britain and Europe, the Middle East, and African countries north of Rhodesia (now Zimbabwe). With the first visit from Henry Ford II, 1948 was a pivotal year for Ford of Britain. It was also allowed to sell its wares in the US but these were at first a version of the 8hp Anglia equipped with the larger 10hp Prefect engine, and the cars were regarded as little more than pocket-sized curiosities. However, within ten years Ford would become the UK motor industry's largest exporter.

It was under the same pressures as the rest of the British motor industry and along with its rivals complained bitterly against the edict to export at least 50 per cent of car production for foreign currency while suffering under a domestic purchase tax rate of 33.3 per cent. While demand for new cars mushroomed, the home market was starved of them. Still, Ford had emerged from the war with very sound finances and was satisfactorily profitable, with an average profit of £663,000 a year after tax. With its 16 factories, the Nuffield Organisation – chiefly Morris – continued to dominate motor manufacturing, however. Next in terms of size was Austin, then the nearest competitors were Standard, Rootes and the other US-owned car maker, General Motors affiliate Vauxhall.

This was the time of the motor barons. The making of cars and commercial vehicles was largely in the hands of a small and powerful collection of knighted men. Standard was

of the Cortina – had also risen to prominence. Hennessy was knighted in 1941 for his work in helping newspaper magnate Lord Beaverbrook, then Minister of Aircraft Production, build up for the Battle of Britain. His connection to Beaverbrook and understanding of the press would later bear fruit when it came to the Cortina's promotion and development. Irishman Hennessy was a Ford man through and through, starting with the Henry Ford & Son tractor works in Cork in 1920 and progressing through the ranks from the foundry there to sales and service at Trafford Park, then to purchasing manager at Dagenham in 1931 and general manager in 1939. Lord Perry resigned as chairman in 1948 as Hennessy became managing director and it was Smith and Hennessy who would guide Ford of Britain into the 1950s, Hennessy being regarded as the most able head of any of the Ford subsidiaries.

Peace also brought about big change in Detroit, as in 1945 Henry Ford finally relinquished control of the company which bore his name. Ford, by then 81 years old and in ill health, had retaken control of the company after his son Edsel had died of stomach cancer in 1943 at only 49. The American giant had been in decline during the Second World

LEFT The 1950 Consul was advanced both by Ford's and its competitors' standards, with chassis-less construction and new engines.

Ford and front-wheel drive in the 1950s

Once the Mini's front-wheel-drive package started to grab the headlines, Ford of Britain became extremely conscious that it looked slow off the mark, an impression only heightened by its awareness that the larger BMC 1100 was in development.

To contemporary critics Ford did indeed seem behind the times, especially when the Anglia and Mini were compared. Yet on both sides of the Atlantic it had already studied front-wheel drive in some depth, especially in America, where as well as the still-secret fwd Cardinal (see Chapter Two), Dearborn had already looked hard at extending front-drive to far larger cars.

In Britain one of the Birmingham test centre's objectives had been to develop a front-wheel-drive car. It is hard to ascertain how far the project got, but according to Terence Beckett it was dismissed after two years by Hennessy. "There came a crucial decision, an absolutely fundamental decision, that it wasn't working out. We couldn't solve either the transmission problem or the universal joint problem. With front-wheel drive you're steering through the front wheels, and you've got two sets of universal joints on each side to accomplish that, and in a small car the angles of the universal joints are really quite considerable. BMC with the Mini never solved this problem. Their driveshafts would typically have a life of about 19,000 miles. Some of them went considerably before that. Anyway, quite pragmatically – and one of the joys of Ford Motor Company Ltd was its pragmatism – it wanted to go to front-wheel drive if it could, but the Mini really forced us to make a decision, a pragmatic decision, that we were not ready to go for front-wheel drive."

A little later in the decade, serious development money was poured into front-wheel drive by the Americans. Confidential internal documents held at the Benson Ford archive in Dearborn reveal a strong appreciation of its benefits. Engineering papers detail a road trip between Arizona and Dearborn in January/February 1958, supplementing the German Taunus 17M testing programme. Five imported European cars were taken along: a Nash Metropolitan, an Opel Rekord fitted with a Taunus engine, a Morris Minor cobbled together with the 1,500cc BMC B-series engine from a Metropolitan, a Ford Anglia (unspecified if this was a prototype 105E) and a German Goliath that would most likely have been the transverse-engined fwd GP900 model. The report described the Nash's pitchy handling, found the Minor very stable, and praised the Goliath for 'remarkably good handling on loose gravel and sand' and being 'very good on curves' and having 'amazing performance for so small an engine.' In fact the obscure Goliath went on to become a development testbed for the Cardinal's front-wheel-drive package. Ford's engineers fully endorsed the increased directional stability, packaging and refinement improvements over a rear-wheel-drive vehicle.

And there were bigger plans for front-wheel drive. With each new US model growing longer and lower, there was a recognition that it was becoming increasingly difficult to provide an acceptable amount of passenger space, especially in the middle seats, in a car with a height of 55in. Front-wheel drive could virtually eliminate the transmission tunnel. It was also recognised that a fwd package allowed flexibility in body types, ease of assembly, and potential cost savings in the future.

From late 1957 intensive studies were made into the durability of constant-velocity joints, traction through front-driven wheels and ride and handling. Two test Thunderbirds were built in 1958 with the aim of proving the technology for the 1964 model year car, seen as the best vehicle to showcase this advanced technology 'because of its low volume and unique position as a vehicle of advanced design'. By 1960 five prototypes were running, and front-wheel-drive

run by Sir John Black, Lord Nuffield (formerly William Morris) oversaw the Nuffield Organisation, and Rootes was steered by Sir William 'Billy' Rootes and his brother Reginald, while Sir Leonard Lord ruled the Austin empire. It was their characters, as much as market forces, that shaped their model ranges and the fate of their companies. Crucially, Hennessy was driven by product and profit. Yet he was also well respected by his workforce, as a benign patriarch, fondly known as 'Sir Pat'. Interviewed in 1984, Cortina stylist Roy Brown recalled Hennessy with fondness. "Sir Patrick said 'Do you know how I judge a man? How does he treat the people that can't affect him at all?' Sir Patrick's best friend at Ford was our janitor in the design studio. We used to sit and have tea."

Hamish Orr-Ewing, who was heavily involved with the first Cortina and later in his career briefly headed Jaguar, was also an admirer: "Hennessy was by far the greatest of the motoring tycoons of the day because he was rational, driven by the objective that a company should be profitable. He had very little ego in the sense of the word of people, unlike people such as Sir John Black, who thought they walked on water. Leonard Lord, whom I was far too junior to know, was a man of undoubted ability, clearly very able, but a very handling was regarded as proven, but the project had cost over a million dollars. While other engineering programmes were looking at new 'trans-engine power packages for the late 1960s' there was no alternative engine for the large cars other than the existing V8 intended for the 1964 Thunderbird. The conclusion was that a fwd vehicle could not be built at a cost and weight competitive with a comparable rear-driven car.

While Ford shelved its fwd Thunderbird and concentrated on churning out conventional successors, General Motors grabbed motoring awards in 1966 with the imposing front-drive Oldsmobile Toronado coupé, but its example was not followed by mainstream American cars.

England looks on

Back in Rainham, Essex, the engineering division had been well aware of the Thunderbird project, witnessed by an April 1959 letter from Jack D. Collins, manager of Ford's advanced car engine and driveline engineering department in Dearborn to Alan Worters, executive engineer of power units, tetchily asking him to return confidential copy 25 of the 'Front Drive Package Program' forthwith. After some difficulty finding it, Worters sent it back by air freight that June.

Grumpy British engineers tried to make their own front-wheel-drive point with a Mini. Hamish Orr-Ewing, like others, remembers that possibly around 1960 Fred Hart, executive engineer for light cars, shoehorned a 105E driveline into a Mini body to show it wasn't necessary to have a transverse engine to get a vehicle of that size with that amount of internal space. "It was a nasty little thing! Frankly it wasn't very convincing. I remember us all standing around with the real Mini and that version, with Engineering making a somewhat defensive presentation."

Three years on, the profitability of the conventional Cortina and Anglia in relation to 1100 and Mini, plus the investment made in the new rear-drive hardware for both models, cemented management's view that there was no point in fwd for English Fords, even if the product planners were screaming for it from a marketing point of view.

This was one of the reasons Hamish Orr-Ewing cites for leaving the company in 1963. "Ford engineering bitterly resisted any concept of Mini-type design layout. I remember being almost in tears over a meeting I had with Vic Raviolo who was the not very inspiring chief engineer who still totally dismissed the front-wheel-drive concept. We'd done a lot of [theory] work in product planning to show that advantages were ultimately overwhelming in our view, and he gave us this lecture and that all this stuff that my colleagues and I had produced was simply missing the point."

Yet front-wheel drive still seems to have been tinkered with in the early to mid-sixties by Ford of Britain. Terence Beckett remembers prototype cars with belt-drive transmission adding to the complication. He also confirms that the V4 engine developed for the Corsair and Transit was conceived with a mind to future front-wheel-drive cars.

In Graham Robson's *Cortina, the Story of Ford's Best-seller* Walter Hayes, the public affairs supremo who joined Ford in 1962, talks of "a little front-wheel drive prototype which we'd built", and of how Hennessy had done all the costings on this prototype. Cortina body engineer Dennis Roberts also recalls being sent between Essex and Birmingham at regular intervals in the mid-sixties for work on the body structure for a front-wheel-drive car similar in size to the 1100, as there was no in-house experience of building such a structure. In practice it would be 1976 before the front-wheel-drive Fiesta would roll off the Dagenham production lines, and that was very much a European Ford product.

nasty bit of work who had really venomous personal fights with people. There was none of that with Patrick Hennessy at all. Leonard Lord was a very dangerous person to in any way disagree with and I think it's true to say that his undoubted ability was hampered by that."

Number one target: BMC

Austin and Morris dominated the British market as well-established national treasures. A merger was debated for many years (prolonged by the strong wills of Morris and Lord) but after protracted negotiations the British Motor

Corporation (BMC) finally came into being in February 1952, establishing a domination of the market that Ford was not to break until the 1970s.

BMC's numbers were daunting. From its very early days the range of cars was vast, not to say incoherent. It spanned Austin, Morris, MG, Austin-Healey, Riley and Wolseley marques, the newly united Austin and Morris dominating the market for small cars, whereas Ford only offered the pre-war Anglia to 1953, alongside the equally upright-looking Prefect. Austin had the monocoque-bodied A30, Morris the slightly bigger Minor and then there was a steady progression to mid-range cars

ABOVE In contrast with the all-new Consul, the ancient Anglia, with its pre-war roots, just kept on providing very cheap motoring. These are of the 1939–48 type, with their characteristic 'coffin' nose.

RIGHT Sitting in a bed of 5,000 roses at Earls Court, the 1954 Prefect 100E appeared a modern car, but lack of funds meant it had an outdated engine design. Ford of Britain's model codes at the time were suffixed with an 'E' for England.

such as the Morris Oxford MO and Wolseley 4/44 and thence to range-topping six-cylinder models. As to the Minor, although 176,000 had been sold from 1948 to 1953 it is worth noting it did take 13 years to reach its only million, in contrast to the four years the Cortina was to take for its first million.

BMC's tactics were the opposite of Ford's. While a certain rationalisation of engines took place as soon as the company was formed, the styles of bodywork they were used in mushroomed. Nuffield had continued its pre-war practice of dressing up its Morrises with a different front to become Wolseleys and extended the process to MG and Riley saloons. After the merger this policy continued and expanded; for example the smaller 1957 Wolseley 1500 and Riley One-point-Five were successfully rebodied and plusher versions of the Morris Minor.

'Badge engineering' picked up on the loyalties which buyers still had to pre-war names and indeed to the same dealer from whom they had always bought their cars. People tended to buy cars locally, returning to the family dealer over and over again. It would be decades before British buyers would comfortably

swap from marque to marque each time they bought a new car, haggling their way into a deal. In the 1950s and 1960s BMC had such a vast spread that the chance of a neighbourhood dealer being in the BMC group was high. By 1962 and the Cortina's launch, BMC's combined total of Austin, Morris, Wolseley, Riley and MG dealers ran to over 5,700 whereas Ford had 384 main dealers and 1,798 retail dealers. Yet while BMC allowed its dealer network to sprawl, Ford did not believe even its much smaller collection was working well and spent the next seven years trying to get a grip on the smaller retail dealers, ultimately axing half of them.

On the surface BMC's strategy worked pretty well, albeit with the exercise becoming more and more cynical – the differences between an MG Midget and an Austin-Healey Sprite were trivial and the only way to spot Austin and Morris Minis apart from a distance was studying their radiator grille. But aside from the fact that the Mini was steadily bleeding BMC dry, the dealers were driving model development from their own micro-empires rather than as a result of any sensible study of the market.

Sir Terence Beckett, the product planner

The man who became known as 'Mr Cortina' is described by his contemporaries as 'not a car man' in factual terms. His focus on costs, planning and business acumen was a major part in Ford of Britain's post-war success, and by 1974 he was Ford of Britain's managing director; he was knighted in 1978 and left in 1980 to head the Confederation of British Industry.

In 1950 Sir Patrick Hennessy had initiated a programme of graduate recruitment, a practice unheard of in the British motor industry at the time but encouraged from Detroit where Henry Ford II had introduced a team from General Motors who were more used to training and development.

Beckett was a professional engineer and had just graduated from the London School of Economics. Even though Ford was one of the very few companies which seemed to be inviting people like himself to join it, he found indifference or mistrust of graduates from his colleagues. Most of the management had worked its way up from the shop floor at Old Trafford and at first Beckett was shipped around the organisation as a spectator, without being allowed to do anything in what was a heavily unionised environment. He was discreet about his background. "Certainly for the first few years in my career with Ford Motor Company I never disclosed to anybody except on the personnel records that I was a university graduate."

After 15 months of boredom he was shipped into Sir Patrick Hennessy's office as an assistant. At first Hennessy was unwell, so Beckett was sent for a six-week stint at the Renault factory at Billancourt, in Paris, where he began to understand the European motor industry. During three years in Hennessy's office he would research product and manufacturing, helping the move towards a company which had genuine long-range planning. In 1954 he became manager of styling at Briggs Motor Bodies and a year later the second manager of the newly created Product Staff, later to become Product Planning.

The brief for the fledgling group of around 60 people was to try to maintain the competitiveness of the product by analysis of the market and the changing models sold within it. Beckett went on to create departments for light, medium and large cars, while an advanced programme looked more than five years ahead.

Beckett cites the 1951 Consul as a perfect illustration of how Ford of Britain needed to get a grip on planning. A small sub-1,000cc car should really have been first into production, but the new model's engine capacity was based on Sir Patrick Hennessy's instincts, Beckett recalled in the 1970s. "The Consul had started out in its development, believe it or not, as a replacement for the Anglia. We were talking about the ideal engine size for that Anglia and there was a lot of concern in the company that we shouldn't go much above 800cc or 900cc because this is what Austin-Morris was doing. Sir Patrick said to me 'What is the most successful car in Europe?' And I said 'Well, it's the Volkswagen.' And he said 'Exactly, this is the size we shall be needing, and in this future engine development I want to go for an 1,100cc car.'"

Even though it was more advanced in its thinking than its competitors, this lack of planning ran to more than cars. When Beckett joined Product Planning in 1955, a new truck was just being announced. This had started off as a three-ton carrier but had been outpaced by wage rates going up, and hauliers wanting to get more truck per man with first a five-ton truck, then a seven-tonner. Ford tried to play catch-up with upgraded axles and frames and eventually gained market leadership until displaced by Bedford in 1960. The Consul MkI and Anglia 105E were successful cars but Beckett still regarded them – not to mention the Classic – as being poorly costed. But they were part of a steep learning curve to the first and most penny-wise Cortina. "It didn't work in the earlier days because we hadn't got a trained team. … It also didn't work because the specific tools that we had in terms of cost and weight control weren't understood."

Again there was a cultural resistance at quite high levels and Beckett was lucky to have the backing of Hennessy: "Men such as Mr Thacker, who was managing director under Sir Patrick, were very much of the opinion that 'there isn't any need you know for product planners if everybody else will do their job properly'. …"

Much of Beckett's time was spent presenting product programmes in America but although those plans were forensically analysed he refutes the perception that everything was dictated from Dearborn. "We created our own products when we were in Dearborn, created our own manufacturing programmes. And, yes we got their agreement, but nevertheless they were our programmes."

RIGHT The newly knighted Sir Terence Beckett poses in 1973 with a facelift Cortina MkIII. He remains the personality most closely associated with the car.

But Britishness mattered, says Harry Calton, who joined Ford in 1952, in the press office, eventually heading the car press department for Ford of Europe in 1985. "There was a lot of room in the British market in those days. Vauxhall weren't quite in it. It was very much Ford v BMC. Ford was admired not so much for styling and engineering but for financial control, in some ways as a more professional organisation, but the British Motor Corporation was regarded with affection – although in some ways it was slightly amateurish, it was seen as having a good British way of doing things, and it had exciting products." In the merger year of 1952 Ford built 93,499 cars, making it second to BMC, but by 1959 this had risen to 314,793 cars compared to BMC's 431,247. Tellingly, on its lower production Ford made £32.2m in profit against the latter's £21.4m.

What of Vauxhall? Its English heritage pre-dated Ford, the first British-built Vauxhall having appeared in 1903. It was bought by General Motors in 1925 after becoming well established as maker of substantial family cars with some sporting pedigree. It was a British pioneer of the use of chassis-less monocoque construction with the 10hp Type H of 1937, and annual output had reached 100,000 by 1953 with a product line which increasingly resembled shrunken Chevrolets and Pontiacs. However, the Luton-based manufacturer did not become a major competitor to Ford of Britain until the 1980s.

The new British Fords

The post-war British Ford offering was initially limited to the large V8 Pilot of 1947–51 (a reworked pre-war design) and to the smaller and more basic bottom-of-range Anglia and Prefect. Ford did not properly counter the Morris Minor and Austin A30 until the all-new 100E Anglia and Prefect family arrived in 1953.

By way of compensation, the first all-new Ford of England design, the four-cylinder Consul and six-cylinder Zephyr saloons of 1950, marked a number of firsts. Bodywork was of monocoque construction and the Consul's four-cylinder 1,508cc 47bhp engine was Ford of Britain's first overhead-valve unit, and additionally had oversquare dimensions, meaning that its bore was bigger than its stroke. Helped by allowing room for larger valves, this configuration made for a more freely revving and responsive performance than was the case with more old-fashioned long-stroke units. The Zephyr and the later and more ritzy Zodiac featured a 2.2-litre 'six' of 68bhp. Independent front suspension

made its first appearance on a British Ford in the form of MacPherson struts, a space-saving combination of a tubular damper within a coil spring, anchored by a single lower arm. The design was named after US Ford engineer Earle S. MacPherson, and was first seen on the Detroit-designed 1949 Ford-France Vedette. MacPherson was based at Dagenham when he designed the strut for the 1950 Consul; he became vice-president of engineering and his strut front suspension went on to become the default system on most cars to this day.

The Consul/Zephyr/Zodiac family enjoyed rapid success in many markets and was joined by convertible and estate car variants bodied respectively by outside contractors Carbodies and Abbott. With very little factory support a Zephyr won the 1953 Monte Carlo Rally in the hands of Maurice Gatsonides and at the end of its six-year run over a quarter of a million of the series had been produced.

The 1953 London Motor Show saw Ford's first 'modern' small monocoque car, the new Anglia/Prefect. Designed in England rather than Detroit, it was styled at the Briggs studio and resembled a scaled-down Consul. The basic Anglia came with two doors, the Prefect with four, and once more there was MacPherson strut suspension. Puzzling some, the 1,172cc engine remained a sidevalve unit. This was in fact an all-new engine but it used a familiar capacity to allow existing production machinery to be carried over, funds being tight after the considerable expenditure on the Consul and Zephyr. "We didn't have the time, the knowledge or the expertise to do a complete new engine at that stage, so we had to cobble the old one," adds Terence Beckett.

Still, the new sidevalve was reassuringly rustic to maintain and Ford now had two offerings in the small-car class: the old 'perpendicular' Anglia was given the original 10hp engine, stripped of much of its equipment, and sold as the Popular 103E, production being transferred in 1955 to the Briggs factory in Doncaster. It found no shortage of takers in austerity Britain as the world's cheapest car, at £391 including Purchase Tax, and ran until 1959, even outselling the new-shape car in its first year of production.

Expansion and a place in Europe

Hennessy had taken over as chief executive in 1950 and was always concerned that Dagenham's near self-sufficiency was most threatened by the outside sourcing of its bodies from Briggs. Although it had been set up principally to build Ford bodyshells, Briggs remained American-owned, with Chrysler

its largest customer. It also carried out work for Austin, Rootes and Standard as well as building bodies for Lanchesters, Jowett Javelins and sub-assemblies for Morris.

Hennessy was immensely concerned that when founder Walter Briggs died a takeover could leave him at a great disadvantage. In the end Briggs died in 1952 aged 74, by which time negotiations to acquire the company had already been underway for two years. The price for the 62 per cent share in Briggs that Ford ultimately bought was a vast $9m (£5.6m), a transaction which gave the British government of the time worries over transatlantic movements of currency. With hindsight it has been recognised that the acquisition was a masterstroke on the part of Hennessy. It prompted BMC to buy Fisher and Ludlow, which in turn pushed that firm's biggest client, Standard-Triumph, into a desperate shopping spree for body manufacturers across the country.

Ford production was already 1,300 vehicles a day when in October 1954 Hennessy, fresh from the absorption of Briggs,

announced a £65m expansion programme to increase capacity over the following five years; in the same year BMC announced a £10m investment in its Longbridge plant. Dagenham's upgrade included a new foundry and press shop and expanded assembly facilities, with the new Paint, Trim and Assembly (PTA) building linked to a re-equipped Briggs works by an enclosed conveyor-belt across a bridge. Further facilities were established around Essex, including in 1957 a giant parts and distribution centre at Aveley. Announcing the plans, Hennessy told the press that the company must lead the market in modern styling and advanced and reliable engineering – while achieving sufficient volume to deal with competition anywhere in the world. He then turned his attention to Europe – without mention of Ford of Germany.

"The UK motor industry has, since the war, secured 41 per cent of the total world export market. We have all read dire warnings of the threat of German competition. Now let's look at the facts. Undoubtedly Germany has achieved a spectacular increase in the output of automobiles since 1948 but the German industry today exports less than half the value that Britain does.

"The chief of the Volkswagen company recently told the Financial Times that their greatest competitor was Ford-Dagenham. That was a gracious thing to say. I return the compliment by saying his judgement is excellent!"

Hennessy clearly did not see Ford of Germany providing much competition. Although management from Dagenham had been sent to Cologne to restart production on the conclusion of the war (the factory had survived bombing well) and in spite of the formation of Ford's International Division of 1949, Ford of Germany and Ford of Britain were pitched against each other in the same markets.

A lack of communication was compounded by the views of the British workforce and management, not least the head of public relations, Colonel Maurice Buckmaster, an Old Etonian who had run the Paris office of Ford of France and went on to head the French section of the Special Operations Executive (SOE) organising resistance against the Germans. "You have to remember that this was only seven years after the war, and there had been little or no communication with Ford-Germany. Buckmaster had a strong dislike of the Germans. It was very much Ford of Britain against Ford of Germany," comments Harry Calton.

This state of mind was embedded in marketing conferences where national sales companies in Europe would pick over the offerings from each factory and compete over which products they were prepared to market and sell. Ford of Germany had been going its own way with a range very similar to Ford's British line-up although lacking much of an offering at either the bottom or the top end of the market. The Taunus – named after a mountain range – was a series of solid saloons, estates and convertibles which initially resembled the MkI Consul before becoming progressively more American in look, with two-tone paint and baby fins. They were available to buy in the UK via Lincoln Cars, whose West London premises also housed Ford's modest competitions department and press garage; the 12M and larger 17M were also exported to the United States from 1958.

Cologne's management enjoyed much less independence from Dearborn, the suburb of Detroit which was home to Ford's headquarters. While Hennessy used the respect he commanded at the parent company to steer Dagenham his own way, Cologne continued to be the problem child. The Cardinal project (see Chapter Two), which was to have a pivotal effect on Cortina development, was Ford of America's biggest effort to boost German Ford production and sales – in 1957 Ford of Britain produced 343,000 units a year compared to Germany's 88,000 vehicles. While Dagenham was left to its own devices, John Andrews was tasked with improving Ford of Germany's prospects. By the early 1960s the Cologne site had grown to 18 major buildings and scores of minor facilities.

Towards a new look

Where styling was concerned, in the 1950s most British car companies were influenced by American trends. Everybody was looking across the Atlantic for confident culture, music and style, in contrast to the bomb-sites and ration books of post-war Britain. Even the thoroughly English makers of Hillman, Sunbeam-Talbot and Humber cars, Sir William and Sir Reginald Rootes, were great advocates of American design and had entered into a contract with the famous Raymond Loewy organisation in 1938.

Over at BMC the podgy little Austin Somerset had given way to the leaner Cambridge, but on the whole BMC stayed away from American-influenced styling, shrewdly farming out the looks of its cars to Italian design house Pininfarina, beginning with 1958's Austin A40 and the bigger saloons that started to be introduced that same year.

With the purchase of Briggs, Ford of England inherited its styling studio, which had already been populated with a team of Ford men before the merger. Nonetheless, as late as 1958 it was referred to as 'the Briggs styling department' and its designers were on the whole adding details to designs which had originated with Ford's stylists in Dearborn. The first Consul and the 1953 Anglia/Prefect fell into this category, as did the longer and wider MkII Consul/Zephyr/Zodiac of 1956, for which the stylists spent hours devising two-tone paint treatments.

Even if the inspiration came from America, Hennessy had a great personal interest in styling and aimed to bring on home-grown talent and ideas. In 1955 he sent Terence Beckett, now styling manager, along with newly appointed chief stylist Colin Neale, to scout round art colleges. As a result, joiners in 1955 included Ron Hickman and Peter Cambridge, both of whom were lured to Lotus before the end of the decade by Colin Chapman. Another notable was Tom Karen, who went on to head Ogle design.

The new recruits were assembled in a modern building hidden behind walls from the rest of the Dagenham complex. Peter Cambridge, interviewed by the author in 2005, recalled

ABOVE Ford of Germany was no less governed by Detroit styling; this 1957 17M resembled a shrunken Ford Fairlane. (Ford-Werke GmbH)

his first impression: "We were all walled-in, in a sort of high-security little enclave. Fifteen people in the room, plenty of room, workstations with compressed air laid-on for airbrushes, plenty of materials that you needed, and adjoining a full-size clay modelling shop was a little courtyard where they could display things. Tacked onto the other end was a large showroom which had a turntable, lighting, curtains – everything for a kind of final presentation to the top brass, every facility you needed."

But there was a long-running distrust between body engineers and stylists. Styling was overseen by engineering and Don Ward, the talented and outspoken chief body engineer, was often in conflict with Colin Neale. With their arts-school backgrounds the stylists were usually seen as effete (*Ford Bulletin* seemed to take pains to mention their marital status) and as they were allowed to spend many hours on space-age airbrush renderings, flicking through the latest styling magazines, and entering competitions, they must have seemed like a bunch of dreamers. As well as being misunderstood by colleagues, they were given no particular support by their American cousins either, as Peter Cambridge recalled. "Every so often we'd get a deputation from Detroit. There was this guy called Elwood Engels [Ford US senior stylist] and Wesley Dahlberg and they were a tough old lot. I wouldn't have liked to have worked in Detroit … we got the opinion that Detroit wouldn't stand any nonsense."

ABOVE When in 1957 the staff of the Briggs styling studio posed with the MkII Zodiac, Zephyr and Consul (left to right), they had yet to truly break from styling dictates from Detroit.

Charles Thompson, who later became pivotal to the styling of the Cortina and Corsair, had been with Briggs since 1947 and worked his way up to styling through engineering. "For a very long time the American company – stylists particularly – looked on us as a little backstreet operation. We were small, we were learning the trade, and it was all very new to us."

Ford of Britain's body engineering in the 1950s could best be described as belt-and-braces. Having moved to unitary construction within the decade, the Briggs body engineers were still learning their way towards a true understanding of torsional stiffness. The first Consul convertible was shown in 1951, but it was not put into production until two years later as it had such problems with structural rigidity that it had to have an extra x-shaped crossmember welded to its floorpan by converter Carbodies. Ford understood how to build cars for harsh climates and started to design its bodyshells to a so-called 'safari spec' which included suspension development in the Kenyan hills as well as at the company's own test track. But of course while the cars grew tougher they also grew heavier.

ABOVE The 105E Anglia of 1959 blossomed beyond its cheap-car roots. This is a 1965 1200 Super, which shared its engine with the Cortina.

When he joined Briggs in 1957, Dennis Roberts, later to be a key figure in taking the weight out of the first Cortina bodyshell, was highly unusual in that he had been trained in aircraft stress engineering. "In those days, automobile engineering and coachbuilding were two totally separate operations. The two really didn't come together. Motor cars were built on the line as a chassis where you put all the bits on, and at the end of the line a body came in and dropped on it. Body engineering was what I would describe as the artisan craft of coachbuilding. When I went into Ford body engineering, I was qualified way above anybody. ... I mean I'm not brilliantly qualified – far from it – but I was still qualified way above them."

Roberts set up a structures-testing department – and struggled, at the age of 26, to be heard. "When I got there, they were talking about torsional stiffness of bodies. They were twisting them but they had no idea what they were looking for, although somebody had convinced them that the torsional stiffness of a body was very important. In actual fact, what they were examining was not the torsional stiffness at all because they had no idea of how a big integral structure worked. When the monocoque body came into

being, all they had done was virtually welded simulated chassis members to the floorpans."

But Ford was not averse to forward thinking. In 1952 it purchased a former glass works at Lodge Lane in Birmingham, the centre of Britain's motor industry, and set it up as the Ford Engineering and Research Centre. The new operation had the advantage of being nearer to the Motor Industry Research Association's Midlands test track than was Dagenham and it was also easier to attract engineers who may have baulked at relocating to the south of England. With a budget of half a million pounds, the Birmingham centre worked in tandem with the Essex engineers developing and testing new components and was tasked with the development of a front-wheel-drive car. Lodge Lane was replaced by the much bigger Dunton research centre in 1966/67.

A new best-seller

The first uniquely British-styled Ford – albeit with heavy American influences – was the new Anglia of 1959, the 105E. Perhaps not a perfect example of product planning, its development was an amalgam of two designs, one from Lodge Lane for a spartan replacement for the ancient 103E Popular, the other a

ABOVE A pre-production Classic sits outside at Aveley. The ritzy saloon was a victim of Ford's big success with the Anglia 105E.

RIGHT The Classic Capri coupé of 1961 was a cheaply designed model which took British Fords into a new part of the market. The registration plate on this styling model is a reference to the Capri's codename, 'Sunbird'.

replacement for the boxy 1953 100E Anglia from Colin Neale and his team at the Briggs styling studio.

The Birmingham project had been started in 1953 as a replacement for the 'sit up and beg' Popular and so was subject to great cost constraints. David Burgess-Wise in his book *Ford at Dagenham* recounts that the team outlined a car with a thin sheet-metal roof welded to the side pressings: 'The same financial restraints also compelled the use of a flat rear window, and the only solution to this problem was to use a daring reverse-rake rear window, which had the added bonuses that it gave a generous boot lid opening and kept clean in rain or snow.'

After the front-wheel-drive car was abandoned, Roy Lunn moved from Lodge Lane to become car planning manager and led the development of what became the 105E Anglia, the true replacement for the 100E. Small-scale models adopted the reverse-raked rear window of the Birmingham car but all the other economy-car features were dropped. Lunn then went on to Detroit and became a key player in the Mustang story.

Elwood Engels is said to have influenced the mini-Thunderbird tail lights of the Anglia, but the overall inspiration for the reverse-rake window has been the subject of much debate. Ford designers of the 1950s say it was Sir Patrick Hennessy's idea after seeing a Farina-bodied Fiat 600 in 1955, buying it and shipping it back to Dagenham. But the reverse-rake window idea was widespread in Detroit, having featured on numerous Ford concept cars across its divisions, such as the 1955 'Blue Job' and 'L'Avion', a 1956–57 Mercury small-car concept.

"All this is fashion," Charles Thompson maintains. "We used to get all the latest catalogues from America and sometimes Italy as well. You can say this or that came from Pininfarina, but quite often it was more subliminal than that, when you were sketching away. Things like that would crop up all the time … you tried every single idea you could think of."

In the long term, the Anglia's styling was much less significant than its new engine, the first of a new family planned to span the 1,000cc to 1,500cc bracket. Ford's studies indicated that the size and weight of an engine for a given capacity could be reduced substantially by adopting 'oversquare' dimensions, with the bore bigger than the stroke. The idea was to produce one cylinder block for several engine sizes, with the bore staying the same at 80.96mm, different capacities being achieved by changing the crankshaft throw. With its stroke of 48.412mm, the Anglia engine had a stroke-to-bore ratio of 0.6:1, which was the lowest of any production car of the time. The engine's three-bearing crankshaft was a new hollow cast-iron design which further reduced the weight of the 997cc engine over the old 1,172cc sidevalve, and another innovation was a combined oil pump and filter unit externally mounted on the block.

The 105E's engine (since known as the 'Kent') only gave 39bhp at 5,000rpm but it soon impressed as a tough, free-revving unit and it was coupled to Ford's first four-speed gearbox – albeit one without synchromesh on first gear. Ford's first eight-port cylinder head (with separate inlet and exhaust ports for each cylinder) gave it instant appeal to engine tuners, as did the strength of the crank and block. It was claimed that it could cope with a driver 'missing' a gear, which could destroy many other engines, and it was also 25lb lighter than its nearest competitor.

The downside of the engine design was less low-down torque, but its liveliness pleased the keen driver. In fact the power unit was so high-revving compared to the wheezy

The long-lived 'Kent' engine

The 105E engine went on to become one of motoring's most successful power units. From 1967 and the arrival of the crossflow redesign it became known as the 'Kent' engine, simply because its designer Alan Worters lived in Kent.

On introduction keen drivers immediately noticed its lively nature and racing-car builders saw it had the kind of bottom end robust enough to allow increased revs for racing without the engine self-destructing.

Starting with the 997cc 1959 Anglia version, it grew to power all small and medium Fords throughout the sixties and seventies, as well as providing the basis of the Lotus twin-cam, Formula Ford racing engines and the Cosworth BDA. Just about every specialist sports-car and kit-car manufacturer made use of a 'Kent' engine, notable examples being TVR and Morgan.

The first major change was the move to the 'bowl-in-piston' crossflow cylinder head (see Chapter Five). Although carburettors and exhaust manifolds were often changed, the cylinder block always retained the original 80.96mm bore.

The next major redesign was in 1977 when the engine was reconfigured for the front-wheel-drive Fiesta, becoming known as the 'Valencia' unit after the Spanish Fiesta plant. Heavily modified in 1995 to reduce noise and harshness, for use in the cheap and cheerful Ford Ka, it was reborn one last time as the Endura-E. By this point the 1,299cc engine was only a distant relation to the first 'Kent', having gone through head, block and piston redesigns, and was considered a bit of an antique with its cast-iron block and two valves per cylinder. Notwithstanding this, it ran until 2008.

Ford and Mini money

As a design, Ford personnel were just as impressed with the Mini as everybody else – even if they didn't admit to it in public. It was about as un-Ford like as it was possible to be without being foreign.

Ford's analysis of the profit BMC was making from the Mini was rigorous and its conclusions famously far-reaching. "It convinced us that the management of BMC were truly incompetent," John Bacchus recalls. He had joined Ford in 1960 as a senior analyst in product planning and like a number of Ford people left for the later incarnation of BMC – British Leyland – in 1968. "It was clear to us that they were very worried about the Mini's ability to be priced reasonably competitively. To have priced it slightly below the 105E, even with its higher design cost, might have been justified to establish such a technically advanced and radically different car in the market, but to accept and live with such a huge price penalty was economic folly and hung a huge millstone around their neck. They then exacerbated the problem by handing their product responsibility over to Alec Issigonis and the die was cast!"

As soon as the Mini was launched in 1959, Terence Beckett got his hands on one from a BMC dealer just for an hour and put it on a ramp. "An hour was long enough. I could see that that Mini was a fine piece of engineering – except as we knew later on, the universal joints weren't up to it – but it was really a complicated piece of work. We looked at it and then a couple of months later we were actually able to get our hands on one and strip it down."

In 1959, the basic Mini was priced at £496 including Purchase Tax, while the nearest Anglia was £93 more. From the strip-down, Ford estimated what it would have cost to build the Mini itself. "It was an expensive piece of work, and the price that they charged for it was quite ridiculous," says Beckett. "They'd priced it down towards the 105E without any idea of what the thing could fetch. By this time we had developed some quite sophisticated market research and we were able to show that BMC could have charged £25 to £30 more without losing any volume. So, it was crass ineptitude."

To be sure of its results, a second Mini was stripped down at Aveley and the conclusions were the same. Ford's price analysis was remarkably profound because it not only examined components and labour but took account of the different manufacturing facilities of Ford over its competitors. For example, the use of aluminium by BMC was quite extensive, but it had an aluminium foundry, which Ford did not. Ford used the terms 'variable cost' and 'accounted cost'. The variable cost was the cost of making that individual unit – that collection of bits, plus the labour cost. Accounted cost was the full variable cost plus fixed costs associated with that particular project, such as factories and equipment.

"The simple conclusion was that 105E Anglia variable cost was lower than that of the Mini by something like 5 per cent," Hamish Orr-Ewing recalls. "But the Mini had a lower market price and without any shadow of doubt the result of that was that BMC made a massive error because they underpriced the vehicle quite unnecessarily."

Far from allowing Ford to bask in the knowledge that every Anglia was profitable, the concern was that BMC was dragging down the entire industry's profitability by pricing so low. Orr-Ewing remembers that Sir Patrick Hennessy rang BMC managing director George Harriman (although David Burgess-Wise says this was joint managing director Allen Barke rather than Hennessy) and said words to the effect of "For God's sake raise the price because you're keeping the profitability of the whole industry down by the fact that you're setting the pace on price at an unrealistic figure." Harriman's reported reaction was to say the product would push the price and you just had to sell enough cars. "That was a fundamental misunderstanding," says Orr-Ewing. "Because you spread accounted cost over large numbers of vehicles and if you got your variable cost wrong the more you make the more you lose."

sidevalve 100E that owners complained that it lacked tractability; magazine *The Autocar* commented that below 20mph in top gear the engine was 'decidedly lumpy'. A modified carburettor was fitted in January 1960 to alleviate the problem.

1959 and a key motor show

There were big plans for this small car, introduced on 23 September 1959, hot on the heels of the Mini's August debut. Ford promoted it as 'the world's most exciting small car' and threw money at its launch.

Overseas Ford executives had first seen the Anglia in July, when entertainments included a fanfare by the Royal Horse Guards army band, tours of Dagenham, and a handling demonstration at London's Crystal Palace racetrack, all of which apparently garnered American orders for 35,000 cars.

At the time Ford boasted that the new Anglia had been given the 'biggest advertising campaign ever' – with lavish

The prediction was borne out by Ford analysts who looked at BMC's profit/loss accounts as they were published year by year and there was an almost exact correlation between the number of Minis, then later on 1100s, that it produced, and its quoted profits. BMC did indeed appear to be losing money – or at best not gaining much – on every one of these cars it produced. Furthermore, the Mini and 1100 had become the core products in the BMC portfolio: there was no modern and nicely profitable mid-range model to add beef to the bottom line.

The Anglia can only have been helped in its early days – and BMC's profits further dented – by the Mini's numerous teething troubles and their fixes slowing its production. According to Mini authority Jon Pressnell in *Mini – The Definitive History*, by December 1959 a 30-page memorandum had been sent to dealers with fixes for dealing with the infamous water leaks alone, and well after launch there were problems stopping the Rzeppa constant-velocity joints making a pronounced clicking noise, plus gearbox troubles and electrical woes.

newspaper spreads, TV advertising 'teasers' and a campaign trick called 'leave it about' where 15 Anglias were driven to busy places in London and the Home Counties and left parked, whereupon crowds apparently gathered. Dealers were deluged with Anglia brochures, scarves, soaps, matchboxes and playing cards with the image of the new car.

The battle lines were well and truly drawn at October's Motor Show. Not only did the Mini make its Earls Court debut but Standard-Triumph showed its new Triumph Herald

with its Italian styling and independent rear suspension, in saloon and coupé forms. Ford was ready with the answers to the anticipated questions, listing them in the *Ford Bulletin* company newspaper. Sticking its fingers in its ears, the answer as to why Ford had adopted a 'more conventional design approach compared with BMC and Standard' was that while features such as transverse engines and independent rear suspension had been studied, the novelty of such technical features was outweighed by the

ABOVE Henry Ford II poses with a 1960 Taunus 17M in Cologne. Ford of Germany was then more of a preoccupation for the parent company than Britain. (Ford-Werke GmbH)

advantages of proven reliability and value for money. The *Bulletin* also supplied an answer as to why there was no Anglia four-door: the market trend in the domestic light-car market had been moving away from four doors and the ratio of two-door to four-door sales was approximately 70/30 for the whole UK market. In any case that niche was soon covered by the announcement, the same month, of the new Prefect 107E, which was the familiar square 100E four-door bodyshell decked out in two-tone paint and given the new 105E engine in place of the sidevalve unit, all at the unchanged price of £621. The 107E was an effective stopgap, and was produced between May 1959 and June 1961. The old Anglia, meanwhile, was rejigged to become the new Popular, finally displacing the 'sit up and beg' version which had plodded all the way through the decade.

The Anglia 105E was an instant sales success. In 1960 191,000 were produced, then a record for a British car. By contrast, with its early production problems putting a brake

on output, a more slender 116,000 Minis were produced the same year. The Anglia range was broadened by the arrival of an estate in 1961, while the 1200 Super of 1962 saw the debut of the still-secret Cortina's engine. In 1963 production transferred to Ford's all-new factory at Halewood on Merseyside. A much-loved car in both domestic and export markets, over a million 105E Anglias were produced, the last in 1967. The small Ford also notched up a formidable circuit-racing career, a Broadspeed-prepared car winning the British Touring Car Championship in its final year of production, driven by John Fitzpatrick.

A classic Ford?

There never was a four-door Anglia, but there was a bigger brother, the laboriously titled Consul Classic 315 introduced in spring 1961. In development since 1956, this was a model badly needed to fill the gap in the Ford range that existed between the Anglia/Prefect and the Consul in the years

before the Cortina. Meanwhile, BMC was busy churning out variously-badged 1,500cc saloons, and Vauxhall had the Victor and Hillman the Minx in this category.

As a premium medium-sized car with fashionable features, Ford hoped that the Classic would rise above the workaday image of its other products. Apart from its reverse-rake window, twin headlamps were boasted as a feature new to the class, as was the standard fitment of front disc brakes. The Classic also had an extraordinarily large boot – helped by the reverse-rake window – which Ford illustrated by sitting a woman on a deckchair in it. Standard upholstery was in two-tone vinyl or a metallic-lustre PVC on the de-Luxe models, with leather at no extra cost, and buyers could choose from seven two-tone or twelve single-colour paint shades. As Ford put it at launch: 'The Classic has been designed for world-wide appeal to motorists wanting a well-appointed car of refined appearance with sparkling performance and all-round economy – a car filling the gap between the four-seater

997cc Anglia and the six-seater 1,703cc Consul – both of which will continue.' Ford of Britain was extremely pleased to report at launch that Miss Katherine Worsley, the future Duchess of Kent, was delighted to have been given a Classic from Ford on her wedding.

Available in four-door and two-door versions, early Classics were powered by a 1,340cc enlarged-stroke version of the Anglia engine, giving 56.5bhp, in conjunction with either a column shift or a floor-mounted gearchange. According to David Burgess-Wise, Ford had experimented with independent rear suspension but finally opted for a traditional live axle and leaf-spring set-up. Ford soon claimed a waiting list for European markets and that the Classic was outselling its nearest competitor by 30 per cent.

But as it emerged later, the Classic was living on borrowed time even before it was launched. The product planners had already realised that it was not going to meet the challenge of the forthcoming BMC 1100, and Cortina

ABOVE **The Anglia made a flying start to a significant motor-sport career with the top three Class B places in the 1960 East African Safari. (Author's collection)**

development was well in train. Ford had in fact opted to make the Classic body pressings on short-life Kirksite tooling, having already lost a year of sales to the Anglia, as Terence Beckett explained in a company interview in 1974: "The Anglia itself did much better than we thought it would. It was decided that we couldn't get any more engines in particular out of the plant at that time, that we were limited as well in terms of body assembly generally, and so although the Classic was supposed to come in 12 months after the Anglia, in fact it didn't. It was postponed so we could get more production out of the Anglia."

September 1961 saw the announcement of a coupé based on the Classic, the Consul Capri 335 – Sir Patrick

having by then insisted that all medium-sized cars be badged as Consuls. The newcomer was described as 'Dagenham's loveliest car' and sported a rakish roofline with side windows that could be wound down to give a pillarless look. At its launch, sales director Allen Barke revealed that the Capri had been in development for two years as a 'personal car', an idea completely new to Ford. It was named after the Mediterranean island of Capri, which Barke hoped would "conjure up something beautiful to the public who will be interested in this type of car". He also commented that due to Ford's dissatisfaction with the recent British budget, sales would be concentrated abroad at first and that UK-market cars would not be available until 1962.

BELOW Much of the appeal to Ford of front-wheel drive, as shown by this 1964 Taunus 12M V4 engine and transmission, was its compactness, which aided shipping and assembly. (Ford-Werke GmbH)

Although based on the saloon, the Consul Capri only sported two full-sized seats, with just a small bench behind. This had been imposed by the slope of the rear window, which in turn owed its look to cost constraints. Designer Charles Thompson played a large hand in the project. "The Classic Capri was Sir Pat's baby. His management was afraid to pay out for completely new coupé but in those days people like Sir Pat tended to rule the roost a bit more and he put enough pressure on for a coupé version of the Classic on the proviso that we had to keep things like the boot lid and that's why they never spent money on proper tooling and it forced us to have close-coupled greenhouse. Ninety per cent was carry-over." This diversion from mainstream production had its bodywork contracted out to Pressed Steel Fisher.

Sir Patrick was also behind the Capri name – although for a time the coupé looked to be ready to go by its project name of Sunbird, an allusion to the Ford Thunderbird. Charles Thompson recalls sending somebody to the London Science Museum to photograph a real sunbird for a badge design.

The Classic gained a reputation as a solid if slow car. The solidity came from what was later realised to be an over-engineered bodyshell, the slowness from the fact that the 1,340cc power unit was not up to pulling 18.7cwt of car at the 'sparkling' pace Ford claimed. Most rivals of similar weight had 1,500cc units – and the new Hillman Super Minx, introduced in autumn 1961, had a 1,592cc unit, while the re-jigged BMC 'Farina' saloons announced for 1962 had their capacity raised to 1,622cc. Hamish Orr-Ewing says the initial judgement was that the Ford engine would not stretch beyond 1,340cc but this was rather more due to the views of engine designer Alan Worters, who capitulated when pressed by Hennessy. A larger unit was duly initiated in 1960 and some accounts have it that Ford had hoped to launch the Classic with this 1,500cc upgrade but missed on timing. Interviewed in 1963, Worters said he was faced with either having to increase the bore – with associated manufacturing problems – or else lengthening the stroke by raising the height of the block slightly. In the end the latter course was chosen, and to overcome anticipated problems of harshness a solid cast five-bearing crankshaft was developed to accommodate the increased 72mm stroke. Announced in both the Classic and the Capri in July 1962, the 1,498cc, 59.5bhp unit boosted top speed on the saloon from 78mph to 82mph and increased flexibility. Another improvement was the fitment of synchromesh on first gear, in reality a curtain-raiser for the Cortina's gearbox.

In September 1962 Ford announced that for about £500 the coachbuilder Hooper would enhance a customer's Capri with leather seats and trim, a carpeted boot and a walnut dashboard with fitted radio. Outside a unique rear light cluster was fitted, the five-star grille was substituted for a single bar and the whole car treated to 14 coats of paint.

In a last-minute performance boost the Capri was bestowed with the forthcoming Cortina GT engine in February 1963. The unexpectedly sporty specification of a twin-choke Weber carburettor, a four-branch exhaust, larger exhaust valves and a Cosworth high-lift camshaft boosted power by over 30 per cent to 78bhp; the package was rounded off with a remote floor shift, servo-assisted front discs, and an auxiliary instrument panel containing an ammeter, oil-pressure gauge and rev-counter. This was but a diversion. In September of the same year, with Cortinas flying off the showroom floor in both 1,200cc and 1,500cc versions, the entire Classic range was discontinued. Just over 109,000 saloons had been made. The Capri continued to be listed until July 1964, by which time 13,145 examples had been produced.

With hindsight, the Classic had proved to be a relative failure in numerical terms. But if it constituted an error commercially, it was a vital error to have made: its over-engineered, expensive body had furnished an important lesson that was duly learnt in the course of development of the Cortina. Equally the Classic had its admirers and it established that there was a clientele that would pay extra for a more upmarket medium-sized Ford; furthermore, it had spawned Ford of Britain's first coupé, something that was a pointer to the future.

Detroit takes control

While American Ford influence had been more or less at arm's length through the 1950s, as the decade drew to a close plans were made in Detroit to rationalise non-US operations and increase flexibility of manufacturing to take advantage of the European Economic Community, or Common Market, which had been formed in 1957 – even though Britain did not join until 1973.

From 1959 plans were put in place for Ford of America to acquire all the remaining privately owned shares in Ford GB, which it finally managed to do in early 1961. Of all the European operations, America had the largest stake in the Ford Motor Company Limited, but Henry Ford II was keen to stress at the time that staffing and model development would still be very much down to Sir Patrick Hennessy. European autonomy was, however, quite some way off.

Chapter 2:
The Cardinal and the Archbishop

GWC 252B

ABOVE This Cortina – or 'Archbishop' – styling clay (with dummy passengers) is nearly finalised by September 1960. The rear 'spears' ahead of the bumper have yet to appear.

Two cars pushed the Cortina into being, the BMC 1100 and Ford-US's Cardinal project, an ambitious American–German car which emerged as the 1962 Ford Taunus 12M. The strong-willed and powerful Sir Patrick Hennessy, Terence Beckett's product-planning disciplines and Anglo-German rivalry were also in the mix.

First, the Cardinal

The foundations of the Cardinal were laid before those of the Archbishop, as the Cortina was codenamed, and they illustrated a profound change in Detroit's thinking. As is well documented, the Volkswagen Beetle deeply troubled US carmakers in the 1950s, taking a relentlessly upward sales curve in a part of the market in which they did not compete. In 1956 Volkswagen sold 50,000 Beetles in the US and 120,000 in 1959, with no sign of slowing.

As well as price and economy, the Beetle's success was founded on deep reliability and impeccable service support wherever you were, a lesson which British manufacturers completely failed to grasp with their offerings. The Renault Dauphine enjoyed a few years of success second to the Beetle, but rusted out of the picture. Ford of England and

Germany also imported their ranges but had nothing to match the Beetle on service support.

The domestic car makers' answer was initially known as the 'compact' car but these were nearer the size of the British MkII Ford Consul and Zephyr/Zodiac ranges. Chevrolet's rear-engined Corvair at first astonished the market but Ford's six-cylinder rear-drive Falcon, a sturdy yet weight-controlled six-seater, cheap to buy and own, was a greater sales success from its 1959 debut, selling a million by 1962.

However, Ford's research indicated that the Falcon would only go so far to stem the tide of imports and that a section of domestic buyers wanted to go even smaller. It decided that a miniaturised Falcon would not compete effectively with a Volkswagen on cost and weight because labour content could not be sufficiently reduced. In June 1959 the Ford division was therefore given the go-ahead to engineer and test an all-new 'Segment 1' car. It was strongly backed by division head Robert McNamara – although he was appointed defence secretary by the new Kennedy administration in 1961 and did not see the project to fruition. Roy Lunn, who had seen the Anglia through development, was also involved.

7-11-61
S-4695-2

US product planners decreed that the new model would have to perform better than European imports, be no longer than a Volkswagen, the same width, and crucially seat four passengers in around the same comfort as the 1960 Falcon. This, they concluded, would lead inexorably to front-wheel drive, which was already being examined. "This was a tremendous amount of innovation for the American system at that time, which didn't generally recognise this sort of development," Terence Beckett says. "It was very far-sighted for the people over there to go for this."

The new small car would adopt Ford's new 'Pony Pac' concept of engine, namely transmission, suspension and steering gear in an integrated unit. This would be pre-assembled as a whole and then bolted to the bodyshell in three places, which would enable faster assembly. Front suspension was by a single transverse torsion bar mounted directly onto the gearbox plus single-arm lower links, with leaf springs suspending the simple beam rear axle.

The debate about front-wheel drive centred around cost, not desirability. Ford of Germany and Ford of England were charged, during 1959, to compare 'Pony Pac' costs using the Anglia 105E driveline as a base. The engineers also

recommended eliminating the engine fan to save power and boost fuel economy. It was an advanced specification for Europe, let alone America. The target weight was an over-ambitious 1,499lb (or 13cwt: the final weight of the Cortina was thought to be remarkable when it fetched out at 15½cwt).

Of course there wasn't a small enough engine in the American Ford range to power a sub-Falcon car, so some thought had been given either to building one from scratch or sourcing a unit elsewhere. In 1959 a report recommended a degree of rationalisation between Ford-US and Ford-Europe in manufacturing. A study using a Renault Dauphine engine (as a representative size and not favouring any one Ford location) had confirmed that a new small engine would be best sourced overseas. Germany became a favoured candidate to produce the new engine because it planned to replace its ancient sidevalve 1,172cc four-cylinder in any case, while Britain had only just introduced the 105E 'Kent'. Engine manufacture in all three locations was judged to be not feasible before 1965.

In 1959 a study concluded that 'The segment 1 car engine seems to offer an ideal test of the feasibility of foreign sourcing.' The new small car project was subsequently named the Cardinal after the bird – a cardinal being smaller

ABOVE A 'Cardinal' mock-up pictured in its final form at Ford's Dearborn styling centre in November 1961. Still destined for US production, it wears 'Falcon V4' badging. (©Ford Motor Co. Courtesy FordImages. com)

BELOW Also believed to date from September 1960, this 'Archbishop' styling proposal is still a conventional offering compared to the Anglia. The tail lights show an influence of the MkIII Zephyr, also being styled by Roy Brown.

than a falcon. Ford of Britain playfully named its competing project the Archbishop, taking an ecclesiastical slant.

Both 60-degree and 20-degree water-cooled 'vee' engines were discussed and Ford of Germany and Ford of Britain were given detailed drawings in October 1959. The range was planned to span 1,000cc to 1,700cc, for 'European considerations'. The engine was also to be short – 14in long in its final incarnation. Once again, a Goliath provided a mobile test bed.

The Cologne Cardinal

At this time, Ford of Germany was being seen as underperforming in a market ripe for growth. Germany's economy was expanding rapidly and something had to be done about Ford's product lines. Ford-Germany had made 112,000 cars in 1958 compared to Britain's 284,000, and in 1959 the Cologne plant was operating at 81 per cent of its maximum capacity, in contrast to a bursting-at-the-seams Dagenham. It was also being out-produced by other car makers across Europe and there was a worry that another American manufacturer might introduce a Volkswagen Beetle or Renault Dauphine competitor in Europe's C-class before Ford did. Any export impact of the forthcoming Anglia 105E did not seem to be factored into the internal document produced by John Andrews to secure investment for Germany.

In the German market the existing 1,172cc Taunus 12M and 1,498cc 15M were doing a fairly good job in propping up sales in the upper price range of the German C-class segment, and a smaller car was in train under the codename NPX-C to undercut both the Beetle and Dauphine on weight, and using either an in-line or V4 engine.

In January 1960 Andrews successfully argued that Ford of Germany lacked the resources to work on a C-class car, so the entire development, including styling, should be carried out in Dearborn, based on the proposals already taking shape for the 'Segment 1' car. Initially there would only be a two-door saloon, with a four-door and a station wagon being anticipated at a later date. Thus NPX-C was stopped. As Germany was already in line to produce the engine for the Cardinal, the 1,200cc German C-class car and the American design became one and the same, albeit with a larger 1,500cc engine for the US version; the four-speed manual gearbox had a column shift, and synchromesh on all four gears.

Eventually the 60-degree V4 won, on refinement grounds, after comparison tests were carried out with a modified Anglia 105E engine, a new overhead-camshaft design by Ford of Germany and a four-cylinder version of the Falcon 'six'. The German ohc engine was of very advanced design, having a rubber timing belt, an innovation which would not be seen on the market until several years later; at the time, doubts over durability prevented its adoption.

The two product programmes became known internally as the Cardinal 'A' (America) and 'B' (Germany). After a fitful evolution, styling was signed off in April 1960, around six

months ahead of that of the Cortina. Given that the front-drive powertrain was a leap into the unknown, a parallel programme was put in place for a rear-wheel-drive version with the 'Kent' unit – deemed the 'lowest-cost, minimum-weight and lowest-risk power plant'. The Engine and Foundry Division recommended it be modified to take advantage of contemporary Ford-US development techniques for lightweight cast-iron manufacturing techniques. Throughout the 1960 Cardinal status documents no mention is made of Ford of England developing its own C-class car: had the front-drive Cardinal been abandoned and rear-drive adopted, there would have been two Cortina-type cars in the Ford empire.

The Cardinal's two-continent assembly was to be equally unconventional and designed to minimise costs on the US side. Germany would build and assemble the 'Pony Pac' transmission units, which would then be shipped to the US to be fitted in trimmed and painted Cardinal bodyshells at the Ford plant in Louisville, Kentucky. A massive investment was made in a new facility in Cologne to build the engines. Complex shipping arrangements were plotted to allow

BELOW This seldom-seen image – possibly later than the black-and-white photos on earlier pages – shows a full-sized 'Archbishop' clay model with the original triangular tail-light design. The rear overhang appears to have been increased.

for strikes in the US and Europe, and directing supplies through Canada.

In sourcing the right components, Ford of America explored some familiar English names. Burman was approached to supply steering gear, at least for the German car, and the same English firm which was making Rzeppa universal joints for BMC's Mini and 1100 was suggested as a possible source for the Cardinal, although US automotive manufacturer Dana had been in line for the job.

By spring 1961, beset by last-minute redesigns and holdups, the Cardinal 'A' was $15m over budget and the 'B' $20m over. Even at this late stage the Dearborn engineers were advising management to consider reverting to a conventional rear-wheel-drive layout.

Ford's internal documents from that year start to reveal some interplay between the Cardinal and the Archbishop, as it still was. In June the committee was asked to explore round tail lamps for the American Cardinal, five months after John Bugas – head of the international division and involved with Cardinal throughout – had ordered the Cortina be redesigned to accommodate them. An indication that Ford of Britain had its costs well in train was given in a Cardinal

'B' cost-cutting document of July 1961, which advised substituting some Archbishop features such as the level of paint finish used and the design of steering wheel.

As late as 1962 a status report listed ten major design issues, termed 'job stoppers', which were considered of major importance by engineering and which had to be tackled and signed-off at a stage perilously close to production start-up. Noise and vibration were in particular still Cardinal bugbears: the alternator leads were breaking under engine vibration, an 'objectionable' steering wheel vibration required a new wheel to be designed, and there was an excessive exhaust note and an engine 'growl' from the balancer shaft at idle, which had to be remedied, respectively, by a new exhaust baffle and the addition of a weight to the pulley. Adding to this catalogue of woes were rear-engine-mount bolt failure, a serious front-spring problem and road dirt interfering with the electrics. The resolution of some of these issues was not scheduled until almost the first cars off the line in June 1962. Such was the difficulty with the original 'Pony Pac' concept that a whole new front end was developed, with the transverse leaf spring mounted to a body crossmember and the original rack-and-pinion steering replaced by a body-mounted recirculating-ball design, which did away with the expense of a flexible mounting for the rack. With the lower links still mounted on the gearbox and dampers above each end of the spring, this became the production specification.

Exit Cardinal 'A'

Something had to be done at the top. Lee Iacocca, with Ford since 1946 and vice-president at only 34 in 1960, recalled in his autobiography a trip to Germany to see the Cardinal a few months into his job and claims credit for knocking the American version on the head: 'Among other problems the Cardinal was too small and had no trunk. And while its fuel economy was great, that wasn't yet a selling point for the American consumer. In addition, the styling was lousy. The Cardinal looked like it had been designed by a committee ... When I returned from Germany I went straight to Henry Ford. "The Cardinal is a loser," I told him. "To bring out another lemon so soon after the Edsel would bring this company to its knees. We simply can't afford a new model that won't appeal to younger buyers."'

Although he doesn't date the trip to Germany, the fact that Iacocca claimed that the car he saw had 'no trunk' might have indicated he saw the 1959 'Hummingbird' (page 42), which was indeed a foot shorter than the eventual design. Given that the Dearborn was still grappling with large-scale production problems so near to the intended 1962 US production start-up, Iacocca may not have had such an instant effect as he claimed.

Corporate nerves probably killed the Cardinal 'A' – and a well-judged shift towards the Mustang followed, led by Iacocca. It would have been clear that it was becoming too great a risk to launch such an underdeveloped car onto the domestic market and Ford would also certainly not have wanted to have on its hands another Edsel – the unwanted new car line which had famously bombed in the 1950s. Some accounts also hold that the dealer network turned against the Cardinal.

The author has not been able to establish when the decision was made to abandon production of the Cardinal 'A', but plans were still active in early 1962, when data given to public relations anticipated an optimistic 50,000 decrease in VW sales in 1963 once it was on sale. Louisville was to stop production of the Ford Galaxie on 15 June 1962 to allow transfer of the Cardinal line by 9 July. Between then

and 30 July, 400 pre-production units were to be built and the first 7,000 cars sold to dealers were to be 'pre-conditioned'. The Cardinal could well have been cancelled with only two months to go.

Enter the Archbishop

The contrast between the Cardinal and the Archbishop programmes was stark. A great deal of thought translated itself into action at Ford of Britain in 1960. Once the Anglia was off to its roaring start, Product Planning broke down the British market into small, family, medium and big cars by share and analysed the market for them.

MECHANIX ILLUSTRATED
THE HOW-TO-DO MAGAZINE

STILL **25c** SEPTEMBER

FORD AMAZES CAR WORLD WITH PLANS FOR REVOLUTIONARY SMALLEST COMPACT

Size Compared To Volkswagen

artist's concept

ABOVE In September 1961 this US magazine mixed well-informed leaks with an image closely resembling a Taunus 17M. No hint of the real traumas of the Cardinal project. (Author's collection)

ABOVE In June 1962 early production Cortinas and Taunus 12Ms await test drivers at the Ford International sales conference at Montlhéry. Its nearest European competitors (before the arrival of the BMC 1100) mingle in the line-up: Renault Dauphine, Simca 1000 and Volkswagen Beetle. (Author's collection)

They decided the Anglia would ably defend the small car territory and that there would thus be no need to build a still smaller car to beat the Mini, a conclusion reinforced by their own cost analysis. A smaller model would not allow them to get much more of that market than the Anglia was already capturing. What they did need was something for the 46 per cent of the market who wanted something in between 'family' and mid-sized cars, given that the 107E was only a stopgap model.

A vehicle sitting between the Classic and Anglia had been on the drawing board, but with little effort expended on it, as Hamish Orr-Ewing recalls. "In my little office we were working on a four-door version of the 105E which in effect was the same thing only bigger. It was something on the same lines, but not with the same styling. We weren't working on it with any radical

departures. It would have been a more or less conventional Ford car, larger than the Anglia and below the Classic."

It has long been held that Sir Patrick Hennessy accelerated the development of this car to match the introduction of the Cardinal/12M, after a trip to the States where it was revealed to him, and that he gave the team their orders in spring 1960. Orr-Ewing confirms this: "It was the fact that the Cardinal was put effectively in the hands of Dearborn engineering and John Andrews that triggered the Cortina. I was at the heart of the Cortina programme and we knew very well that Sir Patrick took considerable exception to this. He was not consulted and he then – and this is I think one of the reasons why the Cortina was a great success – put his full authority behind producing a conventional Hotchkiss-drive front-engined arrangement using the new mechanicals which we had got very recently, first in the 105E, and which were fully capable of being used in a larger vehicle."

However, previous accounts which infer that Hennessy had been unaware of the Cardinal until he saw it on a trip to the States do not perhaps give the full picture of the Ford empire. Although far from integrated in its product planning and production, there was a natural through-flow of information at the upper levels and, as shown earlier, Ford of Britain was asked to work on early elements of the 'Pony Pac' for the front-drive Cardinal back in 1959. Unlike its British contemporaries, Ford was comfortable with a through-flow of information between its divisions. If you provided a good reason for it, people would usually share their plans with you.

Terence Beckett takes a more measured view. "I don't think he [Hennessy] was put out by it. I think he watched what was going on, as we did, and we recognised that they needed replacements there for their old 12M. And we simply said they'd better get on with it. But of course it was, again, a complicated bag of tricks, but while we fully developed our car it was clear that there were problems on reliability with the German car."

A more important driver of the Cortina was the realisation that the yet-to-be-launched Ford Classic would be no answer at all to the technical wizardry expected of the BMC 1100 – on which Beckett had pretty good intelligence by 1960. He had a team of three whose business it was to gather competitive information; they were once caught in the back of a new Standard van at a motor show, measuring it up.

Compared both to the 1100 and the price-band in which Ford wanted to compete, the Classic's utterly conventional layout and sturdy construction would be severe handicaps.

The Classic bodyshell was engineered to true 'safari' spec, with ill-controlled weight and laborious assembly procedures. The Classic in fact looked so far short of the mark that it was nearly cancelled before launch, while a planned estate derivative was definitively shelved. As recounted earlier, it also needed to be up-engined very soon in its life.

Whether or not it was desirable, front-wheel drive was out of the question purely in terms of the development time available to Ford. When the Archbishop was given the go-ahead in spring 1960 it had a 19½-month schedule, when the norm was 30 months from clay model to first assembly. Cortina history dates do vary a little: some accounts put the schedule at 20 months, but an article in *The Motor* magazine at the Cortina's launch seemed to place initial work on the new car as starting in spring 1959. Whatever the case, there was very little room for manoeuvre, with a public launch planned for September 1962 and then the October London Motor Show. Ford wanted 22,000 cars ready for launch and Job Number One needed to come off the line in July, to allow for the annual August close-down while still providing enough cars for dealers to show and demonstrate.

The only way the new car could be made competitive with the 1100 was to offer a bigger car at an unbeatable price, by strict control of cost and weight – the antithesis

of the Classic. The manufacturing concept was simple: the assembly cost of a larger car remained the same, but the profit came from using less material to do so.

Over three months the product programme 'Red Book' was drawn up down to the last spot-weld, by Fred Hart, Executive Engineer, Light Cars, and Chief Body Engineer Don Ward, with Andy Cox. The total budget was £12m, not including the later estates or GT versions. Several of those involved in the project say that only a two-door saloon was sanctioned at first. Although primarily an 1100 competitor, there was also the hope that the new car could out-flank higher-powered models such as the Vauxhall Victor and Hillman Minx, by offering the same dimensions at a lower price. Beckett and two others spent three weeks with seating bucks and pieces of hardboard and cardboard to establish the package and then it was a matter of dressing the contents in a functional yet appealing style.

A new kind of body structure

Although perhaps not appreciated at the time, the choice of body engineer assigned to work on the body structure was pivotal to the Cortina's success. Dennis Roberts, mentioned in the previous chapter, had started his working life with Ford but had left to join Bristol Aircraft's London office, a move which enabled him to train in aeronautics, advance mathematics and aircraft structures. He spent two years as an aircraft stress engineer, including work on an all-steel supersonic aircraft project and the design of a twin-rotor helicopter, until he was recruited to Briggs Motor Bodies in 1957 to set up Don Ward's fledgling structures lab.

It was around mid-1960, when Roberts was working on the MkIII Zephyr/Zodiac, that Ward discreetly asked him to join the Archbishop project, whose styling was already under way, in order to work on the underlying bodyshell structure. "He never discussed my career with me but he must have actually been following it – or managing it in some form – because he obviously knew what my background was and what I'd done in the structures lab," remembers Roberts. "One evening he came up, didn't say very much, but started to talk about this new car, the Archbishop. I knew that they were working on the Archbishop because we were in and out of the styling studio and the clays were emerging, but we hadn't started any real work on it. I went home that night thinking 'Well, where the bloody hell do I start?'"

The point of departure was a Classic bodyshell, made easier to assemble and with 150lb of weight taken out of

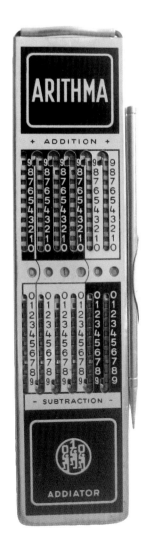

RIGHT **Shot in Scotland, the launch photos covered all markets using rhd and lhd cars – the latter, as seen here, on Cologne numberplates. The obsolete 225 badge is just visible under the Consul tag on the bonnet 'dome'.**

the structure – which Don Ward would later say was to 'eliminate the unwanted passenger'. The aims were to drive down the cost of both manufacture and purchase, and help performance. "There were box members, side rails, and a complicated box section, and I think even young people, who were beginning to study engineering a bit more, began to question why you'd got all these bits," Roberts recalls. "And of course, constructing that reverse backlight was a complicated piece of design work."

Roberts was working in a completely new way for Ford – working theoretically. Established Ford practice was to stretch a part or an assembly until it broke, whether on a test bed, on rough sections of track at Boreham, or on a stretch of Kenyan road. He brought his training into play to work out on paper what stress a structure would withstand, an innovation which was essential to the speed of the programme. The calculations were carried out on hundreds of sheets of paper, using a manual calculator. Familiar with the established

gravitational or 'g' movements an aircraft is subject to in certain manoeuvres, he admits that he had to make an educated guess about which loads would be fed into the new car's fully laden structure in the most realistic situation: a heavy landing after taking off over a bump. He cautiously factored in a 4g vertical stress for the Cortina, whereas the helicopter he worked on was stressed for 2g for areas of the underbody and suspension mounts. Durability was the aim, not crash-testing, which was not required at that time.

Any part in the Cortina's structure which didn't earn its keep was potentially ripe for elimination. The inside of a Ford bonnet conventionally had a pressed inner reinforcement in a cruciform shape and this was replaced by a couple of thin pressings down each side. Roberts also did a lot of work on the door frame where the hinges were hung, which had become over-reinforced because it was believed all the loads of the door had to be taken by the mounting plate whereas they could be distributed around the latch as well. A notable Cortina 'first' was to make the top part of the fuel tank double as a section of the boot floor. The biggest part eliminated was a reinforcement behind the rear bumper which did nothing at all.

"All the books mention 150lb of steel, but what is 150lb of steel? If you take a normal panel, that's the equivalent of about four roof panels. We were constantly checking the weight of the vehicle. We started with the estimate of all the bits, because we started with an idea of what we wanted to do, but I don't believe we said 'Oh, we've got to find another 10lb here.' I just worked on the assumption that I was taking out all the redundant structure that I felt wasn't doing any good. The fact that it came out at 150lb under didn't mean there was a score sheet running along." But the potential manufacturing savings were immense. With the volumes of Cortinas built, the company could save 70 to 75 tonnes of steel a day.

Much of Roberts's design work was subtle. Below the boot floor he calculated that a rear sidemember which also would support a rear spring mounting could be 2.3in deep rather than 3in deep and when his manager and supervisor complained to Don Ward that this would mean adding another bracket he suggested instead making the boot floor longer to compensate for the shallower sidemember. He also argued that if the front wing were to be welded to the front apron it could form part of the structure – although this made life harder for accident repairs. Additionally he reduced the number of spot-welds required, after persuading one of Ford's laboratories to conduct a buckling test to determine the right place for the welds.

There was also a potential read-across from the Cardinal, which had similarly controlled weight. The Falcon had introduced body design which cut weight and cost and this filtered down to the Cardinal. Three body engineers from Briggs under Don Ward were placed in America watching what was happening on the Cardinal project and shipping drawings back to England as they came off the board. So when Roberts and his colleagues in the advanced structures department had the Cortina drawn onto their surface plates (heavy steel plates on which the dimensions of a component or a completed bodyshell could be checked), the plates next to them had the Cardinal details on them.

As a junior employee, Roberts had little idea that such a lot was riding on this new lightweight structure in terms of Cortina profitability or indeed Don Ward's reputation, so he was not present at the first durability test of the two-door Cortina, 1,000 miles of continuous driving on the simulated

pavé and washboard circuit at Boreham. There was a general feeling in body engineering that judgement day had arrived and probably a few who wished to see the work of this upstart fail. In fact the car completed the required mileage without any failure and it was decided to extend the test to 2,000 miles before the hard-pressed drivers were given a rest. Roberts only found this out after the event.

ABOVE AND TOP Early Cortinas had a bare painted dashboard and strip speedometer. Bright metal trim and duotone door panels denote a de Luxe. If a bench front seat was specified, it was a six seater. (John Colley/Magic Car Pics)

At launch Ford claimed that prototype and pre-production models had been run over 20,000 miles of Belgian pavé, 16,000 miles in the Eifel mountains and 20,000 miles of continual running over salt-laden tracks in America and in cold-weather tests at the Arctic Circle. The resulting body structure was without doubt a breakthrough in strength and weight. But was it durable enough to suit all Cortina derivatives in all markets? Accounts differ between Cortina histories and Ford personnel. Hamish Orr-Ewing says that when tested in Australia the front MacPherson struts punched their way through the upper mounting and also distorted the

Roy Brown

The chief stylist of the Cortina was Canadian Roy Brown, who had the distinction of being the first permanent member of American staff to be placed with Ford of Britain in 1959. He also carried some of the fallout from Ford's biggest flop, having styled the Edsel, an ill-judged car from a new subdivision that had been launched in 1957 with vast fanfare only to fail notoriously. "I know I did my job. I don't think I goofed up. I cried in my beer for two days," he said in 1984 when interviewed for Ford's archives. The Edsel was a blip in a very successful career but Brown remained proud of it.

To come to England at the behest of Sir Patrick Hennessy and set up a new design studio was his dream job, made all the easier by the great man himself. "He used to love styling, and come in every Friday morning and have coffee with me. He used to say 'What are we going to sell to the board of directors this week?' and would rearrange everything beforehand; a sort of friendly collusion. He had excellent taste and a very good understanding of design."

Brown's first major task was to bring order to the styling of the prototype MkIII Zephyr/Zodiac, which was running 18 months behind schedule. Initial studies had been rejected as 'too American' and Italian styling house Frua had been asked to produce a further version which was still found wanting. Brown was given two weeks to re-interpret the car and with only 30 staff at the time he resorted to roping in anybody, including dental technicians, to help fashion the clay.

In comparison, the Archbishop/Cortina project was a straightforward exercise, even though under tight time constraints. Brown never expanded much on the inspirations except to say how much he enjoyed the task. "We really started from scratch. It was an ideal situation because by that time I knew all the engineers, they knew me and we respected each other."

Brown's tenure in England only lasted until March 1964, after he had fallen out with managing director Allen Barke. "He talked down to the whole idea of being a stylist. I used to say 'Allen, we're not all sissy guys, there is such a thing as doing things with taste.' And he says 'What, are you trying to tell me I'm North Country?' It wasn't long before he was knocking me to other members of the board."

ABOVE Roy Brown in 1989, pictured in retirement in Florida. He fondly remembered his spell in England. (LAT)

After having prepared a showing of five mock-ups for the Zodiac MkIV, the visiting Americans chose Brown's favoured version, which Barke didn't like and declared he wasn't going to be dictated to by the Americans. Brown was given two weeks to get back to Dearborn. Also, according to Charles Thompson, the same management had not taken kindly to Brown being filmed for a BBC feature on the Corsair explaining the side shape as the male thrusting form and the curves on the side as the female form. Roy Brown returned to the design centre to be executive designer at Lincoln-Mercury and then at the Ford interior studio before retiring in 1975.

bodyshell. He says that a tougher body was required for the Australian market and a young engineer from Ford Geelong came over to England to make sure their vehicle was structurally strong enough.

It has been unclear whether these modifications were built into one single-specification Cortina bodyshell or an alternative 'heavy-duty' shell. Author Jonathan Wood, who produced one of the first histories of the Cortina, states that a second heavier bodyshell was designed for countries such as Australia, and used as the basis of the later GT. However, Graham Robson has also written that the bodies of early GTs would crease in competition use and that as a result the Special Order Vehicle Department made a series of cars available with 'export specification' floorpans.

Certainly, a logical improvement for the hand-built motorsport Cortinas was stronger welding/plating around the MacPherson strut mounts, while the rally workshop at Boreham would also undertake extra seam welding. David Garrett, supervisor of the Light Car Development section on the Cortina programme, confirmed to the author that there was no heavy-duty shell as such, the export specification essentially comprising nothing more than stiffer springs.

Terence Beckett recalls a modification which affected all Cortinas, one which came only nine months before production was due to begin – thus a major upset to the programme – but concentrated on the rear of the car: "We quickly found that it wasn't strong enough in the rear fender area, for these outback roads of theirs, and we introduced some late engineering changes. It was a tremendous risk on a very tight programme but we decided that rather than make a special job for Australia we would put these changes into all the cars." The rear end modification was thus applied to all Cortina shells.

In its production form the kerb weight (unladen but with fuel for 50 miles) of the standard 1200 Cortina two-door saloon was 15.5cwt and as tested by car magazines the kerb weight of the four-door Morris 1100 was 16.2cwt. When compared against the larger-engined Hillman Minx's 19.9cwt the Cortina looked still more svelte, and embarrassed the 18.4cwt Ford Classic. It was still marginally heavier than the Renault R8 and the Volkswagen, but these offered less luggage space. The kerb weight of a Taunus 12M was 16.5cwt without fuel, which blunted its performance in comparison to the Cortina.

LEFT One of two early Cortinas built at the Port Elizabeth plant is shown to South African dealers in 1962. (Ian Goddard/Bobby Keartland)

Styling: no frills

While the body structure progressed at breakneck speed, so did the outer skin of the Cortina. Eight pages of styling objectives covered aspects such as visibility, access and package, a crucial part of which was to be the 21cu ft boot capacity, claimed to be three times the average small-car capacity. In fact, at a nominal 20.9cu ft it rivalled the Hillman Minx and Vauxhall Victor in the class above.

BELOW A left-hand-drive Cortina de Luxe makes its way along the Dagenham production line in 1962. The bright grille was common to the de Luxe and Super models. Even at the Cortina's September launch, 650 cars a day were coming off the lines.

RIGHT AND BELOW
March 1963 and Ford fleet sales manager Gerry Thomas presents some of the 300 base Cortinas ordered by Welbeck Motors (Minicabs). Welbeck had triggered all-out war with London's black-cab drivers, trying to break their monopoly with a fleet of Renault Dauphines you could only book in advance. With its big boot and low costs the Cortina was an even better prospect. A similar theme formed the plot of the film *Carry on Cabby* out that June (pictured). Filmed with the loan of Ford press-fleet cars, it offered the saucy prospect of pretty girls driving cabs. (Adder Productions/ The Kobal Collection/Albert Clarke)

So persuasive was the big-boot argument that the US Cardinal team increased their luggage capacity, allegedly much to the ire of Lee Iacocca. Interior space was to be a key selling point.

The Cortina needed clean, functional styling with no expensive add-ons or quirks. Thus the reverse-slope window did not transfer from the Anglia and Classic as it was more expensive to build and left owners without a parcel shelf.

When styling began in spring 1960, Roy Brown, Ford of Britain's newly arrived head of styling, had little room to experiment. He had a team of one, Briggs-then-Ford designer Charles Thompson, who remembers the project vividly. "It was really a rush job. Roy Brown started off everything, and literally I just went round adding my ideas, cleaning things up and moving things around. There wasn't anybody else involved. It had to be done tomorrow. Roy was the chief and I was like his second hand. There was nothing unique about the aesthetics really, it was purely filling in the lines between the dots."

If there were influences that could be picked out in the Cortina's shape they would perhaps be from the Cardinal and the Falcon, the press soon observing that it was hard to tell Cortina and Taunus 12M apart. The tail was originally designed with arrowhead-shaped horizontal rear light clusters, very similar to those on Roy Brown's first Edsel series. At the front Charles Thompson lays credit to the grille but he recalls that one of the few 'ornaments', the slight bonnet bulge which at first carried a Consul nameplate, was a Roy Brown touch. "It's a nice little feature. The 'in' thing in those days was fake intakes, fake outlets. If you asked what drove the stylists it wasn't so much copying other cars but copying aviation. It probably started off as an intake but we ended up putting a badge on it."

Roy Brown was also responsible for the Cortina's side flute running from front to back, which all agreed helped to increase the apparent length of the body, making the car look as though it were moving even when it was still, breaking up the mass of body below the large window area, and finally adding rigidity to the panel.

Sir Patrick Hennessy was a regular visitor to the styling studios and Thompson recalls him adding his own influence to the styling. "I was working on a clay model of the Cortina, in the early days, and Sir Pat came up to me, pulled out an envelope with a sketch on it and said 'The Cardinal's got a roof line like that', and that's how the rear pillar of the two door turned out – narrow at the bottom and wide at the top."

The biggest styling headache was of course the late change in tail light design. Even though the two-door Cortina clay was signed off in November 1960, in January 1961 John Bugas decreed that the Cortina should adopt round tail lights in the style of those on the current Ford US range. With tooling for the rear panel already under way, this was a significant challenge. It worked surprisingly well in the end, even given that the boot aperture and boot lid shapes could not be altered and thus still followed the line of the original lights.

Charles Thompson mocked up the new tail lamp design in clay and wood. The Y-shaped segments soon became a signature for the car and were likened both to the symbol for the British 'Ban the Bomb' movement, the Campaign for Nuclear Disarmament, and to an inverted Mercedes-Benz logo; it has been said that Mercedes threatened legal action. Thompson's inspiration was in fact purely functional: dividing a circle up into three segments for stop, indicator and reflector lights. He was most concerned that while away from work his first mock-up had been turned into a cheap aluminium casting which he felt meant all the crispness in the shape of the blades was lost.

The Cortina launch build-up

In early 1961, some 18 months before launch, Ford's sophisticated marketing department swung into gear, and coupled to its own research it hired the London Press Exchange to place its advertising. Shortly after, British motor-industry author Graham Turner used the Cortina launch as an example of the state-of-the-art way car makers did business in the 1960s.

Aside from its impact on the competition, there was internal concern that the Cortina would cannibalise Anglia and Classic sales and Ford conducted its own research where representative buyers were shown pictures of the new model and its specification, without revealing who made the car. In all, 40 per cent of the Anglia owners said they would buy the new model next time and 32 per cent of those who owned a Classic said they would. Some Anglia owners, however, thought the Cortina was too large and some didn't like the absence of a reverse-slope rear window. The good news was that 60 per cent said that they would buy it.

But what to call the newcomer? Sir Patrick was particularly attached to the Consul prefix for all medium-sized Fords. The Prefect name was also possible. The first settled name was Consul 225 for the 1,200cc car and Consul 255 for the later 1,500cc model. The final decision was not made until early 1962 and was Terence Beckett's doing.

The Capri coupé of course had a chic Italian-island name and at the time Ford (if not the British population as a whole) was looking forward to joining the Common Market. Beckett also says the one thing the international dealers didn't want was another English name, they being none too keen on Consul. The problem was finding a name that wasn't already owned by somebody else, not least a car maker, and there was quite an industry in registering names so as to extract large sums of money from potential users. A place name had the edge because, according to Beckett, "nobody can really get a corner on a geographical name".

Hennessy apparently liked 'Caprino', which has long been reported as meaning 'goat dung' although if you look it up you'll find it's an Italian cheese. Other histories also report that the Cortina d'Ampezzo winter Olympics of 1960 were an influence, whereas they had actually taken place in 1956 and the 1960 winter games were held in America. But the Cortina games had been notable for being widely televised and the town was a fashionable ski resort, so the name had perhaps already permeated the public imagination. The package holiday was beginning to emerge and European travel no longer seemed the preserve of the rich.

12M, the German orphan

Within weeks of the 'Cardinal A' being cancelled, the American production line was shipped from Louisville to Cologne and the cuckoo was kicked out of the nest, its styling now completely out of kilter with the admired Consul-sized Taunus 17M. A lot more was resting on the success of the new 12M (initially confined to a 1.2-litre capacity for tax reasons) because Ford of Germany had no Anglia-sized equivalent competing below it in the 1,000cc class.

Matthias Horne was a technician working in vehicle development at Ford Cologne when the Cardinal was dumped on their doorstep, having been 90 per cent US-engineered and still full of bugs. "The handling of the car as delivered from Detroit was adventurous," he recalls. "The front-wheel-drive design was too advanced and it had many disadvantages. One of them was the permanent change of the front suspension geometry after over-exuberant cornering or after hitting a kerb or similar obstacle. To overcome this a new front crossmember had to be designed and implemented before Job One. This was mounted on the powertrain and reduced the distortion of the whole 'Pony Pac' to borderline acceptable."

The counter-rotating balancer shaft fitted to smooth out vibration was not entirely successful; *Auto Motor und Sport*

magazine said the 12M possessed a mixture of primitiveness and comfort unlike any other car. To prove the engine's worth, in October 1963 a standard 12M covered 356,430km – claimed to be 15 years of average driving non-stop – at the French Miramas circuit, setting 145 new world records for performance and reliability.

Nonetheless, constant small fixes were introduced until in 1965 the lower suspension arms were attached to a subframe instead of the gearbox, a change accompanied by the fitment of front disc brakes. There were also major engine modifications, not least a move to a 'closed deck' block design. Previously the cylinder walls were not closed but 'open deck' to facilitate casting, and this had led to head gasket failures.

Derivatives almost exactly matched the introduction of new Cortinas. The sporty 1.5-litre 55bhp Taunus 12M TS arrived in January 1963, an estate in March. In September an elegant coupé became the range-topper, unique only above the waistline and so a cost-effective derivative.

Despite its traumatic debut, the Taunus 12M P4 (to give it its full internal identification) became as much a part of the German family-car landscape as the Cortina, although it did not match

LEFT, ABOVE AND BELOW Ford Taunus 12M body styles largely matched the Cortina. The estate, or Turnier, was only a three-door but the range did boast a coupé. (Ford-Werke GmbH)

ABOVE Looking nothing like the 12M, the 'bathtub' Taunus 17M of 1960 was considered the height of modernity and its indicators and upswept bumper featured on successive models. (Ford-Werke GmbH)

BELOW The compact 12M powerpack was used by American Ford engineers to power the mid-engined Mustang 1 prototype of 1962. Despite successful appearances at races, it lent only its name to the final production car, seen behind. (Author)

its export success. By 1966 and the arrival of the new Taunus P6 its sales had totalled around 680,000 whereas the Cortina had run to over a million in the same period.

In contrast to its baby brother, the larger Taunus 17M P3 of 1960 was rather more admired for its looks. The oval headlamps were a 'first' and the radical modern rounded styling earned it the name of *Badewanne*, or bathtub, and contributed to a

claimed 0.40 drag coefficient. The P3 was imported into the UK by Ford's West London Lincoln Cars outlet. Magazine *The Autocar* tested the 17M in 1962 and admired its smooth styling and light weight; but designed for the autobahns of Germany, it remained an expensive curiosity in the UK. In 1963 a two-door 17M saloon would set you back £1,121 – more than a Zodiac, or the price of a Lotus-Cortina with change to spare.

Engines out of the box

From the outset the Cortina was to use the virtually new Anglia/Classic driveline – axle gearbox and engine – for the Cortina. It was that or nothing. The initial engine capacity for the Cortina was set at 1,198cc, halfway between the 105E's 997cc and the Classic's 1,340cc. As per the philosophy behind the 'Kent' family of engines, the same cylinder block was common to all three units and the only Cortina-only components were a new crankshaft (still hollow-cast, as in the Anglia) and longer connecting rods. The cylinder bore remained the same and two compression ratios were offered: 8.7:1 and 7.3:1 for lower-grade fuel, with a Solex carburettor. Net power was 48.5bhp at 4,800rpm on the higher ratio.

It was also an easily maintained engine; the sump could be withdrawn with the engine in place, and the externally mounted oil pump could also be removed without having to drain the engine oil; additionally there were generous 5,000-mile intervals between oil changes. All this was very reassuring to the private buyer doing his own maintenance and to the business user.

The four-speed gearbox was carried over from the Classic 1500 and came with a crucial selling feature for the Cortina, synchromesh on first gear, which meant drivers could move off easily from rest and didn't have to double de-clutch or

'crash' from second to first. This was one technical feature where the Cortina beat the BMC 1100 – at the price of a massive £1.25m investment.

Buyers were offered either a column gearchange when a bench front seat was fitted, or a long floor-mounted lever on cars with separate front seats. The former necessitated an antiquated umbrella-handle handbrake under the dashboard. At launch Ford explained that 96 per cent of British buyers preferred a floor change compared to 40 per cent of overseas

ABOVE While Ford bosses worried that the GT tag was pretentious, in production the Cortina GT was marked only by boot and rear-wing badges.

LEFT As a GT was never planned, a rev counter was sat atop the steering column until 1964.

OPPOSITE The Cortina estate followed the Anglia as an integrated production-line car, as opposed to the Abbott-converted Zephyr/Zodiac estates. The grille is a speaker for the optional radio.

The Red Book

The Red Book was as much a part of the Cortina MkI story as the new bodyshell or the market analysis. It was the statement of the project's objectives in terms of piece cost, investment and weight. It was the Cortina 'bible'.

The entire Cortina product programme was put together in three and a half months. There were detailed and working drawings of each of the 10,000 components, which were given cost and weight objectives. Over 200 cost estimators were said to have worked with product planning, engineering and manufacturing.

Those objectives were arrived at by a process called 'Triangulation' where Ford would fix one point, based ideally on a piece that they were already manufacturing, then fix another on a piece that was being manufactured by the competition as close as they could to the item they were intending to produce. The three sides of the Archbishop triangle were the Anglia, Hillman Minx and Volkswagen 1200.

Terence Beckett was a great advocate of this process. "We got real precision by this triangulation on what the piece cost should be because we knew what steel we'd got to put into it, we knew the specification, we knew the size and we knew the shape and from this we could derive the labour cost, the material cost, the overhead and the weight." Once the person responsible placed their signature in the Red Book as an objective having been met, that objective was their responsibility. "Before 1953 it was the managing director's fault if there was a mess. Now everybody carries his own can," said Beckett in a 1974 interview.

buyers. The operation of the column change was by cables, which enabled an easy swap between right-hand and left-hand drive. Steering was by Burman recirculating ball as on the Anglia and Classic.

Drive was taken to the Classic rear axle via a hydraulic clutch and a single-piece propshaft. Suspension was equally tried and trusted, beginning with MacPherson struts at the front, with an anti-roll bar. At the rear were conventional leaf springs – independent suspension having been toyed with but not tested. However, Ford's attention to detail had resulted in the rear springs being asymmetrically mounted, with five-twelfths of the spring forward of the axle, an arrangement calculated to minimise plunge in the propshaft sliding joint.

Unlike the BMC 1100, the Cortina started life with drum brakes front and rear. Ford put forward that these were more than adequate for a car weighing around 16cwt but it was more of a cost consideration; the eventual fitment of front disc brakes on a Cortina was to take a lot of argument between Beckett and his American masters.

Cortina heads to market

Nine months nearer launch the advertising team were taken to the new design centre at Aveley to view the car alongside the competition, and taken through the market research and given test drives at the Boreham track. Apparently by the end of the day the tagline 'Big-car motoring at small-car cost' had emerged. The launch of the Cortina was the first

overseen by Walter Hayes, recruited by Sir Patrick Hennessy from the *Sunday Dispatch* newspaper to run a new Public Affairs department. He became known as the godfather of Ford's international racing programme, rose to become vice-president of Ford of Europe, then of Ford-US and a director of Aston Martin.

Press officer Harry Calton recalls his boss bringing the company round from its fear that the Cortina was too conventional an offering. "He took the initiative and said we didn't need to apologise for the Cortina and emphasised the convenience and the size. It was sort of the first lifestyle car."

Hayes also immediately changed Ford's facility for press loan cars, which hitherto had been tardily provided by the team at Lincoln Cars who were busier trying to prepare rally cars: "We'd noticed that for the Anglia we didn't get anywhere near the publicity the Mini received. Walter Hayes appeared out of the blue and turned the whole place on its head. He asked for and was given twenty press cars."

As publicity material was commissioned, Ford had to convey two perhaps conflicting themes: upmarket yet affordable. In a break from the usual photos in front of a traditional English setting (usually half-timbered villages in Essex), studio photography was in front of exotic backdrops such as Greek ruins.

Press photography was carried out over two weeks in great secrecy in Scotland in March 1962. They were what would today be termed lifestyle photos. A husband and wife and two or three children were in most shots, which

RIGHT **An early facelift 'woody' estate poses during the December 1964 Cortina trip. By late 1965 the Di-Noc fake wood had been dropped.**

included countryside and beach scenes. In a tradition set by the Classic, a couple was also pictured sitting in the boot of their Cortina looking at a newspaper to show the vastness of the luggage accommodation.

Calton had taken quite some effort to disguise the origins of the new car, including using hired Vauxhalls and transporting the three cars (including one clay buck) in furniture vans. "The only person who found us was the local Ford dealer from Perth, whom I knew," he recalls. "He popped up one evening and said 'What are you doing here?' We showed him the car and said 'You won't be getting this until September and you haven't seen us, have you?'"

It was only towards the end of the shoots that it was realised that the cars did not feature the newly minted Cortina name anywhere on them, being badged instead as the Consul 225 and 255. Charles Thompson was asked to make a set of Cortina badges in tinfoil and was then flown up to Scotland. "I stuck the badges on and took the other ones off, only for the photographers to tell me 'You needn't have done

that you know, we could have changed that on the film. …' Still, I had a nice little three-day holiday."

The first production Cortina came off the line at Dagenham on 4 June 1962. Not only was it on schedule, it was under budget – the exact opposite of the Cardinal – at £50,000 under the £12m target. It was spot-on for weight, £1 under per unit variable cost (the manufactured cost, which was roughly £250) and slightly under on the tooling and investment costs. It was going to be a very profitable car, and Ford had already raised the initial annual production target from 150,000 to 250,000 units.

But before the public saw the new car the Cortina had to win over the international Ford family. In June 1962 Henry Ford II and the vice-presidents and regional directors worldwide convened in Paris and at the Montlhéry race circuit for an international sales conference presenting both the new Cortina and the Cardinal, now only in its German guise, the Taunus 12M. In those days before Ford of Europe, if you were the managing director you went to such conventions, appraised

BELOW The BMC 1100 range may have lacked the breadth of the Cortina offering but it soon mutated into different marques, such as this 1962 MG 1100. (BMIHT/Newspress)

the rival products, and made your decision as to which one to sell. Each territory would place orders based on how it thought the cars would be accepted in its own markets.

This approach was favoured by John Andrews, who propounded the philosophy that two 'fishing lines' would catch more than one buyer. This view was gradually eroded model by model during the 1960s, as it became evident that a shared car could look after the whole of Europe, with considerable economies of scale.

The first 20–25 cars from both production runs were assembled at Montlhéry and both Ford-Germany and Ford of Britain made their pitches. The anxiety that the conventional Cortina would compare badly with the innovative 12M was uppermost in Terence Beckett's mind. "Everybody thought that the German car was going to be the out-and-out winner and that we were coming up with a rather worn-out formula."

In a show of sportsmanship the English team were asked if they would like to 'bat first' and Beckett chose to emphasise that what mattered in this class of car was durability and cost of ownership as well as style, and that the Cortina had a proven driveline. The Germans made their presentation the next day before the circus decamped to the test track. John Andrews later confessed to Beckett that such had been the aggression of his presentation he had been up all night rewriting his for the 12M.

However, in an indication that the Americans had handed over a problem-ridden car to Cologne, the 12Ms had suffered carburation problems, affecting performance and the expected economy, and the night before the German mechanics decided to change the carburettors on their cars. On the day the Cortinas happily lapped the track while the 12Ms stalled or failed, with Ford of Germany's mechanics frantically trying to fix them. Nor were the test drivers that impressed with the front-drive handling. As an added bonus for the British side, the last-minute decision to bring along the prototype Cortina 1500GT proved to be a resounding success – with Mr Ford himself giving it approval, after a white-knuckle ride.

As far as impressing the big bosses, it even seemed as if the decision to match the Cardinal package to that of the Cortina had backfired as far as the styling was concerned: they decided the Cortina looked better.

Back in England the run-up to the 30 September public launch began with a total print-press spend of £175,000 from September to December, concentrating on British national daily papers. Costly television advertising was only to be used on the actual launch night, as it was assumed that the virtues of a car could not properly be explained in a few seconds.

The build-up to the launch to the British dealers saw Ford give its own people a Cortina training course so they could then train the dealerships. Aside from having cars ready for sale, the larger dealers were expected to have 195 Cortina-only spare parts in stock at launch. Throughout September 1962 one-day presentations were given to 800 dealer principals, two days to retail dealer managers, one to 600 big fleet owners and one to the press.

But even though there was optimism about the Cortina's prospects and profitability, the anxieties about how it would appear to the press must only have been heightened from the glowing reception afforded to the Morris 1100, which was launched in August 1962. Although the reach of car magazines was relatively limited, the influence on the trade and industry was significant. In its test of 17 August 1962 *Autocar* magazine ran an 1100 for 2,000 miles and was bowled over by its technical innovation (surmising that there was no reason why the 'superb' new Hydrolastic suspension would be any less reliable than conventional set-ups), refinement, performance and luggage capacity. Although the magazine carped over the lack of synchromesh on first gear, the sign-off was glowing. 'The staff of this journal have never before been so unanimously enthusiastic about the overall qualities of a car,' the test concluded. 'It is obvious that a farsighted and thorough engineering job has been done.'

The Cortina could easily have been regarded as having been beaten on every front before it even saw the light of day. Terence Beckett recalls trying to 'sell' the Cortina to his own dealers: "They thought that we were just introducing the same old thing again. As a matter of fact, this went right the way down through the sales force itself – they felt that. I had two great big meetings with all of the sales force and I took them through what our strengths were versus the Mini and the 1100. And it was an uphill job for a bit of time, and of course the press was similarly disaffected. They were quite convinced that we were still on the old, fuddy-duddy type of construction and it wasn't going to work."

With hindsight, the decision to present a whole different set of virtues for the Cortina was spot-on. The advertising copy was uninhibited in its promises of space, price and above all reliability. If it didn't have any new technology, the Cortina promised buyers a sure deal with a 'Brilliantly reliable 1,200cc engine, developed from famous race-and-rally winning Anglia unit' – and proclaiming that 'Only Ford could have brought Europe this kind of new small car.'

In September the British motoring press drove Cortinas from London to stately home Stanford Hall in Leicestershire, a 200-mile round trip. Harry Calton recalls being ready for the brickbats. "Certainly the engineers, Fred Hart in particular, were known to them and a number of them knew Fred well. So they always wound him up, but he was used to this and knew it was coming. Immediately it was 'Why haven't you got independent rear suspension?' and 'Why are you still on leaf springs?' Fred knew his business, he was able to put up a very good defence. Ultimately he said to them 'Well you've all driven the car today' – the Cortina was a fun car to drive."

Major magazines were of course treated to advanced loans of the car, ahead of the public launch, so that the reviews could be timed to coincide. *Autocar* devoted five pages to the newcomer on 21 September, with cutaway drawings and comparison tables with rivals. It helpfully transposed the Classic silhouette onto that of a Cortina to show it was offering the same space for less money.

England v Germany

Aside from the Classic, to a magazine with a European circulation it was a subject of fascination that the Cortina had been launched just a week after the Taunus 12M and a number of writers had just come back from sampling it in Germany. Now the Cortina was in danger of being rubbished in comparison both to the 1100 and an in-house design that looked superficially very similar. In helping ponder why no single parts of the 12M and Cortina were interchangeable, the respected Laurence Pomeroy of *The Motor* spoke to Victor Raviolo, who had arrived from Dearborn as director of engineering in 1961. His report accurately charted why the Cardinal had been expected to attract Volkswagen Beetle buyers, Ford of Germany's need of help, its own plans for a 'highly advanced' small car in 1959 and the metamorphosis into the Cardinal. Pomeroy found much to admire in the design, but was clearly not privy to its development problems. The reason given for its continuation as the 12M only was that the US small-car market was past its peak and sales would not have exceeded 500 a day over the working year. 'To sum up, the Cardinal project has been a pretty piece of international cooperation,' Pomeroy wrote. 'On the sales and production side it has, at relatively modest cost, been a first-class insurance against a possible swing in the US market.' After detailing the Cortina's development,

he concluded that the relative success of the two cars 'will interest far more than shareholders in the American Ford company'.

The British Ford team had clearly been persuasive in defence of their car. 'Unorthodoxy is not a virtue in itself and the creators of the Cortina were naturally fully aware of what was germinating elsewhere on the Ford tree,' *Autocar* commented. The preface to an exhaustive list of the Cortina's features was that 'the term conventional should not be construed to imply lack of development'. The report also featured images of the four-door promised for sale in November. Of the Cortina's styling it was observed that there had been a reversion to an orthodox rear window – 'perhaps because public reaction to the Anglia and Classic type with reversed rake has not been wholly favourable'.

In Britain it was only a battle on paper. While those who had driven the 12M in Germany generally admired its technical virtuosity and found it more stable in crosswinds than the Cortina – although some reported excessive understeer and found it slower – in the end it was no commercial threat in Britain. The 12M was a bargain in Germany, costing less than its predecessor, at around £475, while benefiting from extra equipment such as the integral heater. 'Our iniquitous taxes would render it somewhat more costly,' *Autosport* magazine concluded. Indeed the only imported German Fords continued to be the larger models.

Facing up to BMC

At launch the Cortina 1200 was listed in two-door standard form at £639 tax-paid and as a de Luxe at £666. The four-door Morris 1100 sold at £661, so prices were roughly comparable. The larger-engined but Cortina-sized Hillman Minx and Vauxhall Victor were both priced at £702, and the Austin A60 at £805. A Classic two-door looked questionable value at £723 and a Cortina 1200 also looked very tempting compared to a £615 Anglia de Luxe. The new, larger Hillman Super Minx was £805.

The Cortina was of course was built down to a price but noteworthy small details such as the zero-torque door latches – which meant doors did not need to be slammed – were dutifully reported by the press. *The Motor* called it 'unskimped detail quality'. The optional heater was obviously fitted to the test cars and praised for its ability to start warming the interior before the engine had reached full operating temperature. Ventilation came courtesy of front quarterlights and on de Luxe two-door models the rear windows were hinged.

Geoff Howard wrote one of the first Cortina road tests, having arrived at *Autocar* in August 1962 as an engineer who had changed direction into journalism. He was allocated the new Ford Consul Cortina de Luxe as his first full road test, for the 28 September issue. The beige test car arrived with the Consul bonnet badge taped over and the F-O-R-D letters sitting in the glove box instead of on the boot lid. He drove it to South Wales from London for the weekend, attracting attention everywhere he took it. Howard joined rival magazine *The Motor* in praising the slick and light gearchange (even with a column change), the ride comfort, and passenger and luggage space. However, he advised readers that the test car's bench seat should be avoided as it felt like 'sitting on an over-inflated air cushion' and also observed that it was

short-sighted not to have included front disc brakes in the specification. At the test track the Ford recorded a top speed of 77mph and 0 to 60mph in 22.5 seconds.

Howard's road test concluded that 'for a family man who wants both space to carry all the impedimenta that seems inseparable from young children and economy of running in terms of fuel bills and reduced maintenance, the Cortina will obviously have a strong appeal. The clean and functional lines, devoid of all ostentation, emphasise the simple and orthodox engineering behind the design, and this naturally reflects in the character of the car. Its performance cannot be termed exciting, yet rather surprisingly a journey from London to the West Country was covered at an average not far short of 40mph, with a consumption approaching 35mpg.

ABOVE Rally cars in preparation at the new Boreham workshop in 1963. The mechanics are standing in the boot-floor aperture where the standard fuel tank was fitted. An auxiliary tank was added ahead of the rear axle and both were filled from behind the rear screen, the original opening being used for extra lighting.

ABOVE Three Cortinas were flown to America to compete in the 1963 12-hour Marlboro endurance race. The key purpose was to beat the Volvos, and the Fords proved ideally suited to the small circuit of 1.7 miles with its 11 tight turns.

This in itself serves as an epitome of the efficiency which has been achieved.'

On 21 September 1962, the public launch day, Ford ensured that there were plenty of cars in stock for sale: it had produced 18,000 cars *before* announcement, in contrast to BMC's practice, and some of the big main dealers threw cocktail parties to welcome the Cortina or paraded them around the streets on trucks. It was party time in London too, where Cortinas were wheeled into Ford's Regent Street showroom the night before, to be unveiled the next day against a photographic background of the Italian town

(claimed to be the largest colour print in the country), where Mayor Amedo Angeli had already been given the keys to his own new car in a jamboree where the tourism officials apparently hoped the fanfare for the new Ford would boost visitor numbers.

Ford's preparation and planning also gave the Cortina a simple and compelling advantage over the 1100. You could walk into a dealer and buy one. Harry Calton says Ford had learnt lessons from 1959. "When the Anglia was launched there was a six-month or seven-month wait and the dealer would only have one car in the showroom. With the Cortina all the main British dealers had about 15 or 20 cars, and this was unheard of. You could go into the showroom, look at a car, and say 'I want that one.' Dealers knew that they were going to get another batch of similar cars in another couple of weeks. When the Morris 1100 was launched I don't think any appeared for about three months."

At the end of September, Ford claimed more than 3,000 Cortinas had been sold in the first three days and that export orders worth £20m were on the books thanks to cars previewed in secret by foreign dealers. Nonetheless, production was not all plain sailing. To Sir Patrick Hennessy's wrath, strike action had actually delayed the launch of the Cortina by two weeks – The Motor wrote that a similar delay was experienced in the delivery of its test car. In common with the rest of the industry at the time, Ford experienced frequent strikes and that October a nine-day unofficial strike at the Dagenham PTA resulted in a production loss of 10,000 cars.

Despite the early sales success, Ford's internal messages didn't let up, and it continued to harangue employees over the wisdom of the apparently unadventurous specification. In December 1962 Ford Bulletin crowed 'So Ford was right after all!' It quoted from a poll of 28,000 people conducted by the Observer newspaper which revealed that all the small car buyer wanted was exactly what the Cortina offered: five seats, a three-box design, rear-wheel drive and – lo and behold – a four-speed synchromesh gearbox and utter reliability. 'True it does not have disc brakes all round,' the writer grudgingly admitted (at that point the Cortina didn't have them at all), 'but it is £60 cheaper than the lowest price the majority of the readers are willing to pay for a new car.'

Faster and more versatile

Strikes notwithstanding, the two-door and four-door Cortina family started to expand in January 1963 with the 59.5bhp 1,498cc Super with the Classic engine, distinguishable by extra bright trim following the line of the side crease, a matching second colour for the roof, fitted carpets, and such interior niceties as a cigar lighter. Once more it was enthusiastically greeted by the magazines, although testers wondered why the 1200 had been launched first, as the Cortina clearly corresponded more to the size of a 1½-litre car.

A week later the Lotus Cortina also made a somewhat premature debut, but the stir it caused can only have helped the standard models along; this model is dealt with in the next chapter. A Cortina also completed a 12,000-mile endurance run from London to Cape Town in the hands of dealers Eric Jackson and Ken Chambers. Described in the press release as a standard production Cortina Super, it was rather closer to the yet-to-come GT specification and took 13 days 8 hours and 48 minutes to make the journey. Despite setbacks such as being attacked by tribesmen, 'the only attention the car needed was the fitting of a fan belt and a light bulb'.

The Cortina had already become Britain's top-selling car abroad: 40,000 of the 67,000 sold since September 1962 had been exported. It had sold twice as well as the Anglia had in its first three months. American magazine Road & Track reported that the Cortina was to be imported to the US through Lincoln-Mercury dealers, with Ford dealers invited to apply. The one-time Cardinal seemed to have already been discounted. 'Ford International has decided that the big push will be given to the new Ford (of England) Consul Cortina. The decision was made despite the fact that the Taunus 12M is now in production and the Taunus was designed (under the name Cardinal) in this country, and with special thought to the American market.'

The writers could only speculate on the reasons for the 12M being passed over, but their take was that 'early indications' showed that the Cortina was a better car, simpler in design and less expensive to produce and service. It was also surmised that other issues might be at play: 'Production facilities of a higher capacity are available for the Cortina; it is thought that the demand for the home market will keep the Taunus in short supply for at least a year.' While the magazine found its Cortina 1200 extremely spartan it did note that it had 'quite possibly the best handling of any Ford product ever'. The large boot and the gearchange quality also found favour and it concluded that 'by and large the Cortina looks very promising to us'. Nonetheless, early US Cortina sales were sluggish, settling at only around 4,000–5,000 cars a year in 1964 and 1965.

The Geneva Motor Show in March 1963 saw the arrival of 1,200cc and 1,500cc Cortina estates. Designed after the saloons, the brief was to offer more space while having a properly integrated and not overly utilitarian shape – something which couldn't quite be said of the Farnham conversions of the big MkII Fords. Illustrating how long the rear overhang of the Cortina saloon was, the wheelbase remained the same and the overall length differed by barely an inch.

The loadbay was designed to offer the maximum possible length and instead of the rear seat squab folding at 90 degrees against the back of the front seats before the rear backrest was lowered, it rotated on itself and its painted metal underside extended the loadbay area to 6ft 5½in, fulfilling the requirement that had been laid down to sleep two six-footers; the more expensive Hillman Super Minx estate could only boast 5ft 3in of load length. The only disadvantage with the Cortina design was that there was nothing to prevent loads from sliding forward and hitting the back of the front seats.

The counterbalanced one-piece tailgate opened to reveal a loadbay only modestly obstructed by the rear wheelarches and with the spare wheel and jack nestling in a bag underneath the rear seat squab. Mechanical changes over the saloon were limited to stiffer rear springs and a 4.44:1 axle ratio in place of the 4.1:1 of the standard 1200. At £683 for a de Luxe, the new model was at launch the cheapest four-door estate car on the British market, by a few pounds.

The de Luxe was available in a single colour or with a contrasting flash following the side flutes, while the Super was offered with a simulated wood panelling called Di-Noc, a plastic film applied to aluminium panels – and also used by Ford stylists to give a paint-like sheen to clay models. While BMC offered timber-clad Mini estates, this was altogether more American; the *Daily Mail* motoring correspondent called it the 'Hollywood look'.

Of more interest to enthusiasts, April saw the announcement of a mainstream 'fast Ford' in the form of the 78bhp Cortina 1500GT. The engine had of course been seen in the Classic Capri GT, but in the Cortina's lightweight shell a 90mph top speed was in theory possible.

Although announced after the Lotus-Cortina (or Cortina-Lotus in Ford nomenclature), the GT had in fact been developed before it and also represented a departure from the established product-planning systems, having never been costed as part of the original Cortina project. Hamish Orr-Ewing recalls it was the brainchild of engineer Ken Teesdale – "a bloody good bloke and a man who loved motor cars" – who was then in charge of the experimental shop. "It was an extremely good piece of one-off 'let's try this' engineering. I think tacitly Ken had the closed eyes of several of the executive engineers, including Fred Hart."

Behind the GT was the old anxiety that the standard Cortina wasn't going to be enough in itself to stir thoughts about performance derivatives. However, by 1962 it was obvious that the 'Kent' engine could give a lot more power. The 997cc version was already established as the standard Formula Junior racing engine because of its 'unburstable' strength and ability to rev, and tuned by Cosworth it was

giving 75bhp, nearly double its output in a standard Anglia.

David Garrett and his colleague and racing partner Brian Peacock were given an old Cortina prototype for three months from March 1962 and more or less a free hand. Garrett remembers that they were pleased when Ford asked Colin Chapman to come and sample the car. He flew into Boreham and tried it out after pumping the tyres up to some 'terribly high pressure' and Garrett suggests these impressions fed into the later Lotus-Cortina.

For powering the GT, it was logical that an early 1,498cc engine be sent to Cosworth, which had been formed in 1958 by former Lotus engineer Keith Duckworth and Mike Costin, who remained with Colin Chapman's company until autumn 1962 as technical director. Duckworth had originally planned his own car based on the 105E Anglia but with a lack of funds had settled on engine building.

The job would cover familiar ground as Lotus had already offered a Cosworth-developed version of the Classic's 1,340cc engine in the Lotus Super Seven. Duckworth had opted for twin Weber 40DCOE carburettors, hitherto used by the likes of Ferrari, and increased the diameter of the inlet valves, boosted the compression ratio to 9.5:1 and fitted a new camshaft. The work for the Capri and Cortina GT followed this specification almost exactly, but with a single Weber carburettor and the requirement that it should be reliable and easy enough to be adopted by the Ford production system. Keith Duckworth sold the design of the high-lift camshaft to Ford for £750. "My input into the GT was minimal," Mike Costin recalls. "Keith designed the camshaft for it, and they paid us for that and talked them into fitting, for the first time ever, a Weber carburettor – a twin-choke downdraught carburettor. That was all we did to the GT."

The Cortina 1500GT's 9.0:1 compression ratio was slightly higher than that of the 1500 and power increased from 59.5bhp to 78bhp. For added durability the engine had stronger pistons and copper-lead shells, while the clutch was uprated and the propshaft diameter increased. The suspension was stiffened and for the first time a Cortina had front disc brakes – 9½in Girling units – while the drums at the rear were the slightly larger units (9in rather than 8in) of the standard 1500/Classic.

The Cortina GT was a very understated car. Inside, a hooded rev-counter sat atop the skinny steering column, and an ammeter and oil-pressure gauge were housed in a console ahead of the shorter remote-control gear lever, but otherwise the interior was standard Cortina de Luxe. A small

‘GT’ badge was placed at each rear wing corner. The new model was greeted with enthusiasm, although *Motor Sport* reflected an anxiety within Ford that it was a little pretentious for the Gran Turismo label to be used on a family saloon. However, the magazine soon came to like the peppy engine and snappy gearchange. Additionally, there were worthwhile improvements an enthusiast could add, such as an ‘uprated second gear kit’ as used on competition cars, which raised the maximum speed in second gear from 42mph to 50mph, plus wider 4½J wheels.

The GT came in two-door and four-door versions and according to records held by the MkI Cortina Owners Club just one MkI GT estate car was released from Dagenham as

a spare car surplus to a 25-strong order for the Nairobi police force, on the proviso the owner didn't put a GT badge on it. The GT proved to be very popular, its sporting allure being boosted by its being faster than the MG 1100 and cheaper than the Vauxhall VX 4/90.

Although for plenty of motorists the first Cortina GT was fast enough and a Lotus-Cortina the ultimate dream, a market emerged for specialist performance conversions of the GT – although if pushed too far you could end up spending the same amount as would buy the Lotus. When the Cortina was facelifted for the 1965 model-year Super Speed offered the 90bhp GTS conversion for £120 over a standard GT, for which price the car received detail work

ABOVE **Exhibited at an American trade show in 1964, the Cortina was the biggest hope of the 'English Ford Line' which at the time included the Anglia-based Thames van and the Consul Capri. (© Ford Motor Co. Courtesy FordImages.com)**

Saxon: the missing link?

In 1962 Sir Patrick Hennessy instigated a two-door coupé styling exercise based on the Cortina. An often-reproduced colour photo of it (below) shows a Cortina-based rear deck and lights but seemingly new frontal bodywork and a unique hardtop design with echoes of the Thunderbird. Its status as a dummy styling model trying out different approaches has been reinforced by the asymmetrical window/pillar treatment (the passenger side has an extra pane). It was reported as being sent to Dearborn for evaluation, never to return.

For many years it has been assumed that the Saxon was a non-runner, but a series of black-and-white photos unearthed in 2010 tell a different story. Believed to have been taken at Aveley in 1962, the images show a functional car fitted with engine, transmission, suspension and fully trimmed interior. The hardtop

matches on both sides and a photo of its base structure shows a cruciform-braced floorpan. As well as a longer exhaust pipe than that visible in the colour image, the car also bears a standard British registration plate of the time.

Several engineers interviewed for this book recall seeing the Saxon as a running car – and one which Aveley would have had no difficulty building. Cortina body engineer Dennis Roberts throws some light: "To the best of my knowledge the Saxon concept car was built in the prototype build area and would have been a combination of some production parts, some fabricated parts and some fibreglass. The durability of the unit-construction Saxon body was never tested but its stiffness would have been more than a match for a similar vehicle with a conventional chassis frame."

ALL IMAGES For a long time the colour image here was believed to show the Cortina Saxon coupé as nothing more than a dummy styling study, an impression reinforced by a differing window treatment each side. However, these previously unseen black-and-white images taken at Aveley in 1962 clearly show a working car (note the engine bay with its Cortina scuttle panel), with a functional interior, matching side windows and a road-legal registration. It is close to Charles Thompson's sketch of a 'sporty Cortina'. (Ford/ Dennis Roberts)

on the cylinder head, carburettor and suspension, plus a higher-ratio second gear. West London Ford dealer and Cortina race-team operator John Willment Automobiles also offered the 92bhp Willment Cortina Sprint GT with a similar bundle of modifications.

A new approach to motorsport

Between 1962 and 1965 the Ford empire's motorsport reputation went from zero to hero and the Cortina played no small part in it. From 1963 to 1965 there was usually a Cortina, either GT or Lotus, winning on track, rally stage or safari somewhere in the world.

Lee Iacocca had come to the conclusion that the new generation of post-war 'baby boomers' was not going to buy a Ford just because their parents had. Ford had an image problem – and to counter this it was time to become a company known for performance cars.

Part of the solution was the Ford Mustang, the other was for Ford to spend its way to the front of the grid in grand prix racing and also to win at Le Mans. In 1962 Colin

ABOVE The 1964 East African Safari winner rests with its laurels at Hughes of Nairobi, one of many branches across East Africa, all the better to provide rally support.

LEFT The publicity value of a win in the East African Safari was healthy sales in a territory where toughness was everything. KHS 600, the Cortina GT of Peter Hughes and Bill Young, went on to win the 1964 event. Only 400 of its 3,000 miles were on tarmac. (Author's collection)

The Crayford Cortina MkI

Despite Sir Patrick Hennessy having a particular fondness for them, Ford of Britain abandoned soft-tops with the demise of the Carbodies-produced Consul and Zephyr/Zodiac convertibles in 1962. If you wanted a four-seat convertible from a mainstream British manufacturer the choice was thus reduced to the Triumph Herald/Vitesse, the Morris Minor or the Hillman Super Minx – and the latter was dropped in 1964.

Established in 1962 by David McMullan and Jeffrey Smith, to make soft-top Minis, by 1964 Crayford Engineering had become successful enough to have 15 approved UK agents and to have secured overseas manufacture under licence in Australia. In 1966 it scooped a rather nice order for 57 convertible Wolseley Hornets which soup-maker Heinz offered as prizes, prompting a move to a new factory at Westerham, Kent.

Crayford saw the gap Ford had vacated and in summer 1964 announced an aftermarket conversion of the Cortina two-door. There were two choices of conversion, at £180 or £220, so you could, in theory, be on the road in a standard 1200 convertible for £762, compared to £643 for a Triumph Herald 1200. Reinforcing plates were added to the sides of the front footwells, sills and rear three-quarter panels.

The Crayford Cortina MkI was a modest success. Around 52 are said to have been made based on standard cars (the existence of any MkI Lotus-Cortina conversions is doubtful) and 30 went to Bermuda as hotel shuttles. The Crayford Convertible Car Club has 17 survivors on its books. The conversions to the Corsair and MkII Cortina proved to be a lot more popular.

LEFT Crayford Engineering (which became Crayford Auto Developments) offered a Cortina conversion from the beginning of 1964. In 1965 it added £180 or £220 to the cost of the car. Around 52 MkIs are said to have been made and 30 went to Bermuda as hotel shuttles.

Chapman's Team Lotus was approached for input into a new state-of-the-art car to shake up the Indianapolis 500; together with star driver Jim Clark, Lotus soon became synonymous with Ford.

In England Sir Patrick Hennessy also admired Chapman's talents. Ford of Britain had fretted over the idea of a two-seater sports car, especially for North America, where BMC with its range of MGs and Austin-Healeys had carved out for itself a very healthy market. Ford had got near to building a Lotus sports car (as detailed in the next chapter), but got cold feet. The 105E Anglia had been making some headway in saloon-car racing and had also gained respectable wins in safari rallying, but the larger Cortina was the car chosen to take up the performance baton in saloon car racing and rallying.

The GT on the track

While the Cortina 1200 wasn't seen as a race car, the 1500 Super was an obvious contender. English driver Jimmy Blumer raced a Super with a twin-choke Weber carburettor before the GT was announced and with Lotus-Cortina assembly at a trickle, the Cortina GT was pressed into immediate service as a 'works' competition car.

Southern England Ford dealer John Willment Automobiles formed a racing team, comprised of Cortina GTs and an exotic Ford Galaxie built to American NASCAR racing specifications. Well known British racing driver Jack Sears was asked to join the Willment team to drive both the Cortina and Galaxie, by new manager Jeff Uren, a touring-car driver later well-known for his V6 Cortina conversions.

Meanwhile, former Ford racer and manager Alan Mann approached Ford of Britain competitions manager Syd Henson with the suggestion he operate a works team. "We were supposed to get Lotus Cortinas," he recalls. "But they were a year late. So Syd said 'Take a Cortina GT and do what you can' and they were quite successful. It was very good, reliable, easy to drive. No big crisis." As well as Willment, Mann ran Cortina GTs with Jimmy Blumer and Henry Taylor in 1963, for the Alan Andrews dealership.

Newly homologated, the Cortina GT made its debut on 6 April 1963 at Oulton Park in the British Saloon Car Championship, and Jack Sears won his class against cars such as the Riley One-point-Five and Sunbeam Rapier. In fact that season Sears won his class every time he raced a Cortina, and won the championship overall in both Cortinas and Galaxie, while other Willment drivers were also often highly placed in Cortinas. Sears was without doubt a star

driver – although perhaps he was also helped by the fact that for most of 1963 the Cortina GT had the field to itself. This was temporary, as BMC had realised that it needed to up its game and pushed forward with larger-engined Mini Coopers, culminating in the March 1964 introduction of the 75bhp 1,275cc Cooper S.

"The crucial thing was that the opposition was a bit tame initially, with things like the Vauxhall VX4/90," Harry Calton recalls. "But the GT never got anywhere near the 1,275cc Mini Cooper S. That always won. We didn't get anywhere near that car until the Lotus-Cortina arrived."

In August 1963 the Willment and Alan Mann teams took three Cortina GTs to America's prestigious Marlboro 12-hour endurance race where they finished first, second and tenth overall and also scooped several other team awards – despite fuel vaporisation in the heat, the throttle linkage in the winning car of Jack Sears coming apart five times, and being hit by an errant Chevrolet Corvair. This introduced Alan Mann to Jack Holman, of Holman Moody, who was developing the Shelby Cobra with Ford-US. "We were met by Holman Moody who gave us all the mechanics we could use. Only after did Holman say 'I was told to give you all the support but still take two cars down to beat you.' Very Ford! But both his cars crashed." Backed by the Ford Division of America, Alan Mann Racing was formed in 1964 and became a factory team through to 1969 with the Lotus-Cortina, the Shelby Cobra Daytona coupé, the GT40 and the Escort.

Sebring was exactly the kind of endurance racing that the Cortina needed to establish an image of reliability for export markets. Across the Pacific, similar efforts were made. In 1963 Ford of Australia managed to assemble a hundred GTs in order to enter the first Armstrong 500 (named after the damper manufacturer) at Bathurst. Pitted against formidable six-cylinder and eight-cylinder rivals, Cortinas came in first and third, helped by their light weight and disc/drum brake combination.

The MkI Cortina GT gave Ford of Britain an impressive foothold in circuit racing until the Lotus-Cortina was homologated and ready to race, which it first did in the hands of Jack Sears at Oulton Park in September 1963, picking up a class win. Sir John Whitmore also wrote, in the *Ford Book of Competition Motoring* in 1965, that long-distance racing had improved the breed. 'An example of this are the radius arms incorporated in the rear suspension of the Cortina GT [from October 1964]; these sprang directly from experience gained on the race tracks, and this is only one example.' Alan Mann, however, has a less favourable recollection of the interest from Ford production engineering:

Stirling Moss's dream?

Perhaps the rarest MkI Cortina arose from the unlikely 1963 pairing of the British Ogle Design consultancy and racing driver Stirling Moss.

Ogle had just begun producing an attractive re-bodied Mini known as the Ogle SX1000 when founder David Ogle was killed driving one in 1962. Former Ford stylist and Ogle designer Tom Karen was drafted in as managing director and chief designer. With loss-making SX1000 production set to end and major client Bush Radios about to walk, Karen was eager for a project to keep the company's name in the press, as was Ogle director and later Lotus-Cortina race driver Sir John Whitmore.

Karen recalls that Whitmore was a huge admirer of Moss, who was seeking to carve a new career following his near-fatal racing accident in 1962. "Whitmore had the bright idea that Moss might get involved with Ogle and become a designer," Karen recalls. "So very briefly this was staged and Stirling was photographed behind the drawing board and all that silly jazz, but he had enough presence to convince Ford they should let us do a special Cortina for him."

Ford director of public affairs Walter Hayes saw an opportunity to add a bit of glamour to the Cortina and a car was supplied to be converted for the October 1963 Earls Court Motor Show. Karen's team removed the rear end of the car, made a wooden structure that defined the shape and the metalwork was contracted out.

Erstwhile coachbuilders Harold Radford, which the same year launched its plush Mini conversions, painted the show car in a 'Moss' shade of metallic green and every modern gadget was thrown at the interior, from a two-speaker radio with automatic aerial to an optional television.

The 'Ford Cortina GT modified by Ogle' was billed as Mr Moss's idea of a practical yet sophisticated GT car 'to carry four people comfortably, confidently, on 500 miles a day journeys with all the luggage they would need'. The notchback 'GT' styling was intended to amplify this effect. Karen was not impressed by the press reaction to the car: "Not being frightfully sophisticated in understanding form, the thing they picked up was that we forgot to put a rear view mirror inside the car."

The car was also exhibited in America in 1964 and in an Ogle brochure replicas of the show car were optimistically offered to the market at £1,390 – when a standard four-door Cortina 1500GT was £767. Whether there were any takers at all has long been debated, but Ogle and Tom Karen went on to greater success with designs for the Reliant Scimitar GTE, the Bond Bug and the Raleigh Chopper bicycle.

LEFT, RIGHT AND ABOVE
The newly completed Ogle/Moss Cortina at Hoopers. The front grille assembly in anodised aluminium incorporates long-distance and spread-beam lamps and its rear wiper and optional Triplex heated rear window were exotic for the time. A Hobbs automatic gearbox was on the options list, as was a Webasto sun roof.

ABOVE There had long been debate as to whether any replicas of the show car were built at all, and the commonest view was just one, but around 2010 this car surfaced in the Philippines, fitted with a Lotus twin-cam engine and non-standard wheels, but otherwise authentic down to its Ogle badges. It looked remarkably sound, including the unique grille and front panel, but the sidelights differ from those of the show car. (Andy Wrightson)

RIGHT Boreham mechanic Mick Jones works on a car for the 1963 RAC Rally. Two electricians had the sole job of making the wiring looms.

"It was very difficult to get much out of them at all. On occasions odd people would help, but it was pretty much a closed shop. There was no obvious interest or enthusiasm."

Rallying gets serious

As far as top management was concerned, every Ford division was expected to play its part in the world performance drive and Europe was thought most suited to tackle the rally championships. This was something Ford of Britain had hitherto neglected. In the hands of Maurice Gatsonides a Ford Zephyr had won the Monte Carlo in 1953, but with a very limited amount of factory support. The year 1962 proved to be a particularly unsuccessful one, with 18 cars prepared for

the Monte Carlo Rally and none finishing in the first dozen.

Rally-car preparation was sandwiched between dealing with press cars and imported Fords at Lincoln Cars until Walter Hayes arrived. Former rally manager Bill Barnett recalls his first meeting with the new PR man, on his second day in the job. "He called me into his office and said 'I understand we do rallying'. So I told him quite bluntly that we were wasting our time. We had all these other teams competing and winning on a very professional basis and we were never going to win anything. We got the occasional class win and team prize but that was really all. He didn't say a lot but later it transpired that he went down to see Sir Pat and said that either we did it properly or we didn't do it at all."

ABOVE One of three
Cortina GTs entered for the
1964 Alpine Rally. Problems
with the durability of the
rear axle were overcome
thanks to a special oil
developed by Castrol.

Without doubt Hayes was an immense driver of the performance programme, as Alan Mann recalls. "He was very good to me, but you had to win. His idea was 'If you can't win, don't talk to me' – which seems pretty sensible. He didn't understand the detail but he understood winning."

Bill Barnett produced a full plan for a purpose-built competition workshop to prepare rally cars at the Boreham testing ground, for £48,000 plus an unheard-off initial staff of 25 people. The building was completed in October 1963 but even while the rally team was still operating from Lincoln Cars, the new GT was scoring highly respectable rally places throughout the year. While the Lotus-Cortina should have been the ideal choice for the new outfit, Colin Chapman's

insistence on a fragile 'A-frame' rear suspension made it too much of a risk for rough roads and the GT was once more the star car for 1963. It was also the test bed for an early try-out of the twin-cam engine in a Cortina in September's Spa–Sofia–Liège rally, driven by Henry Taylor and Brian Melia, who took the car to fourth place. At the end of 1963 Ford was awarded the RAC Manufacturers World Rally Championship.

So was the lightweight bodyshell up to the job? "The one thing that did come out under rally conditions was the front struts were punching up through the inner wing, so we welded in strengthening sections," says Harry Calton. Standard Cortina GTs would arrive at Boreham to be stripped and rebuilt as far as the regulations would allow. Mick Jones, a mechanic at the time, remembers a certain amount of seam welding. Further indicating that Boreham cars were toughened up, Cortina author Graham Robson wrote that in 1963 his shared drive in a private GT ended with creases across the roof and rear wheelarches. To establish how the cars would fare on the roughest ground they were pounded over the Ministry of Defence tank-testing ground at Bagshot in Surrey until something broke. "You could almost call it blacksmith engineering in those days," says Barnett.

With the Lotus-Cortina storming away on the racetracks of the world, Boreham-prepared GTs – and indeed some from other Ford regions such as Sweden – chalked up ever higher rally positions. New talent Vic Elford won the 1964 Alpine Rally and together with teammates Henry Taylor and David Siegle-Morris garnered the Manufacturers Team Prize in the November 1964 RAC Rally, even though their individual positions were not at the top.

The 1964 works GTs were retained, where possible, for 1965 rallies in the knowledge that the newly revised Lotus-Cortina with leaf-spring rear suspension was on the way. Nonetheless, the team picked up a Manufacturers Team Prize in the Circuit of Ireland. Roger Clark, who would later become one of Britain's most famous rally drivers, made his mark in a privately entered GT. But by mid-1965 the works MkI Cortina GT's rally career was virtually over, it having surrendered to the faster and finally durable Lotus-Cortina.

Triumph on the East African Safari

Safari rallying was the one area of motorsport where Ford of Britain had some pedigree. Zephyrs had competed in the inaugural Coronation Rally of 1953 which had expanded to become the East African Safari Rally, some 3,000 miles of mud and dust through Kenya, Tanzania and Uganda. Durability triumphed over speed and the early years were dominated by Volkswagen, with Mercedes and Peugeot close behind. BMC cars were notable by their absence.

In the hands of largely amateur drivers with a reasonable amount of factory support and much more local assistance – such as from Hughes Garages of Nairobi – Dagenham-built Fords turned in ever-improving performances, with teams of Zephyrs winning the Manufacturers team prizes from 1959 to 1962. The over-engineered build of these cars paid off and a lot was at stake when the new construction techniques of the Cortina were put to the test. The 1963 event was a false start, being so gruelling that only 7 out of 84 starters finished and no overall team won. Three Cortina GTs were in

this group and the car driven by Pat Moss and Ann Wisdom had its strength tested most when it overturned.

By 1964 the competitions department at Boreham was fully geared up to support its cars and drivers, one of whom was Englishman Mike Armstrong, who like most safari drivers was a talented amateur, normally working for East African Power and Lighting. Having driven Anglias in 1961 and 1962, Armstrong was struck by the level of support given even before the Safari began, with a man from Boreham flying out to Nairobi followed two days later by a Cortina in which he and co-driver Chris Bates drove the route, trying to exceed the averages and to settle on a choice of carburettor. "After we'd finished, no one touched the car. It was put on the plane and sent back to Boreham for inspection to see what had gone wrong," he recalls. "I couldn't tell how much money they put into it, but the fact that they sent a car out for testing would have cost a lot. I think it was very bold for Ford. We drove those cars hard at Safari speeds at Safari times and didn't let up at all."

For the actual 1964 event, held between 26 and 30 March, the local drivers and six team cars were backed up by rally manager Bill Barnett, two mechanics and a press team. Ford works drivers were John Sprinzel, Henry Taylor and Vic Elford. Cortinas were heavily represented, with eight cars entered overall, and the Lincoln-Mercury division of Ford-US also fielded nine Mercury Comets in its first rally outing.

After 3,189 miles it was undoubtedly the year of the Cortina, with Kenyans Peter Hughes (of Hughes Ford) and Bill Young coming first after only losing 63 minutes from the start, the Armstrong/Bates car in third overall, and the Vic Elford car third in class and tenth overall, with a further Cortina in 15th place. Ford Zodiacs were 5th and 13th and the Manufacturers Team Prize went to Ford. The same month a Taunus 12M won the 1,200-mile Dunlop Central African Motor Rally. Mike Armstrong drove for Ford in a Cortina GT for 1965 and came second in class to Vic Preston's car. Although rewarded by Ford in terms of expenses and hospitality, like many of his fellow Safari drivers there was no talk of going professional.

Rolling changes

Back to bread-and-butter models. By mid-1963 thousands of Cortinas were on the road and there had been plenty of opportunity for any in-service faults to emerge. As expected, the tried and trusted drivetrain and lack of complication largely paid off, but there were some issues around the gearbox.

ABOVE A full-width grille and Cortina bonnet badge denote a 'facelift' Cortina GT for 1965.

The first was a minor fault with a shriek from the synchromesh cones. While this was traced to a poorly designed mainshaft, the cure for the second issue – which also affected Zephyrs – was much more subtle. A sleeve within the gearbox bearings would become loose, start to rotate and would get to the stage where it would seize onto the bearing or the gear. "You'd get a situation where you were driving along quite happily and suddenly the gearbox would just lock solid," recalls David Garrett. The search for a solution was called the T Programme. To avoid asking a test driver to wait until the gearbox seized on him, Ken Teesdale grafted the freewheel system from a Borg-Warner automatic onto the propeller shaft of a test car to avoid this. The solution was simply to put a groove on the inside of the sleeve to improve the flow of oil.

In July 1963 the Cortina 1200's reliability was put to the test publicly by the British consumer magazine *Which?* in a comparison with rivals including the Morris 1100, the soon-to-be-obsolete Hillman Minx 1600, the Wolseley 1500, the Simca 1000 and the Renault R8. Not aimed at the enthusiast, *Which?* bought its own cars anonymously from a dealership, drove them up to 10,000 miles and then compared its experiences with a representative sample of owners. The final report would mercilessly list any faults, right from delivery (usually plentiful from most manufacturers in those days). 'The Cortina did quite well during our mileage while the Morris 1100 gave a great deal of trouble,' it reported, after having had to have a gearbox rebuilt on the Morris. The testers liked the ride, ventilation and enormous boot of its Cortina but also favoured the compact and nicely handling 1100, and so nominated the two rivals as joint best buy. Of the 92 Cortina owners who contributed, none had experienced a failed gearbox.

The comments of *Which?* and of other magazines were taken seriously by Ford. Minutes of the styling committee from January 1964 reveal that the company was looking hard at quality problems: 'Marketing Staff were to be informed of items where we do not propose to come into line with the Morris 1100, with a view to taking marketing action.' A Cortina and 1100 were to be purchased anonymously from dealers for comparison.

ABOVE Visitors to the 1964 London Motor Show were startled to find two dummy passengers in the new Aeroflow Cortina, one of whom was smoking a pipe to demonstrate the effectiveness of the new ventilation system. (LAT)

LEFT The new dashboard of the 1965 Cortina (this is a de Luxe) sported the Aeroflow vents, a glovebox and space for a radio. The bench seat option continued, as before with a column gearchange.

**RIGHT A 2-door Super
of 1965 sports optional
whitewall tyres and two-
tone paint.**

The rest of 1963 saw minor Cortina improvements such as child-proof locks and the elimination of greasing points ('sealed for life' suspension was a big deal in those days) and the October motor show saw the previously rather austere instrument panel with its cheap strip speedometer redesigned with circular instruments in a binnacle above the steering wheel, dispensing with the rev-counter pod on the GT.

A Borg-Warner Type 35 three-speed automatic gearbox became an option on the 1500 in January 1964, but it wasn't the first or ideal choice for the Cortina. Ford of Britain had signed up to take the British Hobbs Mechamatic gearbox, a complex design which differed from a conventional automatic in having hydraulically operated internal clutches rather than a torque converter. It had been designed for series production for 1,200cc to 1,500cc engines and had been adopted by Borgward. "I loved the Hobbs. I thought it was a super transmission," recalls former Ford development engineer

Howard Panton. "It was more economical and it was four-speed. It was a lovely gearbox. I did a lot of work on that. We had it on test in Belgium for 10,000 miles."

However, company politics intervened and Ford of America dictated that Borg-Warner be the supplier. A high-profile legal dispute followed which obliged Ford to continue to source some gearbox parts, including the Lotus close-ratio 'box, from Westinghouse Transmissions, makers of the Mechamatic, which found itself with several hundred spare Hobbs boxes. These eventually found their way onto privately owned Cortinas.

Come 1964, a facelift for the 1965 model year was already well in train. There was to be a new grille but it was decided to leave the tail lamps as they were. The Consul name was to be discarded in favour of Cortina. The debate over whether to spell out the name on the bonnet was resolved by placing it on the 'power dome'.

The biggest change was the adoption of face-level ventilation, which Ford dubbed 'Aeroflow'. Vents on the dashboard allowed cold air to be drawn into the car with the windows closed and aimed at the faces of the front seat passengers while the heater was providing warm air about their feet, plus demisting. The 'stale' air inside the car was extracted by the force of forward travel. Although a similar system is now an accepted part of car interiors, in 1964 it was a major innovation for Ford, although not quite the novelty that the company trumpeted: the 1923 Renault R8 offered face-level dashboard vents, as did the 1961 Triumph TR4. The ventilation system would render noisy front quarterlights redundant and would keep many a sleepy sales rep awake. Fred Hart assigned the project to Ken Teesdale, who was named in the patent application as its inventor.

It was claimed the air inside the new Cortina could be changed every forty seconds, but stale air would probably have exited without a visible vent, through gaps in the bodywork, as it did on the Anglia, which had a small flap in a hole on the floorpan by the rear seat. However, for the best marketing advantage there had to be a visible rear-pillar vent on the 1965 Cortina, contrary to the wishes of the body engineers who were concerned about noise being created right next to the ear of the rear seat passengers. Behind the vents a non-return flap valve in the low-pressure area around the pillar extracted stale air.

Charles Thompson recalls being at the Motor Industry Research Association when Aeroflow was being developed. "We were asked to help design an exit for the air so I came up with these grids. We sat in the car at 60mph with the fan on. They told me later on that we didn't need to put the grilles in because the apertures that existed in the underbody were sufficient to pull air out of the car if there was sufficient inlet force for the air to come in. But management thought

ABOVE A Cortina Super at the 1964/65 New York World's Fair is bedecked with the flags of the countries which had awarded it Car of the Year titles.

LEFT In 1965 the Cortina once more triumphed in the Australian Armstrong 500, in the guise of the GT500 special. The following year homologation rule-changes and a move towards the Ford Falcon curtailed its career.

ABOVE The 1965 Australia-only GT500 was uprated to 98bhp with a new cam and cylinder head and a modified carburettor. It was easily recognised by twin quick-release fuel fillers for the auxiliary and standard tanks. (Garry Saunderson)

LEFT Not unlike the Ogle coupé, Australian company Bodycraft of Geelong developed a Cortina fastback, removing the bodywork aft of the driver and fitting and trimming a new section with a glassfibre bootlid using Anglia 105E hinges and handle. Bodycraft had hopes of Ford of Australia producing the car but neither this nor aftermarket conversions materialised. In the end only four examples were built: two GT two-doors and two four-doors. The car pictured here is the lone 1500 automatic. (Garry Saunderson)

Aeroflow needed to be advertised, as it was a big sales feature, so putting big gaudy chrome-plated grilles on the car said 'we've got air conditioning here'."

Road testers had praised the ventilation of the original Cortina but Aeroflow was welcomed as a further innovation, gaining a safety award from Britain's Automobile Association in 1966 – by which time it featured across each newly introduced Ford car. Some testers even went on to say they would refuse to drive a car unless it had Aeroflow or an equivalent.

The second major change for the 1965 model-year was front disc brakes for the Cortina 1200. Both this and Aeroflow had to be fought hard for in Dearborn, which was very resistant to the extra costs of discs. But perhaps Terence Beckett's case was helped by Henry Ford II having driven an American Ford station wagon over the Alps and coming down the other side brake-less as the fade was so bad.

Fresh air, better brakes and eight other new features were duly introduced at the London Motor Show in October 1964. As well as new seat trims, steering wheel and revised minor controls, the biggest interior change was a third new dashboard with the Aeroflow vents and with instruments fully integrated into the same pressed metal panel. Engines and suspension were left unchanged, save for the GT which received trailing radius arms in parallel with the rear springs to relieve them of drive torque, this paving the way for a revised rear suspension on the Lotus-Cortina.

Undiminished by age

With 1964 having seen the Cortina dominate motorsport across the world and dozens of 'Car of the Year' awards from motoring magazines, sales continued undiminished right up until 1966 when a new version arrived. In April 1966 1,500 Cortinas emerged every day from Dagenham and in November, when the MkI and MkII were selling at the same time, the Cortina achieved a British market penetration of 18.7 per cent, the highest achieved by any car to that date.

European sales showed that Dagenham's salesmen could strike deals in some unexpected places that may have been inclined more towards a Taunus. It seemed somewhat random: even with foreign car imports limited, the Cortina came in third behind Skoda and Tatra in Czechoslovakia and in 1965 sales to Austria jumped 34 per cent over the previous year.

In September 1966, after three years and 351 days of production, Ford trumpeted that the millionth Cortina (a white 1500GT destined for Los Angeles) had been assembled by the morning shift. Over half of all Cortinas had been exported,

earning plaudits from British politicians for the £250m Ford had brought into the country.

Backed by an extensive advertising campaign ('Ford's Cortinas are lowest-priced total performance car'), in 1966 the Cortina became the best-selling British saloon in the United States, with 4,163 finding owners. The MkII would achieve even greater success. But had the Cortina taken the market that the aborted Cardinal was once thought to be able to fill? Far from it. In 1960 Dearborn had projected annual US Cardinal production at 150,000 a year.

And how had the first Cortina fared in the battle with the BMC 1100 range? On the UK market at least, it was the loser. Head-to-head, the 1100 was Britain's best-selling car until 1971, only during 1967 momentarily being supplanted by the MkII Cortina.

A choice of engine capacities did not give the Cortina a decisive advantage. While the MkI soon offered 1,200cc and 1,500cc models compared (until 1967) to BMC's single 1,100cc power unit, the BMC cars instead matched its price range with a plethora of badge-engineered flavours: Morris, Austin, Riley, MG, Wolseley and Vanden Plas.

Even if you added sales of the Cortina-derived Corsair to the mix, the BMC advantage remained. The Ford pair was also competing with the 1½-litre BMC 'Farina' saloons such as the Morris Oxford and Austin A60 Cambridge. In 1965 total UK sales of all Cortinas were 116,985, plus 44,463 Corsairs. This was against 157,679 1100s and 52,503 'Farina' models, plus 22,234 of the new Austin 1800. A similar differential was maintained in 1966, even as the Cortina crossed over to the MkII, but then the gap began to narrow as 'Farina' sales tailed off and the 1800 failed to make its mark.

In truth the first Cortina had created its own market, as a medium-sized car which sat in both the 'C' and 'D' sectors. It had also transformed Ford's image from fuddy-duddy to motorsport champion and fundamentally changed the way in which buyers thought about the company. With the spread of the Cortina range from standard to de Luxe, Super, GT – and Lotus at the top – plus a choice of engines in three different bodyshells, Ford was able sufficiently to differentiate between Cortinas so that the buyer who had paid for a de Luxe wouldn't look at his neighbour's basic Cortina and wonder why he'd paid more for a car which looked the same. Ford ruthlessly kept its eye on making each increment value for money yet profitable, while at the same time not resting on its laurels, working to refresh a successful formula well before it showed any signs of decline.

The Fraud Cortina

Thanks to fairly generous rules, British racing in the late 1960s saw a short-lived craze for amateur drivers putting enormous engines into humble cars. Dr D.P. Merfield – better known as 'Doc' Merfield – was an early pioneer of over-engined Anglias and built himself a 'Fraud Cortina' with a Ford 4.7-litre V8. The idea was adopted by Terry Drury whose 'Fraud' was taken over by Terry Sanger. It too had what was essentially a Ford GT40 engine allied to a Jaguar back axle, the bulkhead being moved back to shoehorn in the engine. Air intakes under the car and behind the doors ducted air to a boot-mounted radiator and a vent in the boot lid attempted to induce downforce above 50mph.

Weighing just 18cwt and putting out 330–440bhp, you had to be brave, as Terry Sanger recalls. "You had to set the thing for a corner and totally commit yourself. You couldn't stuff it into third and slow it down because it would weld the shafts together in the gearbox." His main competition at the time was twin-cam Anglias but Sanger held lap records right through 1967 and even gained his own fan club, winning himself a drive in a GT40 and touring car championships in a Falcon.

BELOW The fearsome Fraud Cortina on its first outing at Mallory Park in late 1966. The air vents at the rear were for much-needed cooling. (Terry Sanger)

Chapter 3:
The Lotus-Cortina MkI

It's the Lotus-Cortina to most people but was always the Cortina-Lotus to Ford, who might have liked a better billing. But the Cortina with the Lotus twin-cam engine did have a Lotus identification number, Type 28. In MkI Cortina production terms it was a dot on the horizon, with only around 3,300 made* in contrast to over 76,000 MkI Cortina GTs. As with the GT, the Lotus-Cortina was never part of the original plan but a late, hastily developed and inspired hunch. But in only three years the white car with the green flash gained a reputation well in excess of its presence on the roads, and achieved an almost instant classic status.

Ford and Lotus

While Ford of Britain had been pottering around the fringes of motorsport and concentrating on making money, Colin Chapman had come from home-built trials cars in 1947 to create Lotus. The little company was soon producing giant-beating and Innovative grand prix racing cars plus the fascinating Seven and innovative Elite road cars. Chapman's effect on the world of motor racing and sports cars was such that he has been credited with inventing the British Formula One industry.

Before Walter Hayes started on Ford of Britain's performance and competition plans, Chapman had already homed in on Ford management to further his ambitions. "He'd attracted the attention of Sir Patrick Hennessy as being a gifted and able man," says Hamish Orr-Ewing. "Chapman was brass-necked if ever there were one, and had no hesitation in trying to contact the Chairman of Ford UK."

The beautiful Elite, despite its groundbreaking all-glassfibre monocoque and class wins at Le Mans, had proved so troublesome in production that it had almost broken Lotus during its 1957 to 1963 production run. One of its least profitable aspects was the use of a single-overhead-cam Coventry Climax engine which was powerful but costly to maintain. From the late 1950s Chapman had been contemplating a low-cost two-seater in the same vein as the Austin-Healey Sprite, using a mainstream production power unit. Until the arrival of the 105E engine, Chapman's involvement with Ford had only been as a small-scale customer of engines for the Lotus Seven, but this new engine and its clear prospects as a solid base for racing units developed by the likes of Cosworth, was another matter.

In the late 1950s Ford had stood by and watched BMC scoop up a large chunk of the North American small sports-car market and had even entertained a proposal from its own designer Ron Hickman for an Anglia-based car. But there was considerable internal resistance to a sports two-seater. Nonetheless, Chapman was keen that Ford would manufacture what was to become the Lotus Elan – with a sheet-metal body rather than one in glassfibre – and release it through the Ford system. While this Lotus-Ford sports car never got even as far as a drawing board, Orr-Ewing was quite closely involved with discussions, when Chapman wasn't dealing directly with Hennessy. But Ford engineers were adamant that it would have to meet normal Ford standards and managed to kill off the idea through sheer inertia, although the official reason was a market downturn.

A legendary engine takes shape

However, the new Lotus sports car shaping in Chapman's mind was certainly going to have a Ford-based engine. For a while he experimented with a Consul engine equipped with Raymond Mays tuning gear but eventually he initiated work on a chain-driven twin-overhead-camshaft cylinder-head conversion to bolt onto the new racing favourite, the 105E engine block. The idea was that this would provide an engine both for the putative Elan and for Lotus racing cars. Chapman contracted Harry Mundy, a former Coventry-Climax engine designer then working as technical editor for *Autocar* magazine, to direct the design of the new light-alloy head. The Lotus twin-cam was developed by Mundy and Lotus engineers Richard Ansdale and Steve Sanville, much improved by Tony Rudd, and its production ran to some 55,000 units. Mundy would often observe that Chapman had been canny enough to pay him a flat £200 rather than a royalty.

As the 'Kent' engine expanded in capacity, Lotus twin-cam development moved with it, first to an early 1,340cc Classic 109E block in 1961, then to the much sturdier base of the five-main-bearing 116E 1,498cc engine. Bolting to the iron Ford block, the Lotus aluminium-alloy twin-cam head featured opposed valves inclined at an angle of 54 degrees and operated directly through inverted piston-type tappets. The Ford engine's con rods and pistons were retained, as was the side-mounted camshaft, fitted with a jackshaft to drive the oil and fuel pumps and the distributor. The new cams were driven by a single-stage roller chain and as the engine was now taller, a new timing cover fitted the forward face of the cylinder block.

A well-worn 40,000-mile Ford Anglia became a road going test bed for the new Lotus unit. Jim Clark recounted in 1964 that in winter 1961 Chapman once insisted he use the Anglia

LEFT **Goodwood 1964: champion driver Jim Clark (in overalls), champion racing car builder Colin Chapman (suit and tie) and a white Cortina with a green flash. The Lotus-Cortina was on its way to saloon-car racing domination.**

when he was short of a car to return to Scotland from Lotus in Cheshunt: "I remember catching up with a Jaguar and giving him the fright of his life by passing him at well over 100mph."

Already developing 103bhp at 6,000rpm, the 1,498cc Lotus-Ford twin-cam engine was first race-tested in a Lotus 23 which had already been entered in Germany's 1,000km race at Nürburgring in May 1962. In the hands of Clark the little car created a sensation by gaining a lap lead of 1 minute 47 seconds ahead of far larger-engined opposition, before the exhaust manifold loosened, the fumes intoxicating him to the extent that he eventually spun off.

The Elan was planned to be launched at the October motor show. Meanwhile, a last-minute change to FIA racing regulations extended the maximum capacity in the 1½-litre class to 1,600cc – which favoured European touring cars – so Chapman took full advantage to enlarge the Elan and

future Lotus-Cortina engine by returning to Cosworth to have the engine reworked.

"After I had left Lotus in July 1962 only a month later I was back in Colin's office on the other side of the table with Keith [Duckworth] talking about what had to be done for a race and road engine," recalls Mike Costin. "The whole project was based on the Lotus-Cortina racing, so it had to comply with Appendix C Group J regulations which stated that you could only modify the cam by starting out with a completely standard, finished camshaft."

As well as Duckworth's new camshaft design, the final version of the twin-cam enlarged Ford's standard 80.9mm cylinder bore to 82.5mm while retaining the stroke of 72.7mm, increasing total displacement to 1,558cc; later racing development took capacity to 1,593cc. The change came so late that 22 1,498cc Elans had already been

RIGHT An early cutaway of the Lotus-Ford twin-cam engine, which transformed the Cortina's racing prospects and powered a generation of Lotus sports cars.

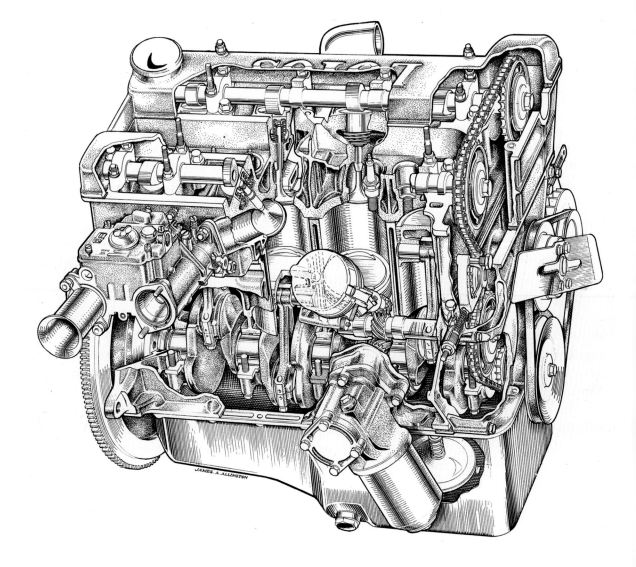

delivered and were subsequently recalled to be fitted with the new engine at no extra cost. Fitted to all Elans from May 1963, the power of the new unit was increased slightly from 100bhp to 105bhp.

Not able to support manufacture of the twin-cam engine itself, Lotus instead assembled them with specially selected blocks from Ford (not every block had enough thickness of casting to withstand the boring-out) and the twin-cam was assembled for Lotus by J.A. Prestwich of Tottenham, North London, famous for its JAP motorcycle engines.

The Consul Cortina Sports Special

While the Cortina was in development, Colin Chapman had already consolidated his association with Ford of Britain, now quite happy to tie itself to the Elan and to Britain's most successful racing team, and in late 1962 the parent company in Dearborn bravely also committed to Lotus designing the

Mk29, a race car to take to the Indianapolis 500 the following year. It was the beginning of a dazzling association for Ford: "This marriage is one of the lasting kind ... there is no question of divorce," said Hennessy in 1963.

Despite Ford's earlier cold feet over producing a sports car with Lotus, it gave the Elan full public-relations support, with an October 1962 press launch at its Regent Street showroom, where Chapman duly thanked the company for the access he had been given to production and development departments while creating the engine. "In a nut-shell we have utilised the highly successful mass-production methods of Ford, with their well-deserved reputation for reliability and precision which has enabled us to offer the car on a performance-per-pound basis that no other sports car can provide," he told the press.

Whether any one person was pivotal in the Lotus-Cortina decision is debatable. But as well as Hennessy's support

ABOVE It looks like a 1962 Cortina de Luxe, but does this photo, found deep in Ford's archive and labelled 'Lotus-Cortina going to Monte Carlo' perhaps show the first Lotus development car, which was indeed grey with a white roof?

RIGHT This somewhat lashed-up binnacle plonked under the standard Cortina strip speedometer did not survive into production. The remote gearshift and centre console also changed.

for Chapman there was great impetus from Walter Hayes, new to the job but actively building up a sporting strategy. It was probably his idea to build a minimum of 1,000 Lotus-engined Cortinas to satisfy motorsport homologation rules. These decreed that Group Two racing saloons based on a production car must have a road-going equivalent, and have very limited modifications from this 'customer' specification.

Then, according to Terence Beckett, there was also that insecurity about countering the technical innovation of the BMC 1100. "We needed something to match all this innovation – a little bit of stardust. People were astonished with Lotus's success – we all were – so Sir Patrick Hennessy and I went to see Chapman. He talked, and talked, and talked to Pat and myself about the importance of getting weight down. It was a sort of holy rite to him. What he didn't fully appreciate was that we had already, in the Cortina, got a great deal of weight out of it."

So when was the deal struck for the Lotus-Cortina? Accounts vary but it would appear that it was around the time the GT prototype was nearing completion in spring 1962. With the lines at Dagenham soon operating at full capacity, the last thing Ford wanted was to deal with a low-volume specialised model with lots of bespoke parts, so it asked Chapman if Lotus could assemble the cars from partially completed Cortina two-doors at his factory in Cheshunt, Hertfordshire. It was a dream deal for Lotus, with the Elite on its last legs and the Elan yet to go on sale, and a new building was erected for the job.

Ford factored in the Lotus-Cortina as one of the three stages of tune for the Cortina 1500: a Ford-developed 75bhp car (the eventual 78bhp GT); a 125bhp competition version (developed and managed by Lotus) and a 100bhp Lotus road car sold through Ford dealers. At the time this was an extremely adventurous departure for any British

manufacturer, let alone Ford, but it was deemed a low-risk strategy according to Hamish Orr-Ewing. "It came across a great deal of design engineering resistance because it did not go through the Ford disciplines but it was a far smaller project [than the sports car plan], and I think the resistance broke down. Because the early cars were built by Chapman, to some extent Ford engineering felt morally they could stand back and say 'Nothing to do with us' if things went wrong."

What must be the fullest account of development from the Lotus side was published in *Thoroughbred and Classic Cars* magazine in 1991 by Hugh Haskell, the engineer charged with the project by Chapman and who later moved to Ford Special Engineering. He was shown the initial drawings of the Lotus-Cortina in July 1962. Years later at Ford he found the original document authorising the venture: 'Ford has decided to dominate saloon-car racing and to this end it has retained Lotus to prepare. ...'

A grey Cortina 1200 duly arrived at Cheshunt undercover from Dagenham and was stripped down with the intention of building a twin-cam car to demonstrate to Ford directors, complete with glassfibre seats from a Lotus Eighteen racer. Lotus had no hoist so the car was rolled onto its side to fit new rear suspension only to flop onto its roof, leaving a dent which was masked by repainting it white.

The one thing at which Chapman had predictably turned up his nose was the Cortina's simple live axle and leaf springs, when all his race and sports cars had fully independent rear suspension. He was convinced that the standard system would result in axle tramp and poor traction when much more power was fed through to it.

But on this principle Ford was not going to budge, as US magazine *Sports Car Graphic* pointed out in its launch coverage: 'Chapman tried really hard to get the Ford chiefs to agree to an independent rear suspension, but in view of the

ABOVE The sole 'production' Lotus-Cortina was shown to the press at London's Dorchester hotel in January 1963. "It came about because of obvious public demand and already we are a little embarrassed by scores of orders from overseas markets," said managing director Allen Barke.

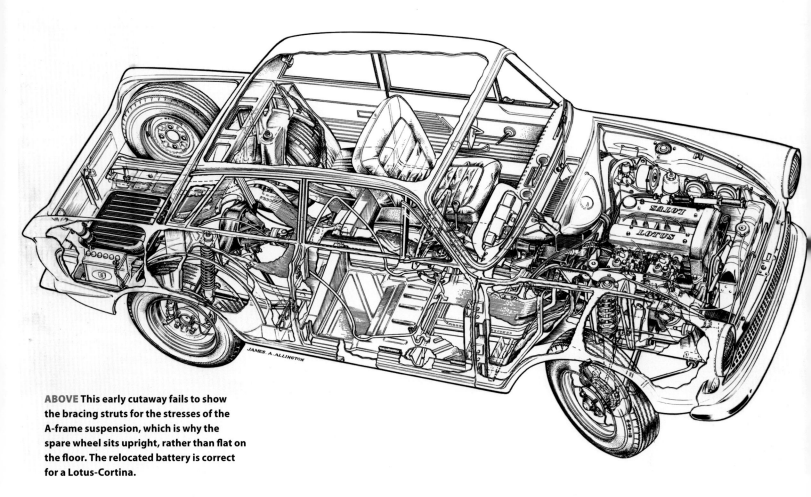

ABOVE This early cutaway fails to show the bracing struts for the stresses of the A-frame suspension, which is why the spare wheel sits upright, rather than flat on the floor. The relocated battery is correct for a Lotus-Cortina.

rigor with which they defended their live axle on the standard Cortina when it was announced, it is hardly surprising that they have stood firm on this point.'

Chapman was determined to improve the suspension, and showed a great deal of interest in the reinforcements built into the rear of the bodyshell to meet Australian requirements and the mounting points for the standard suspension. Accordingly the first Lotus-Cortina ended up with the standard rear suspension layout radically altered by discarding the leaf springs and attaching each end of the axle to links which trailed forward to pick up on the original forward leaf-spring mounting point. Combined vertical coil/damper units took the place of the dampers in the wheelarches and to control sideways movement a triangular A-frame was mounted at its tip under the differential housing with each end splaying outwards to be mounted on the body under the rear seat.

This followed the same arrangement as used on the Lotus Seven S2 but the Cortina was heavier and rolled more than the little Seven. 'Looking back, the rear suspension

question was badly handled,' Haskell wrote. 'For one thing Chapman was undoubtedly the master of single-seater suspension at the time but he was on unfamiliar ground in devising the specification for a much heavier saloon car, and he admitted that the suspension frequencies we were dealing with seemed quite foreign to him.' Haskell revealed that later two experimental Lotus-Cortinas were substantially modified in the boot panelling to accommodate the fully independent rear suspension of the Elan, one of these Cortinas being built as a road car for Jim Clark.

Before production it became clear that in fitting the A-frame rear suspension Chapman had changed the stresses being fed into the rear of Dennis Roberts's carefully designed bodyshell. "When they took away the spring and put in a big coil spring any boot load was not being picked up by side member, it was being picked up by this rear structure," Roberts remembers. "I took a Cortina out with this, took somebody out in it and we found a little hump-backed bridge near Dunton. We just drove it over it and – bingo! – we buckled the quarter panel."

ABOVE A very early Lotus Cortina sits in the newly completed section of the Lotus factory at Cheshunt. The characteristic matt-black radiator sections have been painted over the regular anodised aluminium grille but the Lotus bonnet badge did not stay on the bonnet. The quarter bumpers are from the Anglia-based 5/7cwt van.

LEFT The first production dashboard was a great improvement on the prototype design. The unique wide seats and central armrest meant the Lotus-Cortina had to have the umbrella handbrake of bench-seat Cortinas.

RIGHT **Seen in a Ford film at Cheshunt, Colin Chapman, with his very public profile, only added to the Lotus-Cortina's kudos. (Duke Media Ltd)**

The solution was to add extra bracing struts inside the boot, displacing the spare wheel to lie flat on the floor.

Driving development took place from August 1962 and mostly centred on race circuits, with Lotus engineers joining the future Lotus-Cortina team drivers Peter Arundell, Jim Clark and Trevor Taylor. As well as the road car, more than half the testing was carried out on the hotter engine variants – the Group 2 engine giving 138–140bhp. The schedule was typical Lotus in terms of experimenting and adjusting as it went along. At the Lotus-Cortina launch the following January, Jim Clark recalled trying the conversion for the first time at Snetterton in October 1962, when damper settings were changed, while on his next drive a remote gearchange and new instrument panel had appeared, and on the third day of testing at Silverstone different gear ratios and rear brake linings had been fitted.

Lotus was not on its own during this process. Ford placed George Baggs with the factory at Cheshunt and Hugh Haskell recalled many trips to and from Engineering at Aveley for fixes and advice. During the Silverstone demonstration day where Colin Chapman and Jim Clark terrified various Ford supremos on the track a rear wheel on Clark's car emerged from the wheelarch on its halfshaft as Clark pulled in: the retaining ring had given up. George Baggs designed a heavier-duty ring before production. Ford also later produced a stronger and more resilient pivot for the A-frame.

One of Haskell's jobs was to later estimate the cost of

RIGHT **Pictured in 1966, a new building at Cheshunt housed Lotus-Cortina production and road car development. Stores and workshops were downstairs. Bodyshells would arrive from Dagenham, be hoisted up to the first floor, and remain on trolleys until finished. (© Monitor Picture Library)**

OPPOSITE PAGE **The very full engine bay of a 1964 Lotus-Cortina, with the brake servo on the right-hand side. Observers soon commented on the engine's Alfa-like appearance. The cam covers on the SE models were painted green.**

RIGHT **Reinforcing braces added to the boot during manufacture mean that the spare wheel is relocated. All MkI Lotus-Cortinas have a boot floor hump welded in to accommodate movement of the differential, a necessary modification given the lower suspension of the standard car and the even lower stance of competition versions. (Nick Walton)**

BELOW **Underneath the same immaculately restored car, the A-frame can be clearly seen, as well as the lack of leaf springs. The unpainted alloy parts visible are the differential and the rear of the gearbox casing. (Nick Walton)**

development to Lotus. He dutifully wrote down all the testing, design and prototype building down to the lodging and food allowances. He also obtained a list of tests Ford would expect Lotus to carry out, which was a great deal longer than the one he possessed from Lotus. "I set it all out clearly for presentation to Fred Bushell, the Lotus Company Secretary. He said it looked all right but I should double it. When I sent the final quotation to Ford, the reaction was laughter: 'You cannot possibly develop a car for as little as that!' They doubled the figure again."

It became known to the press that a Lotus version was on the way when the standard Cortina was launched in September 1962. Chapman cheekily took centre stage, as Terence Beckett recalls: "He actually spoke to the press at our launch and I'll always remember what he was going to do with the Lotus-Cortina. He said 'We've had to make one or two changes.' There was an immediate roar from all the journalists, because they thought 'Yeah, you sure would have to with Ford, wouldn't you?'"

An inch lower all round, with stiffer front springs, a beefed-up anti-roll bar and uprated dampers, the whole stance of the Lotus-Cortina instantly set it apart from a standard saloon. The pressed steel wheels were considered remarkably wide for the time, with a rim base of 5½in. To reduce steering effort and stop them leaning out as the body rolled, the camber of the front wheels was reduced to zero by slightly longer and lower forged-steel track-control arms. Steering was, as on all Cortinas, by Burman recirculating ball, but higher geared, with 2¾ turns lock-to-lock. Front-wheel disc brakes were a given and the GT's 9½in discs were used with servo assistance, in conjunction with rear drum brakes from the Classic.

As the twin-cam/gearbox combination was essentially that of the Elan, the Lotus-Cortina shared its high ratios, with first and second very close together, making for vivid acceleration if you were happy to stir the gearbox with its new short lever, situated nearer the driver thanks to a remote extension. However, another by-product of being designed for competition was the availability of three optional final-drive ratios, which made it possible to adjust these characteristics. The clutch diameter was increased from 7¼in to 8in and a thicker propshaft fitted.

To pare down weight for racing – remember these features had to be fitted to at least 1,000 road cars for them to be homologated – the remote gear control casing,

gearbox extension, clutch and differential housing were made in aluminium (this last cast at Boreham) as well as the outer skins of the bonnet, doors and boot. These panels were produced at Dagenham, which stressed the patience of those involved. "They moaned like hell at Dagenham because you couldn't spot-weld them, you could only glue them, and the glue used to come apart," recalls Boreham competition mechanic Mick Jones. A higher reject rate added to the cost of the panels, while owners also had to learn not to slam them, or they would bend.

Lotus estimated that the weight reduction would be around 100lb but the combination of changes inevitably put weight back into the road-ready Lotus-Cortina. 'The

BELOW This Lotus-Cortina in its definitive launch form at Brands Hatch has a grille-mounted Lotus badge. 'FOO' was an Essex registration suffix.

Cortina crime

There was a Cortina which appealed to everyone, including the criminal classes. 'Professional robbers were delighted with the ramming and getaway potential of the Cortina,' wrote journalist and former notorious British armed robber John McVicar, on the 40th anniversary of the Cortina. 'It was fast, roomy, had a cracking gearbox, tight steering lock and a chassis like a bulldozer. It was also easy to nick.'

Naturally, the Lotus-Cortina was the top choice for such a purpose and aside from hallowed race and rally cars, a Lotus-Cortina with a criminal past can lay claim to being one of the most valuable survivors in the world.

The example registered BMK 723A was only the 15th car off the line at Cheshunt and was bought by Bruce Reynolds, one of those convicted for the infamous 1963 Great Train Robbery. Reynolds used the Cortina to finalise the 27-mile route from the train to the

extra weight of the new cylinder head, two-choke Weber carburettors, rear-end stiffening and suspension arms must more than make up for any saving,' *Autocar* magazine pondered in November 1963, when comparing the Lotus to the Cortina 1200. But this was all relative: the unladen kerb weight of a Lotus-Cortina was 16.2cwt compared to 15.5cwt for a two-door Cortina 1200 but then the base car started off extraordinarily light. With a claimed top speed of 115mph, the Lotus was easily the fastest British Ford to that date.

A slow start

At the end of January 1963 the possibly only production-ready Lotus-Cortina was shown to the press at London's Dorchester hotel, just a week after the Cortina 1500 Super had been unveiled. Simultaneously, Lotus announced it was to enter the car in domestic and continental saloon-car racing and rallying.

To the motoring press and enthusiasts it was an unbelievably exotic Ford. The tax-included price of £1,100 reflected the specification and the overheads involved in its gang's hideaway at a farm in Buckinghamshire. In the event the car was never used in the actual robbery and Reynolds, apparently aware that police investigators were then able to match tyre treads, booked it into John Willment's 'Total Performance Centre' to have different tyres fitted.

After the robbery and subsequent arrest of the other gang members, Reynolds fled to Mexico, but was ultimately arrested in Britain in 1968. The Lotus-Cortina was never collected and was impounded by the police until it was sold at auction in 1969, being acquired by a private collector still wearing its original tyres. It emerged at auction again in 1980. Colin Chapman bought the car for £4,500 and it was put on show at the Lotus museum in Norfolk. It was sold again in 1998, fetching in excess of £30,000, and changed hands once more in 2010 for an undisclosed sum.

LEFT The 1963 'Great Train Robbery' Lotus-Cortina pictured in 2010, when it was still showing barely 4,000 miles and wearing its original tyres. (Paul Brace)

RIGHT As the 15th car off the line, BMK 723A already shows a small difference from launch, the metal strip across the glovebox without a de Luxe badge. (Paul Brace)

hand-finished final assembly but it was still considered good value for money. Twin-overhead-cam engines were reserved for the likes of Jaguars, not family cars, and the immediate comparison was with the Alfa Romeo Giulietta, which cost almost a third as much again. The Lotus was soon dubbed 'the British Giulietta'.

There was no British four-seat saloon car directly comparable to the Lotus-Cortina in terms of performance or cachet, especially by October 1964 when the price was reduced to £992 as by then it was sharing more parts with the standard Cortina. In the same month a Vauxhall 4/90 cost £872 but was a much more sedate proposition, while the 1,275cc Mini Cooper S was of course formidable opposition on the track and cheaper still at £778, but less powerful and physically a much smaller car. In the end, the Mini sold more, but the Lotus-Cortina remained a hallowed enthusiast choice.

In contrast to the flood of Cortinas which accompanied the 1962 launch, the Lotus took a long time to be seen. The Type 28 had in any case had to wait until after the Cortina GT had been launched as it used a number of its components.

ABOVE A string of Lotus-Cortinas at Goodwood in 1964, lifting a front inside wheel as usual. Racing Lotus-Cortinas were lightened to the extent of scraping the filler from body joints, removing springs from the passenger seat and eliminating the hardboard from the interior trim panels.

Ford had determined that all it wanted was 15 to 20 cars a day but that was way beyond Lotus production levels and the company was flat-out trying to meet Lotus Elan orders. 'It is understood that over 1,000 are already in the course of assembly', wrote John Bolster of *Autosport* in January, but he was clearly misinformed – no doubt to allay any suspicions that Lotus was nowhere near meeting homologation requirements for the car.

Two-door shells from Dagenham arrived at Cheshunt fully painted and trimmed and Lotus fitted the engine, transmission and suspension. All the cars were white, with the Team Lotus green flash along the side flute – an idea of

Chapman's. Customer cars would go back to Dagenham for distribution into the Ford dealer chain while race cars, built on the same line, were sent to teams – and eventually works rally cars to Boreham.

Relations between Cheshunt and Dagenham became strained as delivery dates strayed. While some accounts hold that production started in February, late Lotus stalwart Fred Bushell told Chapman biographer Jabby Crombac that no cars were produced until May 1963, with deliveries only starting in June. Chapman in exasperation had taken himself off to Team Lotus and promoted accountant Bushell to managing director.

Graham Arnold, the Lotus publicity manager, was not slow to mock up shots of police-liveried Lotus-Cortinas (the green flash was not always present). This image was taken at Cheshunt in late 1963 as 12 dealers handed over cars to police customers. As well as the obvious asset of their performance, it was thought that the Lotus-Cortinas were good for recruitment.

The Lotus-Cortina was meant to race almost immediately and aside from cars for Ford dealers there was considerable pressure to homologate the car for at least part of the 1963 season, something which looked ever more unlikely. 'Manager Syd Henson's chief worry at present is getting the car homologated as touring models', *Sports Car Graphic* reported in March. 'The CSI has laid down four dates on which homologation applications will be considered, the next date being April 25. This means that five important events will be missed, and Henson is trying to persuade the CSI to convene an extra meeting, with all expenses paid.'

"In practice it didn't work out very well indeed. It was twelve months until the Lotus-Cortina came into production and even then they only came out in dribbles," says Terence Beckett. "We gave Chapman a pretty free hand but he had a lot of difficulties getting it into production – the availability of materials he did or didn't want, tapping into a large organisation from a small one. He was developing it as he went along."

This kind of pace was reflected in full road tests not appearing until late autumn 1963, after the car had finally achieved homologation in September. Truly achieved? Current experts maintain that only 200–300 examples were

made in the whole of that year, rather than the required 1,000: an observation perhaps on suspect Lotus record-keeping at the time or that homologation was an understanding rather than a rule.

Hugh Haskell recalled though that the Jaguar E-Type and Mini-Cooper had been homologated with only a handful of cars having been built, but the RAC inspector had been apparently satisfied that the *intention* was there to build the cars in the required numbers. "However, it seemed that the Ford competitions manager was completely frank with the authorities and thus the Lotus-Cortina was not homologated immediately. The RAC inspector could not give his approval once he had been openly invited to collaborate in a circumvention of the rules!"

Press accounts were on the whole glowing, with most concluding that this was an inconspicuous yet deceptively quick driver's car, one made for fast open roads with a slick gearshift that was a pleasure to use, coupled to the other

Cortina virtue of space. It was a car which was set to understeer (as Chapman favoured), with the front wheels running wide, but the skilful driver could hang the tail out by clever use of the throttle.

While the Lotus-Cortina wasn't especially quick from rest, its 105bhp was impressively delivered from 3,500rpm (a weight in the distributor cut the ignition at 6,000rpm). *Autocar* found 0-60mph came up in 13.6 seconds on a wet surface (*The Motor* achieved 10.1 seconds) and 100mph in 43.1 seconds, with a top speed of 108mph. 'The car has an entirely different ride and feel from the standard product', wrote the magazine. 'Everything feels more firm and taut. It is more susceptible to minor bumps; on the other hand it remains glued to the road when driven fast in a way not normally associated with live rear axles.'

The few downsides were reported as a 'painful booming resonance at 4,000rpm' and the inadequacy of the standard eight-gallon fuel tank for a car so suited to long-distance

ABOVE Lotus demonstrator **12 PAR** reappears at the 1964 London Racing Car Show to demonstrate the SE specification; there were 65 factory-built SE models. (LAT)

LEFT Jacky Ickx and Teddy Pilette have their Lotus-Cortina refuelled during the 1964 Spa 24-hour race in Belgium.

touring. In a foretaste of troubles to come, there were a few in-service observations concerning the Chapman-designed rear suspension. *Autocar* in November 1963 found the nuts holding the nosepiece of the axle casing needed checking as they were liable to work loose. But it let Ford off the hook, observing that 'one cannot expect quite the same trouble-free service and reliability normally expected with Ford cars'. In January 1964 *The Motor* addressed the issue, noting that 'any lack of smoothness on the driver's part elicited a clonk from the rear end of our test car which suggests some looseness in the A bracket or radius-arm bearings – the process of locating the back axle has made the drive line much more rigid and much less forgiving of slight clumsiness'.

Circuit champion

Ford operated a two-team strategy to campaign the Lotus-Cortina on the track, signing Team Lotus to run Cortinas for the 1964 British Saloon Car Championship (BSCC) and US work, and Alan Mann Racing – already providing Cortina GT support – to take on European touring car racing (including international rounds in the UK), as well as running Mustangs and Falcons in circuit and rally events plus the Cobras for Ford US. As promised in 1963, Team Lotus drivers naturally included Jim Clark, notwithstanding grand prix commitments, Jack Sears (who had taken the 1963 BSCC title in a Cortina GT), Peter Arundell and Trevor Taylor.

Having won the BSCC in a Mini, Sir John Whitmore was invited to join either Cortina team. 'My first take was to go with Lotus – it was obvious – and be in the team with Jimmy Clark. Then Alan Mann pointed out all I'd ever be was second driver to Jimmy Clark. "What do you want to be, first driver in the European championship or second in the British?" Whitmore joined Peter Proctor, Peter Harper and Henry Taylor, but would occasionally substitute for Jim Clark at Team Lotus.

While 1963 belonged to the Cortina GT, the Lotus-Cortina made a tardy but promising debut in September at the last race of the season, the Oulton Park Gold Cup, in the hands of Jack Sears (on loan from Willment) and Trevor Taylor. Their two cars finished third and fourth, after two Galaxies, but beating the all-conquering Jaguar 3.8-litre saloons. They were first and second in the 1,600cc class. At this time the cars were developing around 145–150bhp.

Jack Sears spent most of 1964 thundering around in a Ford Galaxie or in a Cobra, while Jim Clark simply cleaned up the British Saloon Car Championship in his Team Lotus Cortina, with a class win in each of the eight races he drove

LEFT The 1965 model-year facelift Lotus-Cortina was a far less rarified beast than its predecessor, shedding specialised parts and coming down in price.

ABOVE **Aeroflow vents were incorporated into the new dashboard for 1965, this having a row of extra instruments similar to that of the Cortina GT. (LAT)**

in, including three overall wins (usually when the Galaxies weren't running). In Europe, Sir John Whitmore in one of two Alan Mann Cortinas took five outright wins but encountered more opposition from Mercedes, BMW and especially Alfa Romeo, finally losing out to a 970cc Mini-Cooper S.

This was despite a background of continual trouble with the A-frame suspension. The design put a great deal of stress on the aluminium differential housing, which flexed by a quarter of an inch under load, causing misalignment and wear of the gears, as well as loss of oil. Ford and Lotus were alive to this, and Ford produced special mounting bolts to hold the casing more securely.

Left unchecked this movement could lead to the rear suspension collapsing or the suspension bushes becoming contaminated by oil leaks. The racing teams found that the differentials needed constant checking during a race and would have to be frequently topped-up. The *Motor* six-hour of June 1964 (a round of the European Touring Car Championship) saw Jim Clark's Lotus-Cortina win but was most remembered for the frequent stops for oil. Another example was June 1964's Mont Ventoux hillclimb. Whitmore's car had broken its rear suspension six miles from the top, necessitating a three-day rebuild before going on to the Nürburgring six-hour race later the same month.

Against the background of British and European Lotus-Cortina racing, Team Lotus also raced in the US, hoping to boost those crucial export sales of regular Cortinas – even though the pre-Aeroflow Lotus version was not available in the showrooms. Jackie Stewart and Mike Beckwith

triumphed again at the 1964 Marlboro 12-hours where the Cortinas had won the previous year, with Whitmore and Tony Hegbourne posting second.

For the rest of 1964 the unique Lotus A-frame rear suspension was retained. But the writing was on the wall once the 1965 model-year Cortina GT suspension had been given radius arms, as these could naturally enough be adopted for the Lotus-Cortina. The Alan Mann team did back-to-back tests between both suspension set-ups and there proved to be no disadvantage in times. They were in any case obliged to adopt any production changes Ford made. Alan Mann gives some perspective. "People don't realise that the reason

LEFT Ford dominates the track at a Silverstone race in 1965, when Mustangs (behind the Cortinas) were introduced into saloon-car racing.

the A-frames were giving trouble was because the bending on the rear axle was causing the diff to split and leak oil," he says. "They blamed it on the diff but when they beefed it up it was fine. Being alloy it was lighter, and nowadays they use A-frames all the time."

Sir John Whitmore has his views: "It probably cost Ford a great deal more than it need have done to get the success they had," he once commented to the author. "Chapman was very good with suspension in almost every case but when you're like Colin you're not going to get it right every time, rather like the Lotus 30 sports car – it didn't really work. The A-frame was the same but it certainly wasn't any better."

The 1965 season turned out to be just as much of a triumph as the previous, with Whitmore the overall European Touring Car champion. His victorious Cortina, bored out to 1,595cc, was by then producing 152bhp, all the team's engines being prepared by either Cosworth or BRM with carefully selected engine blocks from Ford. The car featured a Hewland limited-slip differential and was made as stiff as possible by removing some of the rear spring leaves and relocating the eyes. At the front, there was a 15/16in anti-roll bar and shorter front springs. This racer retained all the aluminium parts that had been put on the options list for road cars that year.

ABOVE After a swathe of green-and-white Lotus-Cortinas had passed in front of him, Alan Mann decided that he would go for the more distinctive colour scheme of red and gold. KPU 392C – pictured here in 1965 at Mann's Byfleet HQ – was taken to European victory by Sir John Whitmore.

RIGHT In 1965 Lotus-Cortinas were pipped to victory at Marlboro by an Alfa Romeo Giulia. This right-hand-drive car was piloted by Jake McLaughlin and Pete Feistmann. In the background other foreign imports such as a Mini-Cooper and Renault R8 can be seen.

Jim Clark and Jack Sears scored a one-two in the 1965 Sebring three-hour race and Lotus-Cortinas were also first past the post on circuits in Germany, Sweden and New Zealand. This was often with far less support than the British and European drivers received, but Ford encouraged its local suppliers to develop local talent.

"Spares became a big problem," recalled 1964 South African champion Koos Swanepoel, speaking to the author in 2010. "The only parts that we got were different axle ratios from the local agents. The Cortina rear axle had a high-pitched whine and lots of people weren't happy with that. They would take them out and put a new one in for the customers and we used to have them for nothing as there was nothing wrong with them."

Even though the Lotus-Cortina could only be privately imported into South Africa, Ford of Britain (which at that time ran the South African operations) did ship over two Lotus-Cortinas for Swanepoel and fellow driver Basil van Rooyen. At first Swanepoel found the handling as startling as most

drivers who came across the A-frame car. "It was quite an experience. It was my first drive at Kylami and it was very similar to the Lotus Elite in that it used to go into corners and the front wheel would lift up, but I did two or three laps and I said this car feels like it wants to fall over – it lifts up so high I can't see over the bonnet!"

But there was always support from the visiting teams, and Swanepoel hugely enjoyed sparring with – and learning from – Sir John Whitmore. "You had to have the courage to chuck it around. A lot of people had Lotus-Cortinas and if you had a halfways decent one you'd be pretty competitive," recalls Whitmore. "The national champions in a lot of countries had these Lotus-Cortinas and they use to win relatively easily. But when we went to a foreign country we would always clean up, because they hadn't had to push them as hard as we did – we were throwing them around a lot more – and that helped the local drivers then get quicker."

For 1966 new Group Five rules allowed much more modification, and the Team Lotus racing Lotus-Cortinas

The three-wheeler Cortina

Why did early Lotus-Cortinas only race round bends with the left-hand front wheel off the ground? It was mostly down to the Chapman-designed rear suspension which was relatively soft combined with the much stiffer front suspension. On most contemporary photos the rear wheels seem to virtually disappear into their arches. Indeed, the differential was apt to move around so much the boot floor had to have a 'top hat' in it for extra clearance.

Coming from racing the GT to the Lotus-Cortina, Jack Sears noticed straight away that the GT handled quite differently entering a fast or slow left-hand band (in a right-hand-drive car). Sears remarked how journalists would put the wheel-lifting down to the skill of Jim Clark, whereas it was a natural characteristic. All the same, Clark did use the trick to full advantage, knowing that because the inside front wheel would be off the ground, he could steal a few vital inches off the grass verge with absolute confidence.

Even top racing drivers were puzzled by the car's handling until they got used to it. Alan Mann recounted in 1965 that after Graham

Hill had sampled one of his cars at Goodwood he laid a bet that Whitmore could not equal the lap record in the car. "Although Graham was absolutely confounded by his first drive in a Cortina-Lotus, when he spoke at some length about all the reasons why he found it impossible to drive the car quickly, he was able to find to his amazement that all his lap times were within half a second or so of the lap records. Quiet followed and Graham had to dig deep to buy us lunch all round!"

"Once you got used to them they were great," Sir John Whitmore recalls. "The big issue that the public was impressed by was that on left-hand bends they would lift a front wheel well off the ground. That was because you sit on the right-hand side of the car and the extra weight of the driver on that side of the car made the difference and it used to pick up the wheel enormously on left-hand turns. When you first got into it, it was a bit disturbing on a left-hand bend but they were very good for the day. They were a little twitchy and not very consistent, but they were quite fast round a corner when we got the suspension right."

LEFT Jim Clark rounds a bend on three wheels in this famous 1965 shot at Brands Hatch: the car naturally adopted the pose, the driver controlled it.

ABOVE Sixteen national champions (including a couple of stand-ins), pose for Ford in December 1965. The photo illustrates the peak of the company's worldwide competition effort. Sir John Whitmore, at the rear, stands by the tail of the Ford-powered Shelby Daytona Coupé with British Saloon Car Championship Mustang driver Roy Pierpoint. Around Whitmore's winning Cortina (27) are Italian and Scandinavian drivers. To the Cortina's left is Germany's winning Taunus 12M with driver Alfred Burkhart (with crash helmet) by the door. A young Belgian Jacky Ickx leans against Pierpoint's Mustang, with a Ford GT40 in the front centre.

The MkI Lotus-Cortina as a rally car

Even though the Cortina GT had coped magnificently with rallying, it was eventually going to be out-powered by its rivals. The competitions department at Lincoln Cars and then at Boreham might have hoped that they could have counted on the Lotus-Cortina as a reliable rally car before the 1964 season, but on rough roads or tracks the problem of oil leaking from the movement of the differential was compounded by the low-slung A-frame being torn from the underside of the car.

The first toe in the water was a well-used GT works car, 888 DOO, fitted with a Lotus twin-cam for the 1963 Spa–Sofia–Liège of September 1963 and driven by Henry Taylor to fourth place. Then the first trial of an A-frame Lotus–Cortina was the November 1963 RAC Rally where Taylor and his co-driver Brian Melia by all accounts nursed their car home, to a creditable sixth overall.

The Chapman-designed suspension was simply not cut out for rough rallies, as Bill Barnet recalls. "We did one Scottish rally and at almost the end of every special stage in the Scottish forests the mechanics would immediately find the nearest garage, get the car up a ramp and weld this A-frame back together again. At the end of one rally we got Colin Chapman down, put one of the Lotus-Cortinas on the ramp and it was a mass of welds."

On the other hand where there wasn't very much rough road, the Lotus-Cortina showed more promise and a Boreham-built car won its class in the 1964 Tour de France, finishing fourth outright and also winning the handicap in the 4,000-mile event, driven by Vic Elford and David Siegle-Morris. The rest of the rally victories for 1964 went to the Cortina GT.

With the leaf-sprung Lotus-Cortinas finally ready from June 1965, Vic Elford's car led the Alpine Rally of the following month until less than an hour from the finish part of the distributor fell out. There was a similar let-down when four works cars failed to finish the 1965 RAC. The first works victory came in the Welsh International Rally at the end of the year, with Roger Clark driving a borrowed factory car.

Overall, the performance of the Lotus-Cortina on rallies could be described as patchy compared to its dazzling track appearances, but then it was never designed for rallying and the twin-cam engine was more of a race unit than a mud-slogger. On the Tulip Rally Vic Elford's car suffered a misfire, and his engine blew on the Alpine. Nonetheless, several excellent Lotus-Cortina performances suffered in an era of seemingly unfair disqualifications and scrutineering decisions in rallying.

On the April 1966 East African Safari Cortina GTs finished ahead and just behind their Lotus counterparts and in May three Lotus-Cortinas stormed home in the Shell 4000 Rally in Canada to take first, second and fourth in class plus the Manufacturers Team Prize.

There was another emphatic win in that November's RAC Rally, where Bengt Soderstrom and Gunnar Palm came overall first in an event where conditions were so bad that only 63 of the 144 starters finished and the other works Cortinas were bedevilled by collisions with the scenery (including a crash by Jim Clark) and in one case a blown head gasket. "None of the works-entered Cortina-Lotuses sustained any serious mechanical trouble, and the drop-outs were due to shunts and bad luck," commented competitions manager Henry Taylor.

Even though production of all MkI Cortina variants stopped in September 1966, there was a hiatus before the MkII Lotus-Cortina was ready and while the track teams switched to the new model, the MkI Lotus Cortina enjoyed a rally swansong, with a locally registered non-works car, coming first on the February 1967 Swedish rally driven by Soderstrom.

RIGHT Never designed for rough roads, the MkI Lotus-Cortina had a swansong on the 1966 British RAC Rally.

appeared with BRM-prepared fuel-injected dry-sump engines developing 180bhp and with the MacPherson strut front suspension replaced by wishbones and coil springs. Sir John Whitmore achieved four further wins but the European Touring Car Championship for 1966 went to the Alfa Romeo GTA.

The Alfa was also a key target for Ford in American racing where in 1966 rather than using English drivers and teams, the competitions department shipped seven right-hand-drive Lotus-prepared cars to recognised drivers. They were sponsored in return for a nominal fee of $1, including spares and advice, to contest the 1966 Sports Car Club of America B Sedan divisional championships, and the under-2,000cc class of the new Trans-American Challenge series of endurance races.

Back to standard

As the Lotus-Cortina started to dominate saloon racing, the roadgoing cars began to shed some of their bespoke items and acquire some of the progressive improvements to the mainstream Dagenham cars. From June 1964 a two-piece propshaft was fitted to Cortinas; on the Lotus, being less rigid, it absorbed some of the previous transmission snatch. The cars also shed their aluminium bonnet, door and boot skins, while to the disappointment of some enthusiasts the close-ratio Elan gearbox was replaced by a standard Cortina GT unit with an uprated second gear. This gearbox featured on the new 115bhp (109bhp net) Special Equipment version of the Lotus-Cortina, available from new or as an aftermarket conversion for an extra £95 or £135. The cylinder head was reworked and the camshafts were reprofiled to give better tractability.

Additionally the rear suspension was improved by a move to Armstrong adjustable dampers and revised coil springs. Not that the Great Man was much in favour of this. "The Special Equipment Lotus-Cortina did have adjustable shock absorbers which Chapman hated," former export sales manager Roger Putnam told the author in 2006. "He said 'Why should I allow anyone to play with the suspension on a car that I've designed? They're bound to get it wrong.'"

As Ford became keen to trumpet, 1964 was truly the 'Year of the Cortina' and Team Lotus was similarly successful, having garnered the World Constructors Championship the previous year, with Jim Clark now established as a phenomenal talent. A Lotus-Cortina became deeply desirable but they remained anathema to most Ford dealers, used to shifting vast volumes of standard cars. On the rare occasions they saw a Lotus-Cortina, something had broken.

"The A-frame was a high-warranty item. It wasn't standing up in service," Harry Calton recalls. "But it wasn't making the dealers unhappy: people were buying them, bringing them back and they were being repaired under warranty." When *Autocar* ran a long-term Lotus-Cortina it experienced no fewer than six axle failures.

October's London Motor Show saw the Lotus-Cortina gain the new full-width front grille and the revised instrument panel with Aeroflow ventilation, plus of course that important price cut. Nonetheless, it was still a specialist car with a self-selecting clientele. 'Unfortunately, "Lotus" also spells "racing" to the insurance man,' remarked *Practical Motorist* in February 1965. 'The premiums are pretty high, and there was a lot of truth in the quip heard at the Motor Show – "it's an old man's car. No young man can afford the insurance."'

From July 1965 onwards roadgoing Lotus-Cortinas were produced with regular Cortina GT rear suspension, bringing with it the disappearance of the reinforcing struts in the boot and allowing the spare wheel to return to its original side position. More rationalisation brought the final changes in October 1965, with the gearbox from the Ford Corsair V4 being fitted. This was welcomed for its more sporting ratios, with a much higher first and slightly higher second and third gears. It was considered a good compromise for town and country and the gearchange still had the 'knife through butter' feel. Seats and trim also came in line with the GT.

While enthusiastic owners could find plenty of ways of improving the performance of their 'cooking' Cortinas with better carburettors, cylinder heads and exhausts, there was the snag, if you went too far with a Super Speed or Willment conversion, that you might just as well have gone out and bought a Lotus-Cortina anyway, if you could stand the insurance premium and didn't harbour doubts about the suspension.

The choice and rationale for upgrading a Lotus-Cortina was rather more limited, especially as Lotus itself would upgrade a second-hand car to SE specification. However, once the leaf-spring cars were introduced and were patently so much better, some businesses offered to convert an early A-frame Lotus-Cortina into a leaf-sprung car. Although the Chapman suspension used most of the original mounting points of the early GT, it had to be borne in mind that these cars lacked the extra mounts for the 1965 model-year GT's radius arms.

In 1966 Ian Walker Racing offered just such a switch for £50. Carried out in a day, the work entailed replacing the A-frame with leaf springs and the Lotus coil springs by Armstrong Firmaride shock absorbers (with Selectarides extra), and with the two-piece propshaft changed to a single-piece item. *Autosport* judged the conversion good value, for 'peace of mind'. IWR also went on to offer a similar transformation, plus engine and gearbox upgrades, which when combined with the cost of an older Lotus-Cortina would net an amateur competition driver a very viable car for the price of a new 1966 GT.

Late in the 'States

A left-hand-drive Lotus-Cortina was belatedly introduced officially into the United States in late 1965 in 115bhp SE specification, after the regular Cortina had already been on US sale for three years and the A-frame cars had become a regular feature on racetracks. For the US there was a full-width front bumper, standard reversing lights, four-way hazard warning lights, and seatbelt anchorages front and rear. Cashing in on Jim Clark's victory at Indianapolis in 1965, a Team Lotus badge celebrating this fact was fixed to the transmission tunnel on all cars.

One magazine wit supposed that somehow in the journey across the Atlantic the once-exotic specification had changed and another termed it virtually a Cortina GT with a Lotus engine. Distribution of the new variant was helped by sales of English Fords being switched to domestic Ford dealers, as opposed to being handled, as previously, by Lincoln-Mercury outlets. So unlike anything on offer from Ford before, *Car Life* termed the Lotus-Cortina 'delightful and desirable' while *Motor Trend* dubbed it 'every inch a little tiger'. Some 186 cars are believed to have been imported.

It may have matured to the disappointment of some Lotus fans but 1965 proved to be the best sales year for the MkI Lotus-Cortina, with over 1,000 cars produced according to most records. By now the meaning of ownership was understood: love and hate. *Car and Car Conversions* magazine bought a 1966 example from new, after some effort finding a dealer who could deliver in six weeks. It became a much-modified hard-used and enjoyed track car but like most long-term-test examples of the time, revealed itself to be very different to live with, in comparison to a standard Cortina. The magazine's experience was revealing of how Ford dealers saw these rarified cars, which looked familiar yet were so very different: 'It wasn't until several days later when we'd read the handbook that we realised the oil pressure was lower than it should have been. ... The local Ford dealer protested "Oh, that's OK sir, they're all like that!" We discovered later that he'd never seen one before.'

Notable oil consumption was a familiar part of twin-cam ownership and a new oil pump was fitted to the *C&CC* car, then a core plug blew out of the cylinder block. They put the car in the care of a Lotus dealer. 'Len Street Engineering in London were now looking after the car after we'd written to Lotus complaining that no Ford dealer we could find knew the first thing about the twin-cam engine.' Len Street came up with a whole raft of fixes, mainly to prevent oil seeping from the top of the engine. The experience was summed up thus: 'You don't live with a Lotus-Cortina, it suffers you to exist with it.'

As production of all MkI Cortinas wound down both at Dagenham and at Cheshunt, a new Lotus-Cortina was under development by Ford, and it would be quite a different prospect. Nonetheless, for a hastily developed special, the original Lotus-Cortina had transformed the image of the car and its maker.

* Author's note: The total production figure for the MkI Lotus-Cortina needs to be approached with caution, and annual production statistics from Lotus are possibly open to question. Ford gives a total figure of 3,301, the Lotus-Cortina Register reckons 3,307–3,321 and Ford author Graham Robson 2,894, with annual production equally as variable. Then there is the handful of 'unofficial' cars such as rumoured special-order four-doors and some automatics used by Ford management.

ABOVE September 1966, and Lotus managing director Fred Bushell eases the last Cheshunt-built Lotus-Cortina out of the factory (a left-hand-drive car). He reflected that as well as support with buying, Ford taught Lotus quality control, and virtually forced it into developing a management structure. (© Monitor Picture Library)

Chapter 4:
The Corsair

AVX 127G

LEFT AND BELOW
These early Corsair styling clays show different approaches from Claude Gidman (left) and Charles Thompson (below), incorporating standard Cortina doors with the side 'arrow' mouldings.

LEFT Here's to our lovely new car ... Cyprus was the background for the Corsair's glamorous launch photography in summer 1963. You'd never know there was a Cortina underneath that smart exterior.

ABOVE **The Corsair's extra interior space only benefited the rear passengers. Critics found no more room in the front footwell, complained that the steering wheel protruded too far and that the front seats would not slide back far enough.**

RIGHT **Ford ambassador Jim Clark lent a hand to promoting the Corsair at a government test track in Surrey where he flung it around and praised its general composure as well as its 'Thunderbird' looks.**

The Classic may have been a hiccup on the way to the Cortina but it nonetheless established that there was a reasonable market for a more aspirational medium-sized car. There was no shame felt in continuing the name, either. Styling committee minutes of May 1962 show a detailed discussion tabled on the project code-named 'Buccaneer' being badged as a 'Consul Classic'. It was only by January 1963 that the name was changed to Consul Corsair, ahead of the launch that October.

Funds were released for the new car's styling and engineering in May 1961, with the outline specifications agreed five months later. With product planning now fully functioning, the planners soon knew how much the Classic replacement was to cost, how it should perform, and who would buy it. This was determined to be a man aged 35–55, earning £1,500 or more a year, and most likely to read the

Daily Express, while his wife would have a vacuum cleaner, washing machine and fridge.

The yet-to-be-launched Cortina had set the parameters for the Buccaneer. It had to be much more cost-efficient to build than the Classic yet offer decisively more interior and luggage space than the Cortina without undermining sales of the Zephyr/Zodiac range. Although the project had a tight timetable of 21 months, the car's basic structure and driveline would be Cortina-derived. It was mainly a matter of styling and packaging.

Dennis Roberts, the Cortina's original body engineer, was called upon to lengthen the Cortina wheelbase by 3in, which he did by simply adding 3in of metal ahead of the heelboard of the rear seats. "You have a heel plate and then the rest of the floorpan goes up over the rear wheelarch," he explains. "When it came to Corsair, all we did was move that lot back and put another piece in – as simple as that."

Elsewhere, the Inner engine-bay panels, windscreen and scuttle panel were also shared with the Cortina and the

suspension, the front and rear tracks, brakes and steering from the Cortina Super and GT were all carried over. The Cortina's boot-floor/fuel-tank pressing was also used, so the spare wheel stood upright.

The new wheelbase was 8ft 5in, for an overall length of 14ft 9in, making the car 8¼in longer than a Cortina. In production, a four-door Corsair de Luxe sported an unladen

ABOVE One of Charles Thompson's renderings for a Corsair coupé: one of hundreds of sketches he did. The idea was never seriously contemplated by management. (Charles Thompson)

LEFT Following Classic practice, a two-door Corsair was offered, but it was unclear why such a large two-door was needed. Sales were roughly one-third of the equivalent four-doors, tailing off with the introduction of the 1965 V4. There was no two-door 2000E.

OPPOSITE PAGE Boy meets girl in Cyprus. The Corsair's clean rear styling is uninterrupted by the fuel filler cap, which hides behind the numberplate.

kerb weight of 17½cwt. This was lighter than the outgoing Classic and slightly heavier than a Cortina 1500 Super.

Much resembling a Cortina, the first mechanical prototype was completed in February 1962 to develop the chassis, and the first Corsair-shaped prototype followed in July with eight more cars carrying out durability testing (including one spending three months in the American winter) and plenty of accelerated wear-and-tear testing at Lommel, Ford's Belgian test track.

The Corsair was styled under the direction of Roy Brown, with John Fallis heading the exterior design team. Charles Thompson, who had been largely responsible for finishing the 1962 Cortina, was also brought on board. Who really penned the final shape? It depends on whom you ask. Don de La Rosa has been quoted but Fords were styled by teams rather than one person; Charles Thompson can perhaps claim most credit.

Ford publicity declared eight full-scale clay models were completed before the choice was narrowed down, but Thompson feels this was more likely to have been two double-sided models which each went through a couple of versions. "There were two cars at the end of the day. The process was that rather than one stylist working on one design you had two or three each producing their own ideas. A Canadian, Claude Gidman, did the other one, which looked very much like the old Falcon at that time. Management realised my interpretation was different, and more in line with the brief."

Roy Brown said at the time that he wanted to create a simple, functional and beautiful car. He put a large notice in the studio with the words 'Keep it simple' and, indeed, compared with the fussy detailing of the Classic, the Corsair was a clean design. The exterior stylists were told that it shouldn't look at all like a Cortina but with a telling nod to the cost disciplines that now permeated the company the only visible parts they were initially allowed to change were the bonnet, front wings and tail. At first there was a requirement that the existing Cortina doors, with their distinctive flute, should be used, which immediately compromised the chances of a distinctive-looking car. Thompson did produce an initial design with a flute but management eventually approved tooling for new doors, in which the flute was eliminated. This necessitated new outer pressings but the inner door components such as the Cortina's 'zero torque' door latches and window winders were carried over.

The distinctive pointed nose, with its recessed headlamps, can also be attributed to Charles Thompson. Daring for a

RIGHT **The range-topping Corsair GT was available as a two-door or four-door, the latter being the bigger seller, and like the Cortina only marked externally by badges on the rear wings and bright trim.**

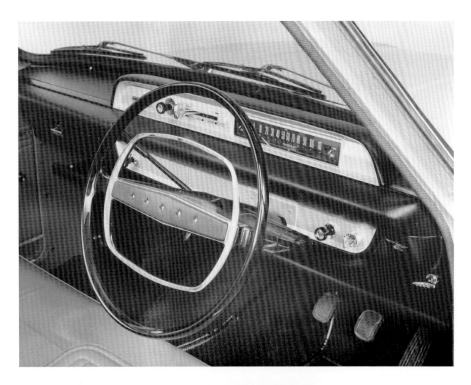

British car, there was precedent within the Ford stable, both in the 'Bathtub' 1961 Ford Taunus 17M and to a much greater extent the 1961 Ford Thunderbird, a link which Ford of Britain happily drew attention to when the Corsair went on sale. While road testers found the sharp-nosed style didn't help stability in crosswinds, it was a slightly more aerodynamically efficient shape than the bluff-fronted Cortina, which *Motor* magazine attributed to helping the slightly higher top speed (83.8mph) achieved during its October 1963 test.

Outside and in, the Corsair differed from the Cortina where it mattered – the parts you could see and touch. The interior contrasted with its cheaper relative by having far less visible painted metal, most surfaces being covered by embossed vinyl, with the lower edge of the de Luxe doors featuring aluminium kick plates.

Eschewing the austerity of the Cortina, the fully padded dashboard featured such niceties as a lidded glovebox, a cigarette lighter and a more sophisticated horizontally marked speedometer than that of the Cortina, with a full

ABOVE *Motor* magazine took a violent dislike to the first Corsair steering wheel, calling the five gold stars set into the steering wheel hub 'unworthy' of an otherwise high-quality interior finish. (Author's collection)

RIGHT By December 1963 Ford was planning a new wheel design, introduced the following October and seen here in a GT: note the console-mounted tachometer, bucket seats and central armrest.

OPPOSITE PAGE By virtue of its extra bulk, the Corsair was largely bypassed for motorsport. Although two Lotus twin-cam Corsairs were built for the 1964 Spa–Sofia–Liège Rally, neither car finished. Boreham mechanics also had V6 Corsair estate 'rally barges'.

A new factory for new times

The growth of the British car market and the success of the Cortina meant that by the early 1960s Dagenham was once more operating at full capacity. However, expansion for new models on the existing site was forbidden by the government of the day, which 'encouraged' growth industries such as car makers to locate new plants in areas of high unemployment. Sir Patrick Hennessy was offered Tyneside, South Wales or Scotland but opted for Halewood, in Merseyside near Liverpool, a 239-acre site some 200 miles from Dagenham, which Ford bought in 1959.

Bringing the factory on stream was a disciplined operation, with a pilot plant at a hanger in Liverpool airport training workers from 1 January 1962, production of the Anglia starting in March 1963, and the first Corsair off the tracks in July that year.

Ford's implantation at Halewood was in complete contrast to the experience of Rootes, which had opened a state-of-the-art factory at Linwood in Glasgow next to the Pressed Steel complex, to produce the daring but complicated little Hillman Imp from 1963. Linwood was some 300 miles away from Rootes's traditional home in Coventry and there was an uneconomic traffic of components between the two locations. Coupled to these unpromising logistics were a fault-ridden car and an increasingly militant workforce. The Imp and Linwood troubles hastened the sale of Rootes to Chrysler and the factory closed its doors in 1976.

Halewood too had its share of industrial unrest and setbacks, but Ford Escort production followed the Anglia until the model's deletion in 1997. With Ford now in possession of Jaguar and Land-Rover, production switched in 2001 to the Ford-derived Jaguar X-Type and the Land-Rover Freelander.

In 2008 both marques were sold to Indian group Tata and in 2011 Halewood was geared up to produce the Range Rover Evoque. Across the river, Vauxhall had started car production at Ellesmere Port in 1962 and was also still making vehicles on the site in 2011. Standard-Triumph, meanwhile, had set up in nearby Speke in 1959, but the plant, a by-word for labour problems, closed in 1978.

With hindsight, the policy of industrial relocation ill-served the British industry in the 1960s, when it needed to rationalise its operations rather than spread them around, and only the strongest survived.

RIGHT When it opened in 1963 Halewood was capable of producing 1,000 cars a day and had cost around £30m. It initially employed 9,000 and at its peak had 14,500 workers. Here Corsair 2000Es come off the line in 1967.

quota of warning lights. A new technical feature Ford boasted at the time was the fact that all the dashboard wiring was connected using a single plug, and that the Corsair was the first British car to use a printed-circuit instrumentation. The steering wheel featured a padded lozenge-shaped centre and a matching chrome horn ring.

The Corsair was sold on its extensive soundproofing, claimed to give 'cathedral standards of hush'. The bulkhead was double-skinned with a layer of glassfibre in between, the carpets had extra soundproofing under them, the transmission tunnel and rear floor were also double-skinned, and the exhaust system had an expansion chamber added to the silencer, on flexible mountings. The engine/gearbox unit was stiffened for both Corsair and Cortina by thicker internal webs and strengthening the engine/clutch flange.

'Job One' rolled off the Halewood production line in July 1963, with a further dozen cars whisked off for more durability testing and brochure photography. Thus the Ford Consul Corsair – Ford persisting with the 'Consul' tag for all medium-sized cars – was publicly announced on 2 October 1963, as a two-door or four-door saloon in standard or deluxe 1500 form with 59.5bhp or as a 78bhp GT model, claimed to have a top speed in the 90s. 'It sells at the same price as the Classic, which it replaces,' Ford's launch copy read. 'It will be bought by the fastidious who want something in between the record-breaking Cortina and the King-size Z cars [the Zephyr/Zodiacs].'

In the UK, starting at a price of £653 including Purchase Tax, the standard two-door Corsair compared to the two-door Cortina 1500 Super at £669, but would only have had much interest in warmer markets as a heater was extra. The range-topping four-door GT was £840 and included a heater and the choice of two-tone paint, as did the de Luxe.

Where a bench seat was fitted, a column gearchange was standard; optional on the de Luxe was a remote change and bucket seats. The Cortina 1500's three-speed Borg-Warner automatic gearbox became a further option soon after launch. The GT featured the floor change and bucket seats, and a column-mounted tachometer, and there were stiffer springs and dampers. All Corsairs had front disc brakes (servo-assisted on the GT) and an eight-gallon fuel tank.

The press greeted the car warmly. In its launch-day test, *Motor* termed the Corsair 'more than just a re-bodied Cortina. A longer chassis has made more room inside and better trim and seats add a touch of opulence and greater comfort.'

ABOVE The Monza
endurance Corsair (see
page 153) in the midst of a
pit stop. The front fairing
with its smaller air intake
was thought to be wind-
cheating and for fun the
registration B007 82B
lost a few digits. Note the
rearranged windscreen
wipers.

But not all that comfortable: testers noted that by putting
the extra inches solely into the rear compartment the space
had not been used very intelligently, with tall drivers feeling
cramped and back-seat passengers having more kneeroom
than they needed yet not being able to tuck their feet very far
under the front seats.

There was praise for the now-familiar five-bearing engine
– 'one of the smoothest fours made anywhere in the world'
– although low-speed flexibility was criticised. As well as an
improved top speed the test fuel consumption of around
30mpg bettered that of the Cortina 1500. While the testers
found the handling safe but unexciting and the steering to be
spongy, the remote gearchange drew praise: 'The Corsair is
not a sports car, yet the gearbox and change would satisfy
the most ardent enthusiast.'

However, the magazine was fairly unimpressed with
the Corsair's interior: 'it appears to be the work of a stylist
rather than a designer, although it is practical and not unduly
garish'. While the dashboard gained muted approval, part of
the speedometer needle's arc was masked by 'an ugly horn
ring shaped liked a television screen'.

Soon after launch Ford announced that it was stepping
up Corsair production at Halewood from 500 to 1,000 cars
a day. Settling into the market with few troubles, the Corsair
received only minor updates and was denied even the most
modest of facelifts during its seven-year career, Ford opting
instead to juggle interior trim and engines.

The V engines

Just two years after launch, the Corsair underwent its most
radical change: a switch to two all-new V4 engines, the first
of such a type on a British car. This also marked the debut of
a new line of engines for Ford of Britain, a related V6 joining
the line-up in 1966 for the new Zephyr/Zodiac range.

The Corsair's 1.5-litre 'Kent' engines were replaced by two V4s, of 1.7-litre and 2.0-litre capacity, moving the car decisively away from both the current and future Cortinas and into the new 2-litre 'executive' territory where the Triumph and Rover 2000s were making headway.

The rationale for a V engine went beyond an increase in power for this weighty Cortina derivative. Ford had wider reasons for looking at a V4 configuration rather than a new in-line 'four': compact packaging for front-wheel drive and for Project Redcap, the new Anglo-German van which would emerge as the Transit in 1965.

"The way we were changing models at that time every four or five years meant we had to look 15 years ahead," said Terence Beckett in 1974. "We thought we really must try to get an engine range which would enable us to take care of front-wheel-drive cars as well as the conventional-layout cars."

ABOVE AND LEFT
The 'Essex' V4 engine was certainly a compact unit, in accord with the idea that English Fords might one day be front-wheel-drive. The panelwork of the Corsair engine bay betrays its Cortina origins.

We've got a V in our bonnet!

smooth, silent V power in the **NEW CORSAIR V4!**

The ribbon? Pure high spirits. But with good reason; because under the new Corsair's beautiful bonnet there nestles a brand new Ford engine—a V4, the first of its kind in a British car. Powerful, silent and smooth as silk, it boosts Corsair's top speed to nearly 90 mph and gives commanding, effortless acceleration. An even faster and more luxurious GT version of the new Corsair V4 is available. And you can specify automatic transmission if you wish, whichever model you choose. Drive a new Corsair V4 soon, and you'll want a V in *your* bonnet . . .

Fresh ideas about ventilation. Ordinary car heating and ventilation systems have no proper means of extracting stale air. Corsair's wonderful new Aeroflow system changes all the air in the car every 40 seconds. Twin extractor vents at the rear take away the used air; movable ducts at either end of the facia control the direction of incoming *fresh* air. To complete your comfort, there are simple controls to adjust both temperature and rate of airflow.

Design for high living. Everywhere in the new Corsair V4 you'll find evidence of the most careful attention to detail and finish. There's a new facia with redesigned instruments and controls; new, elegant trim; a new, deeper front bench seat (bucket seats are optional).
Impressive facts for the hard-headed. Corsair's new engine, with its cross-flow head, short stroke, bowl-in-piston and stud-mounted rockers, extracts a remarkable amount of power from 1662 cc. It also provides the sort of low-speed flexibility which makes traffic driving a pleasure.
You'll find driving the new V4 a pleasure in other ways, too—for instance, a new, more positive gearshift linkage, new feather-light diaphragm clutch and reflex accelerator pedal make for silky gearchanges and less fatigue all round. The front disc brakes are now larger, the rear drums self-adjusting. Maximum speed is 88 mph (up to 100 mph for the GT) and acceleration from 0 to 60 mph takes only 16.5 seconds (14.0 seconds for the GT).

NEW **CORSAIR**

The Transit also needed a short engine to enable easy access to the cab without having a long bonnet. Someone sitting on one side should be able to walk through to the other without having to struggle over a hump for the engine. The V engine also allowed a double passenger seat.

Even though in 1962 Ford of Germany had just started production of its own V4 engine for the Taunus 12M, and would enlarge it to 1.5 litres and 1.7 litres and also introduce a V6 – the 'Cologne' – in 1964, there does not seem to have been much consideration of moving towards common powerplants across Ford's European operations. So it was that in 1963 Ford of Britain chief engineer Alan Worters started work on a British family of 'vee' engines – of course called the 'Essex'. The larger engine was of more relevance, going on to power a much wider range of Ford cars until the 1980s, but spinning a V4 from it allowed the tooling costs to be spread over a wider base. The V4 appeared first in

the autumn 1965 Corsair and Transit, with the 2,495cc and 2,993cc V6s being unveiled the following year in the MkIV Zephyr 6 and Zodiac.

Following the practice of the 'Kent' engines, the cylinder bore of both V4s was the same at 93.66mm, with a longer-throw crankshaft increasing the swept volume. The cylinder heads in both the V4 and V6 were of a new crossflow design with inlet ports on one side and exhaust ports on the other: this was also soon to be seen on the 'Kent' engines. Additionally the pistons were of a new design, with a bowl-shaped combustion chamber machined into the top of the piston. Without the intrusion of a combustion chamber in the cylinder head, this helped power and fuel efficiency by allowing the design of the inlet and exhaust ports to be optimised, and also permitted more space for larger valves. Known as the 'Heron' head after its designer Sam Heron, a similar design had already appeared in the 1963 Rover

ABOVE Here, in 1965, the Canadian Hell Drivers stunt team is entertaining King Hussein of Jordan in Amman. Quite why has become lost to history.

LEFT A more restrained new dashboard with traditional circular instruments and extra crash padding was ushered in alongside the Aeroflow ventilation.

The Crayford Corsair

As soon as the MkI Cortina conversion was off the blocks, Crayford turned its attention to the Corsair, which with its long bonnet and boot rather suited a soft-top. The first car converted in late 1964 was a 1500GT and the last a 2000 de Luxe in 1969. Of the 118 made between 1966 and 1969, 100 were five-seater convertibles and 18 were 2+2 cabriolets. The latter was the more expensive and involved conversion, since in order to allow the hood to sit further forwards – and to be closable by those sitting in the front seats – a well was created behind the rear bench; this was accordingly moved forward, with a corresponding loss of legroom, resulting in the car becoming a 2+2. Bespoke interior trim panels also had to be created. In 1967 a Corsair de Luxe convertible cost £1,100 and the cabriolet added a further £270 to the bill – this when a Corsair 2000E saloon was priced at £1,039 including tax.

ABOVE The Crayford Corsair in cabriolet guise featured two side windows that dropped down if a peg was withdrawn.

LEFT The Corsair worked well as a Crayford convertible and 118 were made between 1966 and 1969. As with the Cortina MkII, it was available with either a coupé or a cabriolet hood. (LAT)

2000, so Ford named its version Bowl-in-Piston, although it became more commonly known as the 'crossflow' engine. A new engine plant was built at Dagenham (with tractor production moving out to Basildon) and a new transmission plant opened at Halewood in 1965.

The V4 Corsair was launched as a de Luxe, with a 1,663cc engine developing 76.5bhp, and as a GT, with a 1,996cc unit pushing out 88bhp. Thus the 1700 version was 30 per cent more powerful than the 1500 'Kent' as well as being 11 per cent shorter overall and running at 15 per cent lower piston speeds. Fitted in the Transit, low-compression cylinder heads allowed lower-octane fuel to be used, while the detuned engines had better low-speed pulling power.

But for press man Harry Calton, the Transit link was not a happy one. "When we were going onto the 'V' our main concern was that we got Corsair out publicly before Transit – the last thing we wanted was a car with a truck engine. In the Transit it worked extraordinarily well: it was durable, it had the torque in the right place. It was much better in Transit than for a passenger car, where it was so bloody harsh."

Ford promoted the new V4 Corsairs as having 'smooth, silent, V power' but this was a little off the mark. The new engine suffered the same inherent vibration problem as the V4 of the Taunus 12M. To damp down out-of-balance forces it required a counter-rotating balancer shaft running at engine speed, which added weight and didn't entirely eliminate harshness. The camshaft and balance shaft were driven directly by the crank through fibre gears, which sadly gained a reputation for premature breakage.

In late 1965 *Motor Sport* magazine ran a 1,700cc Corsair V4 alongside its own Cortina GT for 1,000 miles and liked it a lot less, finding it much noisier accelerating than they had expected and not as smooth-running. The writer looked forward to seeing if the 2.0-litre was an improvement and observed 'I think the new vee configuration of the Ford's latest engines will work out well, with time for development, because at the smaller throttle-openings this 1.7-litre was impressively smooth and the torque was such that very useful top-gear pick-up was there for Mr Disinterested [sic] who so seldom changes down.'

If you wished for a speedier Corsair, on an old-style model you could bolt on the same carburettors and manifolds used by Cortina tuners, but the only aftermarket tuning that appears to have been offered for the V4 Corsair was by Nerus Engineering of Sussex, and brought the performance of a regular Corsair near that of a GT. The V4 Sprint kit was £49,

or £60 fitted, and consisted of two modified cylinder heads – sold on an exchange basis – with flowed and balanced inlet and exhaust ports, a similarly finished inlet manifold, and an adaptor block to take a twin-choke Weber carburettor. You also had to modify the throttle linkage. When tested by *Practical Motorist* in 1966 the Nerus demonstrator was found to knock three seconds off the standard 0–60mph time, despite the presence of a column gearchange, and to have greatly improved flexibility. 'For keeping up with the Joneses it is one of the best value-for-money conversions we have tested,' the magazine commented. One wonders though how many people would have bothered.

With the arrival of the V4, Ford took the opportunity to rationalise the Corsair range, dropping the two-door and four-door standard models, leaving only the de Luxe and GT variants. Externally, there was little to distinguish the new cars, other than chrome Aeroflow vents on the rear pillars; inside they gained an all-new dashboard with circular instruments and Aeroflow eyeballs. You could order an automatic on the GT for the first time and fuel-tank capacity was boosted to ten gallons, with a recirculatory fuel system claimed to eliminate any tendency for fuel vaporisation in hot weather.

A coachbuilt Corsair

There was more Corsair news for 1966 with the addition of an estate, based on the 88bhp 2-litre GT and launched at the Geneva Motor Show in March. Given that this high-end estate was catering to a small market and Dagenham was flat-out producing Anglia and Cortina estates (in 1966 13 per cent of all Cortinas were estates), the Corsair load carrier was a conversion of the saloon entrusted to Ford's favoured coachbuilder, E.D. Abbott of Farnham, Surrey. The styling was nicely harmonious thanks to Abbott using the MkI Cortina estate's rear-door windows, rear side windows and D-posts; as with the company's MkIII and MkIV Zephyr/Zodiac estates, the tailgate was in glassfibre.

The new Corsair estate boasted 59.9cu ft of loadspace with the rear seats folded and could carry items just over 6ft long. The mechanical specification was left unchanged save for stiffer rear springs and wider rear tyres: it was crucial these were kept at the correct pressure, as *Autocar* found in September 1966: 'One short trip with a sack of potatoes on board showed that the steering becomes very vague and the handling unsteady,' the magazine observed.

With a fully carpeted loadbay, this was more of an antique-dealer's car than one in which to take pigs to market,

LEFT Because Abbott's Corsair estate conversion was based on a saloon, the boot's high loading sill was retained, limiting ease of loading and enforcing a shallow load bay. Only the seat back folded flat and a chrome guard rail – just visible here – was fitted to stop objects sliding into the front-seat occupants.

The big German Fords

The Taunus range progressed from the Cortina-sized 12M and 15M to the larger 17M and 20M range, which in P5 form was about 6in longer than a Corsair. This new big Taunus was launched in 1964 with 1.5-litre and 1.7-litre V4 engines and a 2.0-litre V6 – beating Dagenham to a V6 by a year, and with the 20M being promoted as a 'six' for the price of a 'four'.

But in 1967, little realising that bigger was not always better – as could equally be said of Dagenham with the MkIV Zephyr – Cologne rebodied the 17M/20M in a large square-edged style evoking the Lincoln Continental, and dropped the Taunus designation. Critics soon pointed out that the new P7 Taunus offered no more interior space than its predecessor, carried over the same engines, and had no noteworthy changes, apart from a dual-circuit braking system and a safety steering wheel with padded spokes. Performance was actually worse.

The range flopped so badly with public and press that surplus stocks in 1968 ran to around 45,000 cars and forced Ford to introduce a restyled range in autumn that year. Known as the P7(b) model, the new 17Ms and 20Ms were sleeker, losing the 'kink' in the waistline and gaining improved rear suspension with twin radius arms and a thicker front anti-roll bar. There was also an expansion of the V4 and V6 engines into six capacities (including new 1.8 and 2.3 units, the former being the smallest V6 then in production) and no fewer than nine power levels. The 17M/20M was to be the last all-German Ford, being replaced by the Anglo-German Granada range in 1972.

LEFT With its V6 engine, quad headlights and power steering, the 1968–72 26M coupé was the last stand-alone big German Ford.

RIGHT The smart P5 Taunus 20M was available as a four-door, a pillarless coupé and an estate. Ford of Britain sold the 20M through Lincoln Cars but crippling duty priced it above a Zodiac.

RIGHT Each Corsair estate took several days to complete as saloons were stripped out, their roof and rear pillars cut away, a tubular frame put in, and a one-piece glassfibre tailgate fitted, before re-painting and re-trimming. The hinged boot-floor cover conceals the spare wheel.

not least because the loadbay was rendered quite shallow by the conversion from saloon to estate, which laid the spare wheel flat on the boot floor.

At £1,130, the Corsair estate was considered a good-looking, if expensive, conversion, when a de Luxe Vauxhall Victor estate cost £893, and a Singer Vogue estate £960. Ford advertised the Corsair GT as a fast smooth load-carrier whereas *Autocar* considered the GT badges superfluous as the performance was really nothing dramatic. Production of the estate continued until the deletion of the Corsair, but it was a minority interest, and in the end only 940 left Abbott's Wrecclesham works.

The ultimate Corsair

The finale to the Corsair's career was a successful upgrading of both engine and trim. Announced in the first week of January 1967, the Corsair 2000E was both fast and luxurious, and a lower-cost alternative to the Triumph and Rover 2000: at £1,007 tax paid it was several hundred pounds cheaper (£350 in the case of the Rover). "The only thing about it which doesn't belong firmly to the luxury bracket is the price," said Terence Beckett at the time.

Ford was never explicit as to what the 'E' stood for, but it followed the Zodiac Executive and was joined later in the year by the similarly plush Cortina 1600E. For 1967

there was an exciting equipment tally: a standard vinyl roof, reversing lights, Zephyr/Zodiac wheel trims on wider 4½J wheels, radial-ply tyres, fully reclining front seats with standard seat belts, and lashings of carpet including in the boot. The boot and bonnet had their own lights, there were reflectors on the inside corners of the doors, and a dipping rear-view mirror. The walnut-finished dash panel included a standard radio.

The best news was a proper reworking of the 1,996cc V4 to boost power by 9bhp to 97bhp, giving a maximum speed of approaching 100mph. To achieve this a new camshaft was fitted, plus a twin-choke Weber carburettor, a redesigned inlet manifold and enlarged ports in the cylinder head. When road-tested by *Motor* in April, the magazine recognised that Ford had made amends for the 'half-hearted' and now defunct V4 GT – even though the 2000E was 'still a bit noisy' – and concluded that the new model was an 'executive's bargain'.

With high gearing and a relaxed engine, the new Corsair cruised happily at 85–90mph but was still content to slog from 20–40mph in top gear and rev up to 6,000rpm if you could stand the noise. This Corsair was also long-remembered for its gearbox, both for its super-slick change quality and its well-chosen gear ratios. *Motor* called it 'superbly refined' and

ABOVE This 1969 Corsair 2000E is distinguished from lesser Corsairs by its vinyl roof, unique radiator grille, clear indicator lenses and wheel trims.

ABOVE A tachometer, ammeter and oil pressure gauge were added to the 2000E's walnut facia and there was a leather gaiter for the gearstick.

said it was worthy of comparison to that of a Porsche and one of the best gearchanges in the world. It was also soon shared with the 1600GT Cortina.

Handling, aided by the new radial tyres, had also been raised from adequate to good, the testers reported, and larger 9.6in servo-assisted front disc brakes were a further bonus. Suspension was fairly bouncy, as before, but still refined. The new interior also found favour as being suitably more conservative and British than the previous 'stylistic American approach'.

The 2000E proved to be a relative hit, and Ford claimed in 1968 that it was the car with the lowest rate of depreciation on sale in Britain. Only offered for three years, it nonetheless came to represent around 10 per cent of the 331,095 Corsairs built. Alongside the 2000E the previous GT continued, with the 2000E's uprated mechanicals, but renamed the 2000 de Luxe; the 1.7-litre Corsair remained available, as the V4 de Luxe saloon.

Complaints about Corsair V4 refinement persisted. A 2000 de Luxe did not fare well in a June 1968 *Motor* match with a Cortina 1600GT, Renault 16, Austin 1800, Hillman Hunter and Vauxhall Victor. The Cortina came in for a fair swipe for what the testers considered a raucous engine and high wind noise

around the door and window seals, but the Corsair's V4 engine was particularly panned: 'Worst by a considerable margin was the Ford Corsair, which had a rough, boomy exhaust note, although this was for some extent compensated for by lively performance, good low-speed torque and outstanding flexibility.' The test also observed that the overall size seemed a bit too big for the interior space offered.

In mid-1969 Corsair production transferred from Halewood to Dagenham to free up space for production of the Capri, and the final cars were produced in June 1970. With the advent of the slightly larger Cortina MkIII and its new 2-litre overhead-cam engine, the rationale for the Corsair had gone. It was a natural end of the line, as Harry Calton concludes: "Corsair met its targets. There weren't any left lying around on forecourts."

As for its engine, the 1,996cc V4 was to be a relatively short-lived unit compared to the V6 but it had a creditable career and further development in the Capri and finally the 1972 Consul before being phased out of car use in 1974. It also proved popular with boat builders, being short, relatively powerful and flexible: in 1965 there were 51 companies around the world 'marinising' these Ford engines.

LEFT Black PVC was standard trim for the 2000E: the rear seats changed to a pait of bucket seats in 1968.

Cortina and Corsair endurance runs

If you wanted to prove your car was reliable and scoop up worldwide publicity, then racking up an improbable mileage in a short time, preferably via numerous export markets, was a popular stunt for car makers by the 1960s.

Ford dealers and rally drivers Ken Chambers and Eric Jackson undertook a serious of perilous journeys, first in the Cortina then in both a Corsair 1500 and Corsair V4, initially for little more than expenses and glory, although they were given Corsairs after their round-the-world triumph.

Cape Town Cortina

The London to Cape Town Cortina record attempt in January 1963 was suggested to Eric Jackson by an acquaintance who had followed his efforts on the 1962 East African Safari Rally. Jackson then approached Walter Hayes who leapt at the idea. The duo were supplied with a two-door Cortina in the yet-to-be-released 1500GT specification, with higher safari suspension and a full-length sump

and tank guard. The interior was suitably stripped down to take vast reserves of drinking water.

The 13,000-mile route took 13 days, 8 hours and 48 minutes, travelling the length of Africa after crossing from Marseille to Tunis, then round via Egypt. Chambers and Jackson were reliant on plenty of help along the route from passing strangers as well as Ford dealers. Ford was happy to repeat the tale of the duo having to fire at bandits with the guns they had brought along, when they were forced into a 1,200-mile detour through Ethiopia, but Eric Jackson remembers times when the picture got even more desperate. "I lost 20lb and Ken lost 24lb and we got dehydrated. At one time we took 'last' pictures of each other. We got down to drinking soup, and were in a right mess until we came across some French doctors who saved us by offering us showers, rest and some oranges."

Thankfully the engine proved utterly dependable, going without an oil change until 5,000 miles, but the car needed rather more

LEFT The 1963 'Cape Town' Cortina pauses in a foreign land. Local dealers provided some support but for long stretches drivers Ken Chambers (hand on bonnet) and Eric Jackson (under road sign) were on their own, and it nearly killed them.

RIGHT Ahead of their first Corsair epic, Chambers and Jackson inspect their car. The engine was rebuilt and balanced, the high-backed passenger seat could fold down to become a bed, and an electric kettle was wired in for high-speed tea-making.

than the claimed fanbelt and light bulb by the time they reached Kenya and the salvation of Hughes Ford of Nairobi. "Everything was broken," recalls Jackson. "All the sump guard had gone, we had a multitude of holes in the floor, only three wheels with brakes, the battery had broken in half, the radiator had to be replaced – it went on and on. And we had to weld the passenger seat onto the floor."

The triumphant arrival in Cape Town also fell apart. Two hours down on time, after an exhausted stop at Beit Bridge on the South African border, the Cortina crew managed to hit 98mph as to cut weight they threw everything they could out of the car – including spare fuel, as they had mapped all the fuel stops and when they would be open.

Down in Cape Town, competitions manager Edgell 'Edgy' Fabris had, according to Eric Jackson, written them off, so was not at the expected place to confirm their time and officially record arrival to the RAC. The drivers only found Fabris after spotting his white suit as he stood outside his hotel, and crash-landed in a pile of gravel.

"We broke the record by 18 minutes but the tragedy was 'Edgy' should have been in touch with Beit Bridge but he got the idea into his head that as we were throwing things out of the car we'd given up, and he'd not informed Ford. They didn't get the news until the following day, which was the weekend. As a result neither of us got a penny but it made a wonderful difference to the dealership and we did very well out of it."

The Corsair challenges

Walter Hayes soon instigated the next stunt, a round-the-world trip to coincide with the launch of the Corsair in October 1963, the car's arrival timed for the opening of the London Motor Show – some 30,000 miles later. The target was 40 days, but the final tally was 43 days 5 hours.

This was an altogether slicker operation with more support and better communications. Eric Jackson also welcomed the heavier bodyshell of the new car: "I liked the Corsair. It could never have

Cortina and Corsair endurance runs (continued)

BELOW The round-the-world Corsair challenge was better supported by Ford, with numerous photo opportunities. The car's rear seat was removed to allow extra space for water, food and blankets, and the boot carried an extra 16-gallon fuel tank and high-pressure fuel pump.

been a rally car because it was very much heavier than the Cortina – you could tell that when the doors closed. They sold a lot better when we went round the world in one. They were having problems because for some reason the press gave them a bad write-up when they came out."

This robustness was amply tested when the drivers were confronted by two trucks side by side round a bend in Iran and left the road, dropping 150ft and bouncing off a telegraph pole. The fall broke the rear axle and cost them three days.

A relatively banal incident lost them the most time. The Australian service crew were told not to put a thermostat in the cooling system because if they were faulty they jammed in the closed position and so let no water through. But unbeknown to the drivers this had been ignored and when they got to Iran the engine blew a head gasket, leaving them stuck in the desert 100 miles from Tehran.

A more mundane type of endurance run (notably favoured by Austin in the 1950s) was to continuously drive a car at high speeds for as long as it took to amass some records. In 1964 just such a stunt was put to Walter Hayes by Gerry Boxall, whose team had run an Anglia at 83mph for seven days in 1962 and who suggested it should be possible to coax a Corsair GT up to a headline-worthy 100mph.

This was risky because it would have to run near maximum revs. The challenge was to run at more than 100mph for seven days with no more than minimal stops for fuel and driver changes. The chosen car was a two-door 1500GT and the track the Monza banked oval in Italy. The car was little changed apart from a different camshaft profile, adjustments to the Weber carburettor, Lotus-Cortina wheels and tyres, plus a 28-gallon fuel tank with twin fillers. Both bumpers were removed and a fairing put in place at the front.

The six drivers buried the throttle and at times exceeded 100mph, but after 4 days and 18 hours the Corsair's crankshaft expired. Nonetheless, 13 world speed records had been set, the car having maintained over 100mph for 15,000 miles.

The final Corsair challenge for the redoubtable Chambers and Jackson – this time with a two-door V4 2000 in May 1967 – was to 'race' the mail boat *Windsor Castle* from Cape Town to Southampton and beat the Cortina record by two days. A win was chalked up for the Corsair this time, the car covering 9,752 miles compared to the ship's 7,000, at an average speed of 42mph. This time 'Edgy' Fabris had his share of troubles, being detained in the Congo with a party of TV men and journalists, because of suspicion over their aircraft's papers; ultimately the British vice-consul came to their rescue.

Chapter 5:
The MkII Cortina

Although the MkI Cortina continued to sell well in 1966, its successor was on the blocks waiting for October's London Motor Show. The original styling was dating fast, the range had long outgrown its economy-car rôle, and buyers were looking for more power and refinement.

Ford knew that the Cortina was now its most important model. "It became very clear after 12 months that the Cortina was our Crown Jewels," Terence Beckett recalls. "And as Crown Jewels it really had to be protected, so it was very necessary to change, have a new model after four years, and they did this all the way through the life of the Cortina."

When profiling the Cortina story in September 1967, *The Times* newspaper claimed that the MkII had in fact been introduced a year ahead of schedule because overseas dealers were indicating that something more was needed to maintain the Cortina's position as Britain's best-selling export car. The author has not been able to substantiate this. According to the article, the Cortina had initially sold more abroad than at home, but in 1965 and 1966 home sales had exceeded export sales. This was in fact a relief to Ford of Britain, as on account of trade tariffs it was only breaking even abroad in that period.

ABOVE **Carnaby Street-clad 'Cortina Girl' Colleen Fitzpatrick was Ford's symbol of the 'swinging sixties' into which the 1966 Cortina was launched. Her daughter and husband also appear here.**

Money, money, money

Work had started on the second-generation Cortina around 1963. It was decided that there was no reason why the new car could not be based on the very successful platform and running gear of its predecessor, so the project became a careful re-skin and refinement exercise. Nonetheless, the total cost of design and development was set at £12m.

Roy Haynes, a former Briggs interior stylist, had rejoined Ford in 1963 and soon worked his way up to be manager of the medium-car studio, where he was given responsibility for the new Cortina's exterior styling. To see the inspiration,

says Haynes, look no further than Ford of America's wildly successful 1964 Mustang. "There were a lot of fans for the Mustang. If you look at the side of it there's a lot of symmetry with the side of a MkII. The car was very successful. Even down to the little ridge which goes round the backlight – Duncan Macrae [newly appointed head of styling, one of an increasing number of US managers] was very keen on that."

According to Haynes there were two competing designs within Ford's British studios at Aveley, his car and that of fellow Englishman John Fallis, which had a more marked 'Coke bottle' rising curve over the rear wheel arch. This

ABOVE September 1964 and the styling of the second Cortina is largely fixed, although the sweeping wheel arches did not survive.

RIGHT Top Ford management as of January 1965 gathers around another MkII styling proposal. From right to left, figures include stylist Duncan McRae, Bill Batty (who became Chairman of Ford of Britain), managing director Allen Barke (with pipe), chief engineer Fred Hart (with moustache) and finance director John Barber (left, in profile).

mimicked the contours of the famous glass bottle and it had been catching on with American stylists since the 1962 Studebaker Avanti and the Chevrolet Corvair Monza GT design study. However, Haynes disliked the look and his squarer shape won out. John Bradshaw, who later designed the Escort, says the second-generation Cortina was a hybrid of a number of people's designs; his own contribution was the front end.

Although the overall length and wheelbase stayed the same, the new Cortina boasted a 2in increase in front and rear shoulder-room, greater legroom and a little more boot space – Ford claimed 21cu ft to the old car's 20.9 (although measured by the 'real world' test boxes of *Motor* it was 10.1cu ft and still considered 'enormous').

Roy Haynes remembers how each detail was hard-fought with the product planners. "They wanted to control everything, for example the depth of glass. I wanted to increase the depth of glass one inch and there was a glorious row! But I had trained as an engineer, so I could actually beat

them. This began to bite into product planning, so much so that their costings started to be questioned, because they had based it on their previous costs." It was the same for the engineers. Howard Panton was handed the task of final development and testing of the '67 Cortina in January 1965. "It was a crash programme – and a cheap programme. The MkI was a fairly quick programme but the MkII was even quicker," he remembers.

Ostensibly the suspension set-up remained as before, as it was carried over with the understructure of the old car; there was, however, some detailed fine-tuning, Panton being able to make small but important improvements. "I had a personal view, which was shared by some people, that the MkI had a really rather nasty roll-oversteer which was due to the geometry of the rear axle. I got the geometry of the MkII changed in the design phase. It was lowering the rear spring front eye which changed the geometry of the rear axle and stopped the roll-oversteer. We developed it on a MkI by lashing up metal brackets and things to prove it."

The front and rear tracks were widened by 2½in and 1½in respectively. At the front the coil springs of the MacPherson struts were mounted at an angle on each strut to cut down friction – a trick introduced on the Corsair V4. There was also what Ford called a 'compliance' device of extra rubber cushioning where the front anti-roll bar met the suspension linkage, allowing it to move rearwards a little to keep the wheels in proper alignment as they moved backwards under hard braking. At the rear, the GT carried over the twin radius arms fitted to later versions of its predecessor.

Howard Panton also had to fight his corner just for a piece of rubber. "I wanted softer suspension on the front to improve the ride quality and in order to put lower-rate springs on you had to put a rubber bump-stop in the suspension strut to stop it banging. We had to have main board directors appraising two cars I'd set up, one with the original firm suspension and the other the development I'd proposed of lower springs and a rubber bump-stop. I think it was two bob [shillings] a car, something like that."

But then when you were turning out a car in hundreds of thousands, those two-shilling bump-stops soon added up. What to leave out was as well costed as what to put into the new Cortina. In deciding how much more refinement to offer, Ford claimed it had built what it called a 'hushmobile' – a development car fitted with every possible piece of soundproofing and rubber damping, with no heed to weight, fuel economy or performance. This provided a base from which to compare what could be done with more scientifically applied soundproofing. But if an element cost too much it was left behind.

"There was a bit of a struggle the whole time," Panton recalls. "Particularly on things like insulation materials inside, you had to really demonstrate a benefit. There were other things that were developed and didn't get approved. The automatic had a nasty boom-period at 40mph and I tuned it out with a resonator on the springs, but that did cost a bit of money and so wasn't adopted."

Front disc brakes were standard fitment from de Luxe models upwards, with those on the GT being slightly larger.

ABOVE This 1966 cutaway shows little rear wheelarch intrusion for rear passengers in the new cabin, although the wheelbase was unchanged. At 14ft, the new Cortina was marginally shorter than before.

LEFT A 1965-registered MkII prototype is tested at Bagshot in Surrey, its true rear light shapes obscured. This was a tank-testing circuit where rally cars were driven until they broke.

ABOVE Painted metal on this export-model dashboard means it's a 1300; more expensive Cortinas had a PVC covering. Aeroflow ventilation was now claimed to be 25 per cent more effective.

RIGHT A very early MkII in a tight bend: the angle looks precarious, despite the roll centre of the rear suspension having been improved.

The brakes were self-adjusting, as was the new diaphragm-spring clutch, cable-operated as opposed to the hydraulic operation used on the MkI. By necessity, more attention was paid to built-in safety features, a number of which were imposed by new rules. For example, American GSA (General Services Administration) regulations for 1966 dictated that rear lamps should be visible from the side, hence the new Cortina's wraparound lenses.

In the four years following its launch, the Cortina's competitors had grown in both dimensions and engine size (save for the BMC 1100), and with the extra refinement deemed necessary for the new car, an increase in engine capacity and power was inevitable. Additionally the 1100 and 1300 Escorts were being readied to replace the Anglia and would occupy some of the territory of the previous Cortina.

Thus the 1,198cc unit gave way to one of 1,297cc. Ford was keen to stress this was not merely a stretch but a new unit with a unique cylinder block supporting a four-throw crankshaft in five main bearings. The flywheel was made heavier to smooth out variations in engine torque.

The new 1300 gave 53.5bhp (net) to the old 48.5bhp. The 1500 engine was carried over virtually unchanged; it developed 61bhp as used in the Super (or when optionally fitted to the de Luxe), or 78bhp in the GT. In standard 1300 and 1500 tune it went over to Ford's own make of carburettor, while the GT stayed with a twin-choke Weber. The Cortina 1200 didn't entirely vanish, being available for some overseas markets where there were higher taxes on larger engines.

Gearboxes were largely carried over. This wasn't universally well received: the ratios of the GT's box, inherited

from the MkI 1200 and 1500, appeared too widely spaced for a sporting car, with a gap between second and third gear which *Autocar* said 'made driving a misery'. This was remedied in early 1967 with a swap to the Corsair GT's ratios. The Borg-Warner three-speed automatic could now be specified with the 1300 engine.

The 1966 Cortina didn't put on much weight compared to the slimline original. When tested by *Motor* the new 1300 four-door weighed in at 16.6cwt, compared to 15.8cwt for 1962's 1200 four-door. The extra power more than made up for the weight and there was an 11 per cent increase in torque at lower speeds. On test, acceleration from standstill through the gears was very much the same as a 1965 Cortina 1200, with an 80mph top speed being recorded; with a calculated touring consumption of 33.7mpg, the car was judged reasonably economical. All of this was delivered in very much smoother manner, the magazine found, thanks to the five-bearing crankshaft.

'New Cortina is more Cortina!' was the slogan at the October 1966 launch. The eight-model range was fuller from the start, with two-door and four-door versions of the de Luxe, Super and GT on offer. Estates and a new Lotus-Cortina were not available until 1967. Prices started at £668 with tax and ran to £834. Ford had priced its new car at just £8 more than the old one, even at a time of economic gloom in the home market – at the motor show Sir Patrick Hennessy lambasted the UK government over hire-purchase restrictions. There was plenty of choice on options and for the first time Cortinas could be specified with two shades of metallic paint, Blue Mink and Saluki Bronze, which sadly gained a reputation for losing their shine – indeed adhesion – rather rapidly.

With so much familiar material under the smart new bodywork, Ford could not expect the rapturous reception of 1962, but the 1966 Cortina was well received and the press gave Ford credit that after only four years with the MkI it was not resting on its laurels a little longer. After quite some chin-scratching and hopping between an earlier 1200 and the new 1300, *Motor* arrived at a list where gains outweighed the losses, deciding that 'numerous small improvements make the 1300 a significantly better car'.

Its verdict was finely drawn. In-gear acceleration was much the same, the steering and brakes had become heavier, but there was a much more comfortable ride and better roadholding. The new Cortina was roomier, quieter and a 'very sound, sensible car'. The best thing, though, was the price. 'Where else can you get so much for £669?'

LEFT Available from February 1967, the new estate was a formidable load-lugger; the completely flat floor was protected by a rubber mat on the Super.

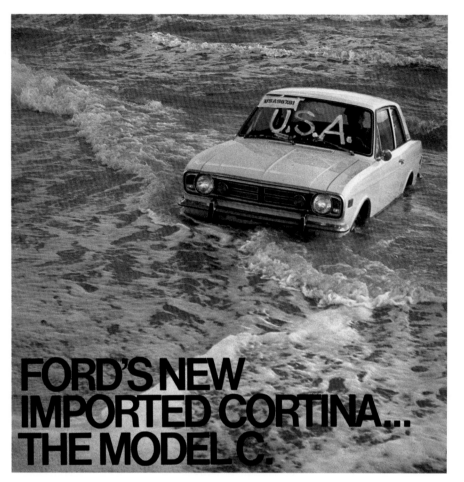

FORD'S NEW IMPORTED CORTINA... THE MODEL C.

ABOVE No wonder they rusted … 1968 model-year US Cortinas sprouted an inelegant solution to lighting regulations. The central amber lamps are indicators and the former indictor/sidelamp units are reduced to sidelamps only, while reflective markers are fitted aside each front wing. (Author's collection)

Nonetheless, this time competition was stronger, 1966 seeing the introduction of several similar noteworthy alternatives in and around the Cortina's size and price-class. The Simca 1301/1501 and the Fiat 124 were new in 1966, perhaps not serious volume competitors in the UK, but bearing a distinct resemblance to the new Cortina. The groundbreaking Renault 16 had been on sale for a year, as had the front-wheel-drive Triumph 1300. Also launched at the October show, Vauxhall's second-generation Viva was admired for its big-car looks and rose up the best-seller charts in the following years to give the Escort and lower-priced Cortinas a run for their money.

The most direct domestic challenger, introduced early in 1967, was the Rootes Group's 1½-litre Hillman Minx, based on the 1,725cc Hillman Hunter, which had been the first in a series of models replacing all its earlier Minx-derived cars. With its MacPherson strut front suspension (a first for Rootes) and a light, strong bodyshell manufactured by Pressed Steel Fisher, it was a whole hundredweight lighter than its smaller predecessor. By badge-engineering this 'Arrow' range of

cars into Hillman, Humber, Singer and Sunbeam saloons and estates (plus the Rapier/Alpine coupé), healthy sales followed – but not enough to save Rootes from a full takeover by Chrysler US in 1967. With money fast running out, the Arrow cars were only allowed mild facelifts and sales tailed off as two further Cortina evolutions passed it by before production finally ended in 1979.

BMC was not now competing directly on engine size with the new Cortina, and its larger-engined cars were up against the Corsair, but nonetheless the 1100, with its multiple badge-engineered derivatives, was still Britain's best-selling car in 1966; a 1,275cc engine finally arrived the following autumn.

New Cortina sales took off at a great pace. In 1967 alone 290,972 were assembled and in Britain – for that year only – it knocked the 1100 off its perch, capturing 14.9 per cent of the whole market with 165,300 cars registered. In subsequent years, once you added the sales of the Escort, the 1100/1300 was still roundly beaten year-on-year, and the Cortina was to reign supreme for much of the 1970s. Business liked the new Cortina too; fleet orders included 450 for Tupperware area managers plus hundreds of Cortinas for hire companies Godfrey Davis and Hertz.

A capacious purpose-built estate (with minimal wheelarch intrusion thanks to lever-arm instead of telescopic dampers) arrived in February 1967. It was available with both engines, but automatic transmission was only an option with the 1500 because of the prospect of heavier loads being carried in the estates. A bench seat and column gearchange could also be ordered on the 1500, as well as on the 1300.

In the same month Ford of England launched a determined assault on the US market with the new Cortina, flying 260 US dealer principals and 50 journalists to London with a great deal of fanfare, to sample the cars and be wined and dined. Such was the importance of exports that there was a message of support from the Prime Minister. "We believe there is a big potential for the new Cortina in the US – especially the GT version – and we are prepared to spend a lot of money to open up the market," enthused Ford Division executive Matt McLaughlin.

Slotted in with the Falcon and the Mustang as part of a trio of 'economy' cars, in the States the Cortina was dubbed the 'Model C' in an attempt to evoke instant heritage. Against a sales target of 15,000 compared to the previous year's 10,000 cars, by year-end 16,193 MkIIs had been sold to US buyers. The economy-car tag now held true, as a US Cortina came in under the important $2,000 barrier, thanks to

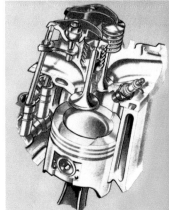

ABOVE Ford's use of the 'bowl-in-piston' design was the most widely manufactured application of the 'Heron' concept at the time. The combustion recess in the top of the piston is shown here.

a pound devalued by 14.3 per cent. All the same, Ford was careful not to flood a market with cars which would not meet 19 new safety standards looming for 1968, plus stringent exhaust emission controls. March saw the eagerly awaited introduction of the new Ford-built Lotus-Cortina, fully covered in the following chapter, but this was not exported to the States, presumably to allow Ford to concentrate on modifying the mainstream models to meet the new standards.

New show, new engine

One wonders if the buyer of a 1967 model-year Cortina might have been somewhat irked to find that in September 1967 the range was fitted with the crossflow engines – not least as the cheeky advertising showed a 1968 model overtaking a 1967 car, with the legend 'The new ones go even faster without being more thirsty.'

Foreshadowed by the 'Essex' V4 and V6 engines, the crossflow design improved power and fuel economy – especially important ahead of anticipated American anti-pollution regulations. The design was a welcome enhancement of the high-revving oversquare Kent engine, which soon became regarded as the best standard engine in the business. But it wasn't the only interesting British power unit that year. The new Vauxhall Victor FD, bigger than its predecessors and with pronounced 'Coke bottle' styling, boasted all-new 1.6-litre and 2.0-litre belt-driven single-overhead-cam engines, a 'first' for a British car and considered very advanced for the time. The Victor would be a major influence on the following Cortina.

The smaller Cortina crossflow engine retained the 1,298cc capacity but with the new head power rose from 53.5bhp to 58bhp. The bigger power unit grew to 1,599cc, however, with a deeper cylinder block and up to 88bhp in GT

ABOVE Looking very Jet Set here, the desirable 1600E sat 1in lower on chrome-and-black sports wheels, and had fixed twin spotlamps and a subtle blue or gold coachline. Unlike the other 'E' cars, a vinyl roof was never standard, although it was a popular option.

RIGHT The 1600E interior boasted reclining front seats, a leather-covered aluminium steering wheel, a clock, leather gearlever gaiter, walnut door cappings, and veneer applied to the GT dashboard. On later models the extra instruments sat lower within the dash.

tune. Having been development-tested in 50 Cortinas run by Ford employees, the company claimed that the new units were faster yet no less economical than their predecessors.

If it seems odd to effectively relaunch a car a year later, it could have been that the crossflow engine and the new Cortina were originally planned for introduction at the same time. "The problem is you have to align your production facilities with your marketing programme," observes former *Autocar* editor Ray Hutton. "They were going to change the model at a certain point because the life cycle had been defined, and if engineering and production couldn't keep up with that, then too bad, they'd do it later. I think it was simply that they hadn't got all their ducks in a row."

Not just a Cortina ... a 1600E

As well as the new engines, the 1968 model-year Cortinas were treated to a selection of minor interior improvements. Of rather more interest to enthusiastic drivers, the GT now came with radial-ply tyres as standard, while the Super was given

the GT's remote-control gearchange.

Then, without much fanfare, a new type of Cortina, the 1600E, appeared at the September 1967 Paris Motor Show. Following in the tracks of the Zodiac Executive and the Corsair 2000E, the humble Cortina now got the luxury 'E' (for 'Excellence', 'Executive' or whatever you prefer) treatment. With no alternative marques to pull out of the hat, in the fashion of BMC and Rootes, the 'E' Fords were a concerted attempt to widen the market, develop a measure of prestige and hopefully steal sales from the likes of Rover and Triumph. It also gave the fleet manager a range of Cortinas to please junior sales reps or managing directors.

Based on the newly crossflow-engined 1600GT, the new model was offered in the UK only as a four-door, although a handful of two-doors were produced for Ford UK management and some two-doors were built for overseas markets, notably left-hand-drive cars supplied to Ford-Amsterdam as Knocked Down kits, for assembly for the Benelux countries and Switzerland.

**ABOVE The very rare
2-door 1600E was not sold
in the UK.**

The 1600E was a combination of Cortina features that owners could not specify themselves: a cocktail of Lotus-Cortina suspension – which made the car 1in lower – with the standard radial-ply tyres of the GT and Lotus, plus a walnut dashboard encompassing the GT's extra instrumentation, along with wood door cappings and extra carpet and soundproofing. It also managed to retain the rear radius arms which the GT lost for the 1968 model year. Another quirk, unearthed by author Graham Robson, is that suspension settings varied over the years, and did not in fact always match those of the Lotus-Cortina.

The wood had been a bit of a struggle to get through, Terence Beckett recalls. "We couldn't get our own engineers to be interested in this, and in the end we found a man up in Coventry who was fitting these panels on a sort of 'one-off' basis. We got one in a car and brought it down to Dagenham and showed them how easily all these extra fittings could be done, and what they did to enhance the value of the car."

The 1600E's unique 5½in chromium-plated Rostyle steel wheels came from Rubery Owen and were similar to those

fitted to Jensens and Rovers. They gave the impression of being spoked by the depressions being painted matt black. Perhaps not as expensive as they looked, they became quite a target for thieves over subsequent years – as indeed the whole car did, for its interior trim.

Copious standard equipment included a radio, twin reversing lights, and two Wipac spotlamps permanently wired into the main light circuit to give the 1600E a four-headlamp system. Dual-tone horns told others to move out of the way, even though with the standard 88bhp (net) it only looked faster than the GT.

At launch the Cortina 1600E was priced at £982 tax-paid, £98 more than an equivalent GT and £86 less than a Lotus – exactly the gap Ford wanted to fill. All the same, *Autocar* could not quite see the point at first. 'It's hard to see where the Cortina 1600E fits in at only £47 less than a Corsair 2000E, except that there is a very real £1,000 barrier which the Cortina slips under and it has slightly less status attached to it than has a Corsair,' wrote the magazine.

The Taunus P6

In contrast to the cautious evolution of the Cortina, the Taunus 12M was radically rethought in September 1966, retaining front-wheel drive and V4 engines but adopting MacPherson strut front suspension and rack-and-pinion steering. The new car was 2½in longer than the original, and like the Cortina boasted more interior space through the use of curved side glass.

While still badged 12M, the engine was enlarged to 1.3 litres and the 1.5-litre version saw the reintroduction of the 15M designation (although confusingly, you could still get a 12M 1500), based on the same bodyshell but with square headlamps and a different grille. The 15M dropped the earlier combined heating/cooling system for a conventional front-mounted radiator. Designed to bridge the gap between the 12M and the ever-growing 17M range, a 1.7-litre joined the 15M range in January 1967 and this formed the basis of the sporting 15M RS coupé. It was hardly surprising there were no English takers; when listed in the UK, a 12M came in at little less than a Lotus-Cortina.

Production was centred on Cologne and the new Genk plant in Belgium. The P6 proved a reasonable seller, with 668,187 built to 1970, a figure in line with that for the earlier generation but not very impressive compared to the Cortina. It was to be the swansong for the all-German front-driven Ford.

In a historic footnote to the 1950s Cardinal project where Saab test mules would run around Dearborn proving front-wheel drive, Ford of Germany supplied the 1.5-litre V4 for the Saab 96 from 1966, replacing Saab's dated two-stroke units. It would continue to power the 96 saloon and related 95 estate until their demise in 1979, and was also installed in the Saab Sonnett sports car.

ABOVE The 1966 Taunus 12M range expanded to include the 15M, distinguished by its own grille and rectangular headlamps.

LEFT The 15M continued the tradition of a coupé cheaply spun off the saloon with a new roof and rear window glass. (Ford-Werke GmbH)

Crayford and the Cortina MkII

With the advent of the MkII, Crayford was at the zenith of its Cortina conversions, offering both soft-top options and engine upgrades on it and other Fords. Crayford's relationship with Ford was firmly established and a convertible was exhibited with the new range at the 1966 Earls Court Motor Show, work having been carried out in secret in previous weeks by Jeffrey Smith. The roof of a two-door Cortina was removed just behind the windscreen pillars and at the back at waist level. The interior was gutted and extra internal boxed sills added to the floor and vertical reinforcements to the door pillars, which were braced by a bar running across the car under the dashboard. Steel plates were welded around the rear seat pan to stiffen the rear end. As with the Corsair, there were two types of Cortina conversion: on the 'convertible' the hood folded down to sit on top of the rear seat just ahead of the front edge of the bootlid, while the more costly 'cabriolet' hood sat further forwards, entailing a larger panel between the front of the boot and rear edge of the hood, which folded flat into a well added to the rear compartment, this entailing a narrowed rear seat. About two cars a week were converted.

By 1969 Crayford was converting the Cortina, the BMC 1100/1300 and the Vauxhall Viva. The usually outspoken *Car* decided it should sample a Viva and a Cortina for its July issue. It was not impressed by the Ford. 'Quite frankly the Cortina seemed to bear out our worst fears about this type of conversion because it rattled and banged, the steering wheel shuddered, the hood flapped and the visibility with the hood up was extremely poor', wrote the magazine. Having put off any potential buyers, it did observe that Crayford could only work with the material it was given, and that 'Ford are not noted for the heavy gauge of their body metal or outstanding rigidity in the chassis stiffness of their unit-construction motor cars.' Luckily for Crayford, *Car* found the newer Viva to be much less prone to scuttle shake and rather preferred it to look at as well as to drive.

"I cannot remember a single car ever returned by a customer complaining of body shake, weird though that may seem," David

ABOVE While in 'cabriolet' form the hood packed down neatly, when it was up there wasn't much rear-quarter visibility. All-in prices in October 1966 ranged from £917 to £1,069.

LEFT This prototype Crayford convertible was finished hours before the 1966 London Motor Show opened and 17 days after Ford had given Crayford the GT it was based on. It was the first Ford convertible at the show since the MkII Zephyr in 1962.

RIGHT This handily labelled group of Crayford's 1969 fast Fords purported to include Cortina 'Diplomat' models ranging from the fuel-injected 1600 Diplomat Junior (A and B) to the V6 Cortina Diplomats in the foreground, complete with Vauxhall Victor FD grilles and lights. The bloated Escorts (D and F) are 2.5-litre and 3.0-litre V6 'Eliminators'. (Giles Chapman Library)

McMullan recalls. Geoff Howard also offers a plea in mitigation: "All the top-cut convertibles of that era were very floppy. The tin roof was a vital part of the unitary structure then and even adding great big beams in the sills did little to help. They all shook and rattled, twisted and bucked whenever they came near a bump or steep road camber. If you look at the press packs of the '80s you see torsional stiffness figures and improvements quoted as enormous achievements, so the likes of Crayford were really biting off more than they realised."

Crayford generally worked with cars that were on paper secondhand, although this would amount to the owner buying the car new and then taking it for conversion for £200–£350 more. If you bought the car new you paid tax on both car and conversion, meaning that in 1969 a Cortina 1300 two-door cost £809 but rose to £1,323 when chopped. Despite the premium and its structural

wobbliness, the Crayford MkII sold well, with 400 soft-tops built in total, of which 20 were based on the Lotus-Cortina.

Crayford engine transplants

As well as the convertibles, Crayford Auto Developments also offered engine upgrades for Fords, although these were short-lived. A V6 conversion with the 3-litre Zodiac engine was offered from 1968 to 1970. You could also have a V6 convertible for a heady £1,902. In 1968 Crayford claimed its range was a '14-point attack on the 1969 European market', making the company 'the largest manufacturer of Ford-based variants in Europe'. There are no sure numbers, but the bulk of these V6 Cortinas appear to have gone to Spain – where Crayford had strong business connections – and don't appear to have been heard of again, although four are said to have survived, two of which were running in 2011.

ABOVE Spot the difference. The Hillman Hunter was followed by the smaller-engined Minx in January 1967. 'Neat but anonymous' said *Motor* of the front grille – which was not much different from that of the Cortina and Taunus, and of Vauxhall and Volvo models of the period. (Author's collection)

As might be expected, *Car* was much more forthright, after spending ten days in a 1600E in summer 1968. While the testers viewed the 'Executive idea … with its social-climbing overtones' to be 'so very repulsive', they did concede that by offering extra trim with the Lotus suspension and GT engine the 1600E was more than just a cosmetic exercise and that the soundproofing did a good job at calming down some of the harshness for which the heavier-pistoned crossflow unit was becoming criticised; wind noise from the window frames, meanwhile, was a problem shared with other Cortinas. 'The faster you go the worse is the noise,' the magazine remarked, observing that 'above 80mph the radio is inaudible and conversation becomes too much effort'.

On top of this, *Car* said that the reduced suspension travel of the Lotus set-up seemed the worst idea for an 'executive' car, especially if you were in the back seat. The handling was good but the ride was awful: during the course of a journey through Switzerland the magazine reported one seasoned traveller being sick and the driver left exhausted by the constant jiggling and the heavy steering.

The Cortina's fussiness at high revs and elevated levels of wind noise – especially when experienced in the higher-priced versions – started to be regular gripes in road tests. In a *Motor* comparison test of March 1969, a 1600E Cortina was matched with an identically engined new Capri 1600GT and found wanting: 'Ford's NVH treatment has obviously paid off,' commented the writer, as the engine was now 'quiet and remote compared to the 1600E.'

But what did Terence Beckett care of the critics? The 1600E made far more money than posh Zephyrs or Corsairs,

he points out. "You could get extraordinarily good volume on this car, while at the same time the relationship of cost and price was such that we made a good unit profit on it." There certainly was volume. Orders taken at the motor show led to the doubling of planned 1600E production for 1968. The new variant had struck a section of motorists as a deeply desirable car. "People who bought them weren't buying a Cortina, they were buying a 1600E," says Harry Calton. "It sold like it was going out of fashion."

"The 1600E was the one everybody wanted to have," Ray Hutton recalls. "Ford combined luxury with sportiness, and gave it some of the Lotus bits without the twin cam. When I went to work for *Motoring News* in 1970 they were renowned for paying no money but giving everybody decent cars. There was a discussion about what was a good car up

to the limit the boss would pay and the 1600E was one of those, even though it was coming to the end of its life. There was a lot of bullshit about it really, because it wasn't anything very special but it looked quite nice."

There were a few adjustments to the 1600E for 1969, including twin rear bucket seats apeing those of the Rover 2000, with a centre armrest plus more stowage, and a matt-black finishing panel between the rear lamps. The chrome plating on the wheels was replaced by aluminium paint. Being GT-derived, it also received the GT's revised instrument layout, with the auxiliary dials migrating from their dash-top pod to the centre of the dashboard.

Sold for just under three years, with a total production of 58,582 cars, 1600E sales built year-on-year, with a monthly peak of 3,054 in June 1970, just two months before MkII production ended. The car remained a much-admired model long after its demise in 1970, and became the first Cortina to have an owners' club, in 1976. The 'E' designation was further applied to the Capri and Escort and reappeared on a Cortina in 1973 but the badge was ultimately dropped in favour of the spurious Ghia denomination, which was applied to both English and German Fords.

There was no 1600E estate but the rare 1600GT estate was pretty close mechanically. This did not appear in the catalogue but if you asked a Ford dealer nicely you could order one. It had the full GT suspension and interior package – although retaining the estate's lever-arm rear dampers – and *Autocar* found that although expensive for a Cortina, at £1,137 tested, none of its rivals could better its performance.

Cortina conquers America (a little)

Bedecked with extra lighting, GT40-style stripes and safety gear, 1968 was to be the Cortina's finest year for American sales. With Anglia production having ended in 1967, 26,000 Cortinas were sold as the sole English Ford on offer, with Dagenham maintaining that the number could have been higher but for strikes. The base 1300 was never offered, nor was the 1600E or the Lotus, and true to sales predictions the GT proved to be the most popular model.

The enthusiast magazines loved the Cortina's small size, reasonable price and perky nature. 'Always interesting in any Ford of England is that swinging engine. The Cortina engine is to England what Chevy's small V8 is to the United States,' said *Car Life* in 1968, full of praise for the design of the crossflow head. 'It is surprising to find a smog pump on this ultra-modern engine,' it commented, all the same. 'Most US manufacturers have found ways around them by better mixture control and optimum spark advance … We suspect that it was an economy move. Ford markets this car, and the smaller Escort, all over Europe where smog control is not yet required.' This was true. For an engine which had not been designed for the air around Los Angeles the smog pump – or air pump – was indeed a bolt-on fix for many importers, injecting extra air into the exhaust system to reduce carbon monoxide and hydrocarbon emissions. The pump and plumbing inevitably sapped a little power.

The Cortina's US career was already drawing to a close in 1969 when Ford US introduced the smartly styled Maverick compact as a prelude to the 1970 Pinto (see Chapter Seven). Ford of Britain optimistically thought US buyers would come to look at the Maverick in the showrooms but go for the

cheaper Cortina, but the Maverick finally killed sales. The numbers sold had been the biggest-ever for a British Ford, but the Cortina's entire American sales career was a drop in the ocean compared to the 500,000 or so VW Beetles imported each year – and nor was quality and durability at the same level as that of the Volkswagen. 'As with so many other English machines of the era and origin, it was fraught with issues. The Kent's distributor was susceptible to condensation; sadly, typical electrical and rust gremlins often followed', wrote Jeff Koch in 2008, in *Hemmings Sports & Exotic Car*. While 1970 spelt the end of American Cortinas, Canada, which had posted sales at roughly half the amount, took the Cortina MkIII until 1973.

V6 will go …

By the time of the MkII Cortina, a host of aftermarket tuners had sprung up to make the cars go faster. Ray Hutton recalls one of his first jobs was to test a Taurus conversion, which was a modified cylinder head and camshaft supplied for £39. Super Speed and Chris Steele Engineering also offered engine upgrades. On the whole, tuning a Cortina was fairly predictable. "They liked to work on the 1600E because like the GT it had a Weber and it wasn't too difficult to fit a bigger one, so quite a lot of people did that. The performance gains were not as great as you might think – the car was quite fast by standards of the time. In those days nobody cared about torque, so if you got a bit more speed out of it that would do. Quite a lot of people were using various shortcuts to get a bit more performance."

There was rather more scope for complete engine swaps on the MkII Cortina, now that the compact 'Essex' V6 was available. LuMo Car Products in Bedfordshire offered the Lotus twin-cam in a 1600E for £1,399, but the biggest bang-for-your-buck was always going to be shoehorning the 3-litre V6 into the engine bay. Such conversions were already unofficially being carried out within Ford of Britain – the competitions department created their own V6 Corsair rally-support estates and boss Henry Taylor had his own V6 two-door Cortina, along with Walter Hayes. However, Dagenham was too busy pumping out regular Cortinas to be diverted by building such a hybrid, which would doubtless also have poached sales from its larger cars. Instead, it looked on with interest while others set to work.

The Cortina Savage, offered by Race Proved of Hanwell, West London, was the best-known conversion, and nearest to being endorsed by Ford of Britain. The business was run

RIGHT A 3-litre V6 plus Cortina equals Savage: a scene in Uren's Hanwell workshop, photographed by Ford in 1968. The Zodiac carburettor was retained but with a shallower air cleaner.

ABOVE No two Savages were alike, and there were thus around 142 unique examples. This painstakingly restored 1969 1600E-based example wears the 'S' bonnet badge and Dunlop alloy wheels. It is fitted with optional overdrive. (Rob Sargant)

by Jeff Uren, one-time Ford racing-team manager with the Willment Group and a former Ford rally driver The degree to which Ford tacitly approved of the Savage remains a little foggy. "Ford discreetly gave us their blessing and a lot of test information that helped us brace the body correctly for the extra loads … what sort of extra welding would be needed in the chassis side-rails, that kind of thing," Uren (who died in 2007), claimed in a 1986 interview with Jeremy Walton for *Classic & Sportscar*.

Much was made of the fact that the 3-litre 136bhp (net) Zodiac engine was unmodified – therefore implying that it was still warranted by Ford; in any case, once freed from the weight of a hefty bodyshell no further tuning was required. When a development Savage was tested by *Autocar* in August 1967, the figures were astonishing for the day: 0–60mph in 8.8 seconds and a mean top speed of 104mph, with equally impressive in-gear urge. The driver could burble around town in second and fourth gears, and third and fourth on the open road. 'Although this car is so docile and well-behaved in town, it really does hitch up its skirts and get moving on the open road in a manner that will leave practically everything else standing,' enthused the magazine.

From summer 1967 a complete Savage from Race Proved was offered for sale for £1,365, based on a Cortina 1500GT minus engine. Future production was then based on the 1600GT, the Lotus, and the 1600E after its introduction later that year. On the whole Race Proved preferred to convert new Cortinas, but some used cars were up-engined.

It was not a simple conversion. The front crossmember had to be modified to accommodate the deeper sump, new engine mountings welded in, and an adaptor plate fitted between clutch and gearbox, the latter being the standard item, with Corsair 2000E ratios. The battery was relocated to the boot, a new wiring loom fitted, plus an alternator, and a very necessary second eight-gallon fuel tank was fitted behind the rear seats.

A Salisbury Powr-Lok limited-slip differential and thicker half shafts were very necessary axle modifications. The Lotus final-drive ratio of 3.77:1 was later joined by an optional 3.55:1 as the Savage was regarded as too under-geared to achieve its true top speed. Wheels were 5½in wide and shod with radial-ply tyres. The aim was to produce a potent car which was nonetheless civilised to drive and would put its power down without yards of axle tramp. Road tests reflected a well-tamed car, but heavy steering was the price to pay for the big engine and wider tyres.

Between 1967 and 1968, much effort was made to sort the suspension and braking to cope with the power, the Savage clearly being a work in progress. The *Autocar* test car, XJH 234F, boiled its coolant after a long drive and Uren altered the position of the thermostat to the electric radiator fan. When *Car* published its test of the GT-based car in January 1968 it said that 27 suspension settings had been tried before Uren reckoned he'd got it right – but he wouldn't specify how.

Uren said that the Savage had a particular appeal to press barons and the aristocracy, who wanted speed in a discreet package and that this encouraged Walter Hayes to supply an early batch of 1600Es to convert, because it put Fords into the hands of a different class of buyer – this while dealers were still waiting for their first 1600Es.

In January 1968 Race Proved was gearing up to produce ten cars a week, the order book was filled for months to come, and the 1600E was now the basis of what was known as the Savage II. Although Uren also produced tuned versions of subsequent Cortinas, the MkII Savage was by far the most successful, making up the bulk of the 1,000 Cortina conversions built by Race Proved between 1968 and 1974. The overall total of uprated Fords passing through the

Uren workshops totalled 1,700 and included V6 Escorts, V8 Capris and even V6 Transit vans.

Ray Hutton recalls that this constant exchange of engines had some side benefits. "I don't think Race Proved were allowed to be delivered cars without engines, but they had a kind of deal where they took the cars in. They usually had a load of new-ish 1600 engines which would unofficially be put into Anglias. I always fancied one of those because there were Anglias with 1,340cc engines which had come out of the Classic but a 1600 Anglia was going to be really good." Geoff Howard did exactly that, obtaining a redundant 1600GT engine from a contact within Ford and persuading Uren to build him an Anglia 1600GT. "With its new engine it pulled like a train in every gear including top," he remembers.

The South African cousin

There was never any intention to go racing with the Savage, but in South Africa the Cortina Perana V6 had road and race success in its sights. Unlike the Savage, the Cortina Perana was a fully warranted part of the Ford of South Africa line, sold exclusively through Grosvenor Motors of Johannesburg, which in 1967 had commissioned well-known tuner Basil Green to develop the conversion. It also became a response to the Holden Monaro in domestic racing.

Green started development with a MkI Cortina fitted with 2.5-litre and 3-litre V6 engines supplied by the factory in Port Elizabeth. He found, as Jeff Uren did, that the main problem was the weight of the engine, sitting further forward as it did. "With a lot of change in different areas we came up with a package which seemed exceptionally good," he told the author in 2010. "Grosvenor Ford went to Ford Motor Company and said 'We would like to sell this as a new vehicle' and Ford said 'No way. What are you going to do about warranty and legal ramifications?' But in the end they gave the approval to go ahead because they were so excited about the performance on the race track."

The Cortina Perana was a very similar conversion to the Savage but based exclusively on the Cortina GT, as the 1600E was not officially sold in South Africa (although small numbers were imported for individuals). As with the Uren cars, it also needed work to the front crossmember, and the suspension was lowered, with strengthened front struts and Koni or Telaflo dampers at the rear. The 9½in front disc brakes were claimed to stop the car from 100mph in six and a half seconds.

A Corsair 2000E gearbox was imported especially for the Perana, which ran with the same back-axle ratio as the

ABOVE The South African Cortina Perana was available in red or silver with a distinctive 'rally stripe' around the nose, similar to that on the Chevrolet Camaro. (Basil Green)

RIGHT Cortinas roll off the line at Dagenham PTA in 1967, the year it first out-sold the BMC 1100 on the British market.

Savage and was similarly criticised for being under-geared until a 3.5:1 option was introduced. It was not fitted with a limited-slip differential but had a larger 12in-diameter clutch than the Savage, to help cope with racing starts.

Tested by Ford over 3,000 miles and on sale from summer 1968, Cortina Perana production was set at 300 cars for that year. Magazine testers were just as awed as their English counterparts, not least because the Perana both out-gunned the Lotus-Cortina and cost less, because it avoided punitive import tax. It too was aimed at discreet but hurried business-types. Basil Green estimates 200 to 250 Cortina Peranas were eventually built.

The Perana's racing career – in the livery of the Gunston cigarette company – began in 1969 after 100 units had been built, with Bob Olthoff driving. Although Basil Green's later V8-engined Capri Peranas have tended to

overshadow the success of the Cortina version, August 1970 provided a memorable finale for the latter, as Koos Swanepoel vanquished the 5.7-litre V8 Holden Monaros in a surprise win at Kylami, thanks to deft driving and correctly calculating that the Perana's brakes would outlast those of his heavier competitor.

Leave them wanting more ...

With buoyant sales of the MkII, the Cortina was now so much of an institution that Ford of Britain declared 2 September 1968 National Cortina Day, with a host of events at Mallory Park race circuit, from Ford-related race turns by Graham Hill and Jackie Stewart to a performance by a pop group called *The Cortinas* – not to be confused with the punk band of 1976. One lucky visitor was to go home with a new Cortina if their programme number was drawn out of the hat by Mr Hill.

Capri: a Cortina under the skin?

Although it shared many parts, the 1969 Ford Capri coupé was much more than a dressed-up Cortina, and it certainly only shared a name with the Classic-derived two-door of earlier in the decade. But did it matter that it was derived from the best-selling saloon? After all, the Cortina was part-Anglia and the Corsair was part-Cortina.

The Capri's origins lay in the success of the 1964 Mustang, a four-seater 'personal car' based on existing parts and which buyers could tailor from a long (and profitable) options list. Encouraged by its US bosses and the acceptance of its more sporting and luxury models, Ford of Britain's product planners reasoned that a more aspirational Ford could succeed. Unlike the Mustang, a convertible was not on the cards; in any case a conversion was made more difficult by the thick rear buttresses, although both Abbott and Crayford carried out such an exercise.

An early styling clay, dubbed GBX, was shipped from Dearborn in 1965 and provided the essential form for the end product, although details changed. Early mock-ups were anonymously shown to buyers in customer clinics across Europe and final sign-off came in July 1966.

Dennis Roberts's team conducted the 'pre-programme assumptions' for the Capri. These anticipated the number and cost of essential body panels. "I've no doubt that the assumptions for Capri were exactly the same as Cortina," he says. "How it finished up I can't remember. There was no reason to be otherwise."

Development started on a MkII Cortina base, but the final Capri floorpan featured a number of important differences to suspension mounting points, while the steering was by rack-and-pinion, as ushered in by the Escort. There was also a major difference aft of the axle, as the Capri fuel tank was above the rear axle with the spare wheel in a well in the boot floor.

As for dimensions, compared to the MkII Cortina the wheelbase of the Capri was almost 2in longer, the front and rear tracks were wider, but the car was the same length and only fractionally narrower. The sleek looks, however, meant that 3in was shaved from the overall height.

Location of the leaf-sprung rear axle was helped by twin radius arms, and as travel had been much reduced and stiffer springs used, beefed-up bushing and bump-stops were fitted to provide an acceptable ride.

Capri production was split between Britain and Germany (with unique engines for both countries in the early years) to spread the investment for what was still a niche product. Both British and German engineers worked on the development and proving programme. Launched in January 1969 with the memorable tag line of 'The car you always promised yourself', the only Capri competition on the British market in the same price bracket was the Sunbeam Rapier and – from later that year – its lower-priced Alpine derivative. The MGB GT only had a token back seat, and the 1970 Triumph Stag was to be a premium product.

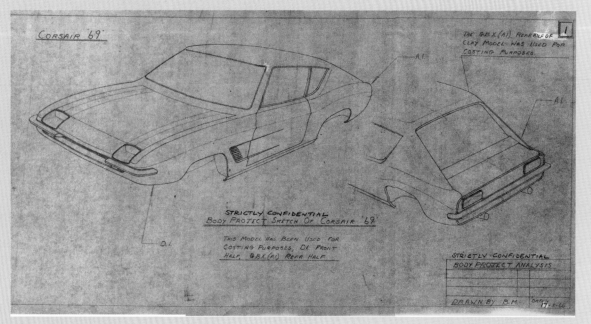

LEFT Early 1966 'pre-programme assumption' drawings for the Capri body structure show it as the '1969 Corsair' and feature recessed headlamps and split bumpers, later ruled out on cost grounds. The swept-up rear side window survived almost until production but potential buyers found it made the back seats claustrophobic. (Dennis Roberts)

If a 26-model range wasn't enough temptation, Capri buyers could specify one of five 'Custom Plans' with any of the six engines. So even if you were determined that you could only afford an £890 Capri 1300 you might still be persuaded to buy an 'L Plan' including overriders, wheel trims and a locking petrol cap, or just go mad and have all the packs combined – the 'XLR Plan'.

Any differences from the Cortina in the driving experience were not apparent to *Car* magazine when it got its hands on one of the first Capri 1600s: 'It sounded the same, it rode the same, the gearbox felt the same

– in fact to sum it up we felt it was just a Cortina with a different body ... a subsequent check on the GT confirmed our suspicions that any Capri version is a slower car than the equivalent Cortina.' But on closer inspection the testers found the Capri a lot quieter – as indeed it was – and equipped with better seating.

Even if it was a bit of a fraud, the MkI Capri was a wild sales success and as bigger-engined and more overtly sporting versions appeared it gained a formidable competition reputation. Three generations later, production ended in 1986, four years after the Cortina.

ABOVE The Capri was a Mustang in miniature, down to its fake cooling ducts ahead of the rear wheels. The Ford salesman's mission was to make you walk out of the showroom having spent at least a little more than had been the original intention.

LEFT The dashboard of this 1967 US Cortina GT was dubbed 'Lifeguard Design'; the car featured a deep padded steering-wheel hub and dashboard, front and rear seat belts, and hazard warning lights.

RIGHT The matt-black grille and extra Ford badges mark this GT out as a 1969 model; that was the extent of the MkII's facelift. The centre badge no longer obliged car thieves by opening the bonnet.

LEFT For 1969 the 1600E, GT and Lotus gained a new instrument panel with integrated dials and full crash padding. Fully reclining bucket seats gained deeply embossed PVC trim.

RIGHT Rear passengers in 1969 were treated to Rover-like twin bucket seats.

ABOVE **Mini Cortina? As soon as Ford stylist Roy Haynes transferred to British Leyland he set to work on the new Mini Clubman. As well as the frontal aspect, BL also adopted the wood-effect Di-Noc plastic first seen on the MkI Cortina estate, as a way of dispensing with the real wood on Mini estate cars.** (Author's collection)

RIGHT **The very rare Crayford V6 coupé – advertised as the Lotus eater – was said to have a rear window made of a Cortina windscreen.** (Author's collection)

The MkII Cortina GT on the Safari

Now a mainstream model, the Cortina GT wasn't required to do much more than mark time on a few events while the Dagenham-built MkII Lotus-Cortina (see Chapter Six) was readied for production. With the MkI Lotus still very competitive with non-factory teams. the Cortina's sporting honour was maintained through autumn and winter of 1966–67.

Four new GTs were prepared for the March 1967 East African Safari, with tyre testing on a ploughed field in Essex and full preparation at Boreham. A revised head gave 97bhp and other mud-proof and dust-proof measures included twin fuel pumps, a double windscreen-washer system, front and rear jacking points and a heavy-duty sump shield. The GTs were supplemented by a MkI Lotus-Cortina for Roger Clark and Gilbert Staeleare, with a further Lotus entered by Hughes of Nairobi.

It was another good East African Safari for Ford, with the GT of Henri Greder and Jack Simonian only missing an outright win thanks to an 80mph detour into the bush to avoid hitting some errant wildlife. As in 1964, the team prize went to the GT and one of the obsolete Lotus-Cortinas in the team still took a class win.

In 1967 a Ford win on the Safari against the 'Big Three' of Mercedes, Volkswagen and Peugeot was still a big sales-boost. Kenya was an especially important territory where buyers with large families often went for Cortina estates. These were usually 1,500cc rather than 1,300cc cars, as much of the country is at high altitude and carburettors had to be adjusted to cope. Kenyan Cortinas also had extra sealing against roads made of volcanic dust. In 1967 business was booming for Hughes of Nairobi, with sales up by 20 per cent – helped by a government contract for 3,000 cars. However, Japanese manufacturers were already starting to make headway and the mid-'60s proved to be the golden days of Cortinas on the East African Safari Rally although a Taunus 20M RS won in 1969; thereafter the event became Peugeot and Datsun territory.

RIGHT With the Lotus-Cortina not quite ready, the MkII GT almost triumphed on the Easter 1967 East African Safari (with a MkI Lotus for company); the cars were painted white to keep the cabin cooler, the bonnets black to reduce glare.

ABOVE This fleet of eight US-specification Cortinas ran continuously at Boreham from May to September 1970 to test the engines for emissions standards. They sported yet another rearrangement of indicator lights. But given that this was the last year of American Cortina sales, were they in fact testing 'Kent' engines for the new Pinto?

There wasn't much to report for the 1969-season Cortina, but then why change a winning formula? There was a matt-black grille, a fully fused electrical system for the first time and a bonnet release operated from inside the car (a belated anti-theft measure). The biggest mechanical changes were a single-selector-rail remote gearchange and a pull-up handbrake for the GT and 1600E with a restyled centre console. There were new front seats in the upper model ranges, the individual rear bucket seats in the 1600E, plus some colour-coding to the interiors and – as discussed earlier – a revised dashboard on the GT and 1600E, integrating the auxiliary dials previously mounted in a pod on top of the dashboard. Metallic paint had proven such a popular option that seven different shades were offered for 1969.

As the 1960s drew to a close, buyers continued to be happy with the Cortina MkII – although Escort sales were perhaps starting to poach its buyers, the smaller Ford taking third position to the Cortina's second place in the 1969 charts. Then again, the Cortina was being exported to 145 different countries.

As to the whole UK market, Ford continued to post second place to the new and vast British Leyland empire (formed in 1968), which now included Rover and Triumph alongside the former BMC marques and Jaguar/Daimler. For 1970 Ford of Britain captured 26.5 per cent of the UK market, much the same as 1963 and the first full year of Cortina sales. BL had 38.1 per cent of sales. Beating BL was the number-one priority for the surprisingly different Cortina which would emerge in autumn 1970.

ABOVE A contract in 1968 to set up Cortina production in Korea created the mighty Hyundai car company. Here, a Korean Cortina cruises the streets of Seoul. The deal, also to build Ford trucks and vans, was worth a considerable £8m for British exports. (Ford Motor Company Ltd collection, Benson Ford Research Center, the Henry Ford Museum)

LEFT Like many fledgling car industries, early Hyundai Cortina assembly was labour intensive, but production climbed from 5,000 to 7,000 Cortinas in just the first year, and successive generations of Cortinas followed. (Hyundai)

Ford of Europe

Despite Ford International's existence, for much of the 1960s Ford in Britain and Germany competed against each other with similar cars which shared no components (witness duplicate V4 and V6 engines), and were sold by separate dealer networks. "There was no attempt made at controlling and making sure we did the same thing," recalls former Ford engineer and eventual boss of Special Vehicle Operations Rod Mansfield. "We scarcely spoke to each other. I couldn't understand why we had a 2.8-litre and a 3.0-litre V6 or two 1.7-litre and 2.0-litre V4s. It seemed so silly to us at the coalface."

But while the 'two-fishing-line' sales approach continued to operate (for example, in France in 1964 a Taunus 12M and a Cortina 1200 were identically priced at 7,760 francs), John Andrews, the American head of Ford of Germany, commissioned studies on how Ford could compete in a future European Common Market, and whether cross-European operations could be centralised.

Project Redcap, which became the 1965 Transit van, gave a taste of how increased Anglo-German cooperation might work. Built in Britain and Germany, the hugely successful Transit was a small step towards rationalisation, although the 1.7-litre V4 engines were not common.

Ford bosses continued to regard the lacklustre sales performance of the Taunus range with concern. One worry was that the 12M – and especially the 1966 12M/15M – was also too large to compete in the sector where Ford of Britain already had the Anglia. A prototype Taunus 10M two-door was seen in 1964, looking very much like a 12M minus a foot of length, and was said to have a V4 of 1,000cc; but nothing became of the project. Thus although entirely British-developed, the Anglia's replacement, under development since 1964, was selected for pan-European production and given the less Anglocentric Escort name.

Ford International continued until 1965. The case for further integration between Britain and Germany had become emphatic, and finally the corporate entity of Ford of Europe came into being with great speed. Hotfooting it to Paris after the GT40 win at Le Mans in June 1967, Henry Ford II met Andrews, Stanley Gillan (American managing director of Ford of Britain since 1965) and Walter Hayes and effectively told Europe to manage its own affairs.

It meant a dramatic split of responsibility. Ford of Britain's modern offices, opened in 1964 at Warley in Essex, were to be the headquarters of Ford of Europe, and the new Dunton research and engineering centre also took on a wider European rôle.

Manufacturing and purchasing processes were integrated and a company airline was set up to link Dunton and Merkenich. The test track at Lommel in Belgium, opened in 1965, became the default proving circuit. The new structure of specialisation meant that no one country had the autonomy of parts to build a complete car, thus minimising the prospects of a complete shut-down.

The reform happened so fast that within months there was a marked exit of senior managers, notably to BMC, among them Roy Haynes. Ford of Britain's stylists would henceforth only devise interiors (although the advanced styling studio remained), while Merkenich near Cologne would take on exterior styling. "There were grumblings in some areas," Charles Thompson recalls. "Some guys this side of the channel would have liked to have done some more exteriors and some projects still lingered for both sides. But if you went into the studios in Germany you'd find Japanese, French and Italian stylists – they weren't 'Germans' as such. They were much more cosmopolitan than here."

Introduced in January 1968, with UK production at Halewood, the Escort was also built in Genk, Belgium, in an almost identical range of engines and trims to British cars. The new small Ford was an instant hit across Europe, helping Ford of Germany gain 2.2 per cent of the market by the end of 1969. Cologne also took on Capri production in 1969. This all took place as the third-generation Cortina development got under way; yet, as detailed in Chapter Seven, that car wasn't quite the model of rationalisation it should have been.

Ford of Europe was an early multinational. Engines were largely German, a transmission plant in Bordeaux, France, was added in 1973, and a new engine plant at Bridgend in Wales in 1980. Spanish Ford production started with the Fiesta in Valencia, Spain, in 1976. Dagenham ceased to produce cars in 2002, to concentrate on diesel engines, and Ford of Europe had its headquarters in Cologne, rather than at Warley in Essex.

"I think Ford of Europe worked quite successfully," said Terence Beckett in 2010. "Nationalism was there in the companies, but broadly it was overcome and I think broadly we succeeded. Our problems in Britain were our industrial relations and the fact that management had to spend so much time putting out fires, coping with emergencies, that they weren't able to keep their eye on the ball in the same way that the Germans did on quality. It's since been handled, for example, by specialising in particular things. I think it was almost inevitable this was going to happen."

ABOVE The first German-built
Escort rolls off the line at the new
Saarlouis plant in June 1970. It
was a much-needed counter to
domestic small cars such as the
Opel Kadett and the Volkswagen
Beetle. (Ford-Werke GmbH)

ABOVE In a memorable publicity coup, each member of England's 1970 World Cup football team was loaned a white 1600E, still a desirable car in its last year of production. GWC 10H was captain Geoff Hurst's transport. Around 10 of the 30 cars are thought to survive.

RIGHT July 1970 and the one millionth export Cortina, a white 1600E, is delivered by helicopter to a customer in Ostend, Belgium. At roughly the same time the two millionth Cortina was made. The home-to-export sales ratio was then 50.2 per cent to 49.8 per cent.

RIGHT 1969–70 Cortina 1600Es featured a matt black panel between the rear lights.

The MkII Cortina 1100

While others were usually keen to insert larger engines into Cortinas, Ford of Britain's Special Vehicles department busied itself with downsizing engine capacity for shipments to countries where there was a punitive tax on larger engines.

In 1969 the base Cortina engine for the home market was a 58bhp 1300 but for Uganda, Tanzania, Kenya and Greece Ford produced a very basic Cortina with the 1,098cc 49.5bhp crossflow engine from the Escort. It rode on stiffer export springs and had a bench front seat with a column gearchange. *Autocar* magazine managed to sample a nicely run-in four-door demonstrator destined for a Greek dealer, and found it highly intriguing. It was of course a whole lot slower than a 1300 crossflow Cortina. Top speed was 12mph down, at 71mph, and 0–60mph took nine seconds longer, at 27 seconds.

A comparison with test figures from a 1962 MkI Cortina 1200 with its three-bearing 1,198cc 48.5bhp engine was inevitable, as the two cars weighed about the same. The 1100 was slower by such a margin that *Autocar* wondered if it was 'off colour' in some way, as it took 24 seconds longer to accelerate from rest to 70mph.

To help wring out what little performance there was, Ford fitted the lowest-possible back-axle ratio, and the driving pleasure was further diminished by a bouncy ride with the export suspension and a stiff column gearchange. Fuel economy fell below 20mpg during performance testing.

But on the bright side, even if it did have the performance of a Volkswagen 1200 the testers conceded it did have much more space, and for these hotter climates the Aeroflow ventilation and export-only opening front quarterlights were an added plus.

Chapter 6:
The Lotus-Cortina MkII

RIGHT The sports pedigree was alluded to but there was to be little factory-backed racing. A green flash and door stripes were optional.

The Lotus-Cortina disappeared from sale between October 1966 and March 1967. While Ford was busy introducing the new Cortina in autumn 1966, Lotus was in the midst of a major relocation to a purpose-built factory at Hethel, near Norwich in the East of England. Assembly of a new Lotus-Cortina did not figure.

Encouraged by grants on offer to attract new business, Colin Chapman had acquired the Norfolk site in 1965 and by November the following year the move was complete, allowing Lotus to bring into production the additional Europa and Elan +2 lines. Even if this had been thought desirable, continued Lotus-Cortina assembly would have been hampered by distance alone.

Would Ford have even wanted it? The Lotus-Cortina MkI had been a great image builder for Ford and the entire Cortina line, but it had only really started to become reliable as it was being phased out in 1966, once it had abandoned the fragile A-frame rear suspension Chapman had demanded. Although Lotus-Cortina production was tiny, it represented a niggling gap in the regular Cortina's reputation for durability.

Nothing wrong with the Lotus name of course, but for the Lotus-Cortina MkII, bringing production in-house was the only way that Ford quality standards could be applied. When it was launched in April 1967 the underlying message, that it resembled its namesake in performance, not problems, was clearly expressed: 'Now, after an 18-month test programme the '67 Cortina-Lotus bows in – constructed almost entirely on Ford production lines and powered by an engine developed by Ford, Lotus and Cosworth … subject to the same stringent quality checks applied to all vehicles that come out of Ford's British plants.'

Although Dagenham would now be turning out these dependable new fast Cortinas, Lotus still supplied the engines. The Hethel factory had given Chapman the chance to bring complete assembly of the twin-cam in-house, still based on 'Kent' engine blocks supplied by Ford. That's not to say that Ford didn't make changes. A development story in *Motor Sport* magazine in May 1967 recounts that quality-control issues had demanded at least a dozen improvements: 'Engine durability testing revealed piston failure, which has been cured by new specification, and the throttle linkage has been made heavier and stronger.' A lot of detail development, it was said, had been to stop oil leaks.

While Ford was preparing to go across to the crossflow engines, with their new cylinder heads, pistons and taller 1,599cc engine block for the 1600, the Ford/Lotus twin-

APRIL 1967   1s 6d

FORDTIMES

*This month: anatomy of the new Cortina-Lotus/
Derek Jewell on Goodwood/James Wentworth Day
in Dorchester/Harry Loftus on motoring prosecu-
tions/PLUS Joe Lowrey, C. H. Rolph, Tony Brooks,
John Blunsden, Oliver Stanley, Tom Hutchinson in a
brighter, busier, better-than-ever new-look magazine*

UEV 629E

**ABOVE Ford emphasised
that this 'Cortina-Lotus' was
a mainstream production-
line model, and contained
a reassuring amount of
'normal' Cortina in it.**

**RIGHT Lotus boss Colin
Chapman (left of group)
looks happy enough with
a prototype Lotus-Cortina
MkII in 1966. Running
left from the car are Ford
competitions manager
Henry Taylor, Lotus liaison
engineer George Baggs
and possibly a visitor from
Ford-USA.**

cam was already set at 1,558cc and bored out from the shortly-to-become-obsolete 1,500cc cylinder block. This made Lotus well aware that it could not depend on Ford for engines to power its entire range. Accordingly it started development on its own 2-litre 16-valve unit for the luxury Lotus cars of the 1970s. "We had to thank Ford for a lot of the successes we had with the twin-cam but we never knew how long they would continue to be available," Fred Bushell told Chapman's biographer Jabby Crombac. "There were difficulties in boring out the blocks, because of which there was a tremendous scrap rate and unless there was pressure from very senior management it was highly likely that they would cease production altogether, so we just had to have our own engine."

Compared to its 1963 ancestor, the 1967 Lotus-Cortina had a far less rarified specification for the simple reason that it had to come off the same lines as regular Cortinas; it was in essence a Cortina GT with a Lotus engine and bespoke suspension. There was also less need to rush it onto racetracks, with bespoke components, because the Cortina's competition pedigree was now well established and the smaller Escort would soon be taking over its mantle.

Motor Sport readers were told that towards the end of the Cortina GT's trials in April 1966 two new cars – based on heavy-duty export bodyshells with stronger welds around the front strut mountings – were fitted with the 109bhp (net) Lotus twin-cam (the old car's SE-specification engine), and then turned over to the competitions department, who pounded around a succession of proving grounds to select the damper settings and spring rates. In complete contrast to 1962 and track development at Silverstone, the car was thus tested by rally engineers. "They were looking for a more reliable car," former competition mechanic Mick Jones recalls. "We did a thousand miles at Lommel, a thousand miles at MIRA in the rain, in the fog – days and days of it." Each car was said to have travelled 25,000 miles and helped counter some of the feeling that the MkII was not a pale imitation of the old car.

The new body was ¾cwt heavier than the previous shell, with the kerb weight of the car fetching out at 17.8cwt, compared to 16.5cwt of the 1963 original. With this extra weight, and with the rest of the Cortina range boasting power increases, a higher-tuned engine was inevitable. Power figures were quoted by Ford this time, not Lotus, so maximum power was an honest 109.5bhp net, with the gross figure being 115bhp at a higher 6,000rpm. A distributor cut-out at 6,500rpm prevented over-revving, though the tachometer was calibrated to 8,000rpm. *Autocar* achieved a mean maximum speed of 104mph, so performance was not a major improvement on paper but torque had been raised by 2lb ft to 106lb ft at 4,500rpm.

As this second-generation Cortina was essentially a reskinned version of the last one, suspension and steering was familiar, only retuned to suit the wider track. Radial-ply tyres were standard, on 5½in rims, and the suspension was close to that of the Cortina GT: at the front stiffer springs and a smaller anti-roll bar, at the rear twin radius arms and softer springs. The distinctive stance was maintained by a ride height 1in lower all round. With Chapman's stress-inducing A-frame suspension long gone, there were no stiffening braces needed in the boot and the spare wheel sat upright;

ABOVE The engine bay was dominated by the large air cleaner, developed over several months to reduce induction noise.

RIGHT Unlike its predecessors, the dashboard was a straight lift from the Cortina GT. Some testers found the central armrest got in the way of gearchanging and drove with the lid up.

as in the first car, the battery was displaced to the boot, because there was no space in an engine bay filled with twin Weber carburettors and a brake servo.

The gearbox was also a carry-over gearbox from the 1966 Lotus-Cortina and was shared with the new GT. It used the same ratios as the Corsair 2000E, harmonised before the introduction of the Lotus, and thus had a higher second gear; mated to it was a new and sturdier 8in diaphragm-spring clutch with reduced pedal pressure. Close-ratio and Hewland five-speed gearboxes were later listed as racing options, available from the Ford Performance Centre. The propshaft was a two-piece item to reduce vibration from the higher-revving

engine and was allied to a 3.77:1 axle ratio. Benefiting from mainstream Cortina improvements, the brakes were now self-adjusting; the 9.6in front discs themselves were unchanged.

Inside, all was standard Cortina GT, without even a wooden gear knob, and you even had to pay extra for a Lotus wood-rimmed wheel. Outside, you could now order your Lotus-Cortina in any one of the standard Cortina colours. Nonetheless, Harry Calton decided that for the launch press fleet a green stripe should be sprayed on to play up the heritage, and Ford duly offered this as an accessory. The smooth sides of the MkII Cortina had no pressing onto which a green flash could be painted and perhaps the idea had become a bit devalued anyway once

ABOVE Playful Ford advertising – with no mention of racetracks – sought to sell this Lotus-Cortina to the family man who wanted performance with a big boot. (Author's collection)

RIGHT The MkI Lotus-Cortina remained competitive well after it was obsolete. Here at Silverstone in 1967 an ex-works car tails a new model driven by Lucien Bianchi.

accessory manufacturers had discovered a healthy demand from humdrum Cortina owners for self-adhesive items – if they hadn't simply painted on a 'Lotus' flash themselves.

The UK press concurred that the new Lotus-Cortina was still a desirable car, but on different terms. *Autocar* said that sometimes a car was so different from its predecessor that it was a shame to continue the same name. The MkII was 'immensely better, and is now a thoroughly satisfying high performance car', it wrote. Ford was credited with having made the Lotus-Cortina perhaps less raw but a lot easier to live with on a long journey, the vast new air cleaner making such an effective job of muffling induction roar. The magazine concluded that the 1967 car would be 'the best engineered and most reliable yet'. Ford had also pegged the price at a highly competitive £1,068, compared to £1,499 for an Alfa Romeo Giulia Super – although buyers may have been tempted by the all-extras-included Corsair 2000E for slightly less.

In its July 1967 test, *Motor* reported that the new air cleaner had 'virtually eliminated' intake roar and that what the car lost in character it gained in refinement (although at high speeds the wind howl from the redundant quarterlight windows was now more obvious). 'We enjoyed the previous Lotus Cortina simply because you could chuck it around on opposite lock in complete control, even though its cornering powers on cross-ply tyres were not all that high', wrote the magazine. 'You now get the best of both worlds plus an important additional bonus in that there is no longer any vicious bump steering.'

ABOVE **West Sussex police traded up from MkI Lotus-Cortinas to six of the new cars. Police specification included a heavy-duty battery and zip fasteners in the roof lining for the blue light and box.**

It has been said that four-door versions were available to special order. It was long thought that this was a myth, but in fact the Mid-Anglia Constabulary, based in Cambridge, specially ordered two such cars in 1970, because it considered two-door cars were not fit for transporting errant drink-drivers away from the scene.

A short competition career

The Lotus-Cortina MkII's only major factory-backed track campaign was the British 1967 season, with cars run by Team Lotus and Alan Mann. The generous Group Five regulations allowed some examples to use the newly developed 16-valve Cosworth FVA engine (FV for 'Four Valves' per cylinder) which Keith Duckworth had developed as part of Ford's £100,000 V8 DFV engine contract. In fact most of the Ford competition money for 1967 went towards the Cosworth Formula One and Formula Two engines, so major international track work with the Cortina was not envisaged.

Based on the 1,499cc pre-crossflow 'Kent' engine block, the FVA easily developed 210bhp when fitted with fuel injection. The engine was in theory an optional extra for road cars and supposedly you could buy one if you had contacts in the right place and enough money; it is unlikely, though, that anyone ever did.

Total Performance

Ford had begun sales of go-faster accessories and competition parts in 1964, and by 1967 the Ford Performance Centre was doing big business, with a turnover of £130,000. These lucrative aftermarket goodies were sold through Ford dealers at first, but a parts counter was set up at Boreham in 1968 for devotees to visit the 'Mecca of Motorsport'. If you were lucky someone would give you a selective guided tour, while those who couldn't run to a £125 Hewland five-speed racing gearbox, could always join the FordSport Club and follow the adventures of the works drivers while wearing their club tie or rally jacket.

In theory all the mechanical parts used in competition cars and sold to the public had to be homologated – at least 500 had to be produced. Former competitions manager Bill Barnett recalls the visits from the Fédération Internationale de l'Automobile (FIA) official to check this was the case. "Because Switzerland weren't car manufacturers the usual bloke who came round to check on us was a Swiss delegate of the FIA and we had to prove that 'x' number of gearboxes and back axles had gone into cars, 'x' number were still in the stores, and show the invoices and show him to whom all these parts had been sold."

"We used to make a load of bits for us and a few to sell and if we hadn't made enough we used to fill the box up with nuts and bolts and put the right parts on top," Mick Jones confesses. From the early 1970s the Performance Centre was subsumed into the RS accessories range masterminded through AVO, but Boreham continued to be a Ford motorsport hub until 2004.

LEFT Whether Lotus or GT, as this car is, you could treat your Cortina to everything from engines to alloy panels and competition seats.

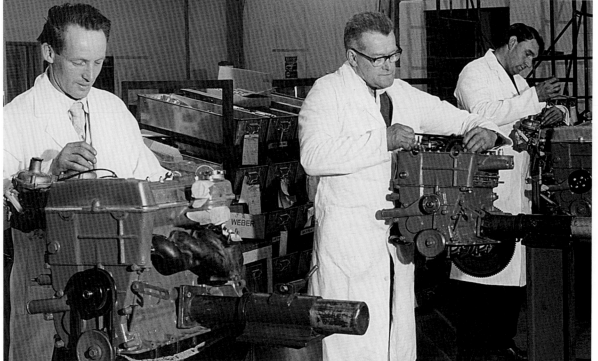

ABOVE Roger Clark hurls his MkII Lotus-Cortina to victory on the 1967 Scottish Rally. He would, however, find fame with the Escort.

LEFT With the move to a new factory, Lotus installed new machinery to assemble both heads and blocks for the twin-cam engine. This photo was used to emphasise a drive for quality. (Author's collection)

RIGHT Steaming after a rough trial in England, a Lotus-Cortina is prepared for the 1968 London-to-Sydney Marathon.

The Escort Twin Cam and RS 1600

By late 1966 Ford competitions manager Henry Taylor had realised that he needed a competition car that was both lighter and faster than the next-generation Lotus-Cortina. Yet there was no thought of putting a Lotus twin-cam into the forthcoming Ford Escort. While a 1,300cc Escort GT was always in the product mix and would be available for racing, anything faster was not initially considered. However, as the competitions department was on the same site as development-testing for the new car, all Ford histories credit chief mechanic Bill Meade for spotting that the smaller, lighter Escort would 'go like hell with a twin-cam engine in it'.

"This was a very clear initiative from the motorsport guys," says Rod Mansfield. "Why do we have to drag a Cortina frame around with us when we could get away with an Escort? It'll be lighter and smaller." Henry Taylor managed to convince Walter Hayes that such an Escort might be the right car to take on ever-increasing competition which now included the Lancia Fulvia and Porsche 911 as well as the Mini-Cooper S.

Approval was given in January 1967 – and suddenly it was 1963 all over again and a frantic rush to develop and build 1,000 Lotus-engined Fords for the Escort to be homologated. At this stage it was not even known how hard it would be to shoehorn the running gear from the Lotus-Cortina into the smaller Escort bodyshell.

While most of the components could be fitted to the prototype car – based on a strengthened shell adjusted with the aid of a large hammer – the width of the engine initially proved a major problem, until the battery was relocated to the boot and the nose of the engine set slightly at an angle to the transmission line.

As with the first Lotus-Cortina, there was again great internal resistance within Ford to disrupting the Escort line at Halewood with a specialised car which had never been planned to be built there. This time, however, a compromise enabled production to be kept in-house: the fast Escorts went down the normal production line until mechanical components were needed, when they were pulled off into a separate workshop.

Roger Clark took a Lotus-engined works Escort to its first international victory on the April 1968 Circuit of Ireland (as a non-homologated prototype) and the new car soon began to dominate both rally stage and race track – it being a more effective rally weapon than the Cortina because of its size alone. The bodyshell was narrower, so the wheelarches were widened to accommodate a track that would fit the furrows ploughed by tractors on British Forestry Commission land. "Jim Clark crashed on the RAC Rally in a MkI Lotus-Cortina because he had two wheels in the track and it flipped him over into the trees," recalls Mick Jones. "The Mini was dead right for the forest but the Cortina was too wide, and it was riding up the whole time." Roger Clark also observed that when you got them sideways the Cortinas felt a bit too big.

After taking the rally world by storm, Ford offered a limited run of cars to private customers 'who want to sharpen up their daily driving with a weekend Autocross'. But Graham Robson, in his RS Escort history, recounts that 'the factory rather lost interest in the Twin Cam as it was rather a difficult car to "package" for the general public and it was a car many Ford dealers did not even try to understand, or to sell'.

The big-engined Escort was clearly a winner, but Walter Hayes and Stuart Turner, Ford's competition chief from 1969, looked to Keith Duckworth of Cosworth, rather than Colin Chapman and the Lotus twin-cam, for a new and more powerful engine to keep up with motorsport competition.

The inspiration was the state-of-the-art Cosworth FVA Formula Two engine, which in having four valves per cylinder reflected the way Cosworth had changed its ideas to combat the racing threat of the likes of Honda. Duckworth was commissioned to design a 16-valve conversion based on the 1,599cc Cortina crossflow engine block but driven by a reinforced rubber cogged belt (hence BD for 'Belt Drive') rather than the noisier chains of the racing FVA. Duckworth in any case needed a production platform for the racing BDA to be homologated. "Getting something done by Cosworth was really a no-brainer," says Mansfield. "I was closely involved with that and they were just the obvious people to go to. They were good to work with because in the racing field they were used to putting things right in a very short space of time. We didn't really have any troubles with them at all."

The BDA was such an efficient design that even road-going versions considered as mildly tuned were developing 120bhp at 6,500rpm – a comfortable improvement on the Lotus-Cortina. The first roadgoing Fords to feature the BDA were actually a handful of Capris built for the press launch in 1969 but never put into production.

The 1970 Escort RS1600 was more or a less a re-engined Twin Cam and it ushered in a new Ford brand, Rallye Sport, set up to produce specialised versions of mainstream Fords and sell parts and accessories. Ford had tired of letting the market for go-faster parts and high-performance production cars such as Alfa Romeo, BMW and Fiat pass it by. In 1968 the European market for such

ABOVE This 1971 Escort RS1600 was effectively a re-engined Twin Cam, retaining its bodyshell and quarter bumpers.

cars was 125,000 a year and the Lotus-Cortina was taking about 1.4 per cent of it.

The idea of a new facility to build specialised cars away from the main production lines was suggested in 1967 and approved in late 1969. As Ford's European motorsport activity was very much an Anglo-German concern, Ford Advanced Vehicle Operations assembled and developed cars at Aveley in Essex and in Cologne, where there had been RS Fords since 1967.

Bodyshells would arrive at AVO from Halewood and BDA engines initially from Harpers of Letchworth. After a year, AVO was building more than 100 cars a week on a unique production line of cradles which could accommodate small runs of completely different models. The first Escort RS 1600 came off the line on 2 November 1970.

Overlapping for a while, before the Escort Twin Cam bowed out of production at Halewood in April 1971, the RS1600 was already the new darling of the motoring press. 'It is hard to think of a sporty driver who would not be completely delighted with a 1600 RS', wrote *Autocar*'s Geoff Howard. 'Away from speed limits it streaks along with a rare dash of vigour and all the right sounds to thrill the enthusiast.' It was to be the first in a long line of sporting Fords that were to be even more successful than the Lotus-Cortinas.

ABOVE Crayford convertible Lotus-Cortinas are the rarest of all, and few survive: only 20 drop-top MkII Lotus-Cortinas are thought to have been built. (Author/Andy Morrell)

For that season Graham Hill, Paul Hawkins and Jacky Ickx took Lotus-Cortinas to four UK class wins, but it was a quiet end to the track glory days and the Ford and Team Lotus Cortinas were sold off to private teams at the end of the year.

Meanwhile, the rally circuit saw a little more use for the MkII Cortina GT and the Lotus, with a slimmed-down works team of Roger Clark and Bengt Söderström, supplemented where necessary. Having notched up an outright win in the Swedish Rally driving a MkI Lotus-Cortina, Söderström and co-driver Gunnar Palm gained third place in May's Acropolis Rally, Roger Clark won the Scottish Rally in June, and the Canadian Shell 4000. Ove Andersson was the outright winner in the third International London Gulf Rally, again in June '67, and a team of three fuel-injected Lotus-Cortinas were all set for the 1967 RAC Rally when the whole event was cancelled in the midst of an outbreak of foot-and-mouth disease.

These cars were the pinnacle of Cortina rally car development. In March 1968 *Car and Car Conversions* was loaned Graham Hill's RAC-prepared car for a few days. The specification made them drool: Goodyear Ultra Grip tyres for optimum mud-plugging, a Salisbury limited-slip differential, and above all that Group Five twin-cam with Teclamit-Jackson fuel injection, putting out 137bhp.

The next year belonged to the Escort Twin Cam, but five Lotus-Cortinas were fielded for the epic London-to-Sydney Rally in late 1968; there were also three Taunus 20Ms from Germany and three Australian Falcons, all managed from Boreham. Billed as 'the greatest rally of the century' and including a trip through India and the Australian outback, the event turned out to be traumatic for both people and cars. Bill Barnett and Gunnar Palm nearly didn't survive the Australian recce alone, when they wrecked the steering on their loaned

Cortina GT and had to drive 26 miles in reverse through the Nullabor Plain. It was after crossing this stretch on the event itself that Roger Clark's leading car burned a piston out, and after that was replaced the rear axle failed.

Internal competition

As soon as the Escort Twin Cam was announced in early 1968 it became a must-have car for enthusiasts, but a waiting list soon built up as production was slow. The Lotus-Cortina continued, cannily offered at exactly the same price of £1,163 including Purchase Tax in 1968 – although the Escort price came down in time – and catered for those who wanted a bigger car.

When the mainstream Cortinas went over to crossflow engines in late 1967 the Lotus underwent only minor changes, in particular gaining the GT's centre console with integrated

clock. Additionally the car was now listed as a Cortina Twin Cam, a move signalled by the 'Lotus' bootlid badge giving way to one reading 'Twin Cam'. A new single-rail gearshift system was introduced in October 1968 – along with the restyled dashboard described earlier – and the umbrella-style handbrake was belatedly replaced by a floor-mounted item in a revised console.

By the time production ended in July 1970, 4,032 MkII Lotuses had been made, yet again a drop in an ocean of ordinary Cortinas, but making the car a much more commercially successful model than its predecessor. With a new line of sporting Escorts produced in-house at Ford Advanced Vehicle Operations, the Lotus-Cortina was no more. Its achievements as a vehicle to redefine the company's image had been immense, but there were to be no more Lotus-engined Fords, or indeed serious British competition Cortinas.

ABOVE This 1970 left-hand-drive Cortina Twin Cam is discretion itself. When given full road tests by Britain's two main magazines, the non-striped press cars were hard to tell apart from a regular Cortina 1300 – and maybe that added to the appeal.

Chapter 7:
The Cortina MkIII

ABOVE The new lower and wider Cortinas sail round Ford's Belgian test track in summer 1970. For the first time two headlamp arrangements were offered: the GXL sported twin quartz-halogen units.

Sure enough, come autumn 1970 a new Ford Cortina appeared. But this was not just a new Ford Cortina, this was an all-new Ford Cortina: new styling, new floorpan, new engines, new suspension. And at first it seemed as if it was all too much, as the car floundered in a sea of quality problems and hold-ups. Yes indeed, in Cortina terms the 1970 MkIII got off to a shaky start.

A collaborative Cortina

As work on the third-generation Cortina got under way, so did the creation of Ford of Europe. British collaboration with Ford of Germany had already been shown to work with the highly successful Transit van and the Escort was adopted as a Euro-Ford, set to be manufactured in England, Belgium and

Germany. It was inevitable that the Cortina and Taunus 12M could not continue as completely different product lines, so Ford of Germany abandoned its front-wheel-drive V4 engines in favour of a new series of overhead-cam units powering the rear wheels. Once considered a handicap, the conventional Cortina model had finally won out.

The new car was known internally as the 1971 TC, for 'Taunus-Cortina'. While the vast majority of the mechanical parts were shared, the two cars ended up with subtly different styling but with the underlying body structure common to both cars. Because of this commonality – and with Britain's hesitant moves towards metrication – the MkIII was also designed to metric dimensions.

It is important to note the turbulent environment in which the project was initiated. Throughout 1967 and 1968 there was an exodus of British Ford personnel unhappy with the abrupt changes brought upon them by the formation of Ford of Europe. The short-term solution was for the American bosses to ship in more personnel from Dearborn, especially stylists to replace the likes of Roy Haynes and his several colleagues who had decamped to BMC/BL.

One of the replacement designers employed in the US-led team at Dunton was a young Frenchman, Patrick Le Quément, who had been working at Simca, then freelancing for a time, until he joined Ford in June 1968. He was later to become head of design at Renault. In those early days of his career at Ford he found an immediate resistance to European harmonisation, which explains why the twin cars were not identical. "There was a lot of protective decision-making, with people saying 'Well you know German taste is very much different from British taste.' That was a kind of unconscious way of preserving job authority and a dual management – exactly the reason why Ford of Europe was created, to break through that cultural difference."

The stylists make their mark

When Le Quément arrived, exterior styling had just been signed off and it was a radically different – most said Americanised – interpretation of the Cortina. Early styling clays appear to have surfaced around 1967, with a slight 'Coke-bottle' effect of a rising curve over the rear wheelarches giving a coupé-like rear profile. This idea may have been pursued both through a devotion to American styling and a desire by the stylists to please their US managers.

In any case, 'Coke-bottle' styling was very much in vogue as the Cortina TC was being developed and was clearly thought to be capable of going into the 1970s. The MkII Cortina had soon been joined by a new Vauxhall Viva and Victor, both larger cars than their predecessors and both with curved waistlines, and if there was one car maker Ford took notice of it was General Motors, the owner of Vauxhall. In

ABOVE AND LEFT
These rare photos from a book by Ford US stylist Bob Thomas show the MkIII's Coke-bottle profile and prominent centre grille emerging in a 1967 study. (Bob Thomas, 1984)

ABOVE Harley Copp, the American chief engineer at Ford for much of the 1960s, pictured here with a model of the independent suspension for the MkIV Zodiac, had a defining influence on the 1970 Cortina.

fact the comparison between the MkIII Cortina and the 1967 Victor extended beyond styling to its wheelbase, overhead-cam engine and wishbone suspension design. Many viewed the Cortina III as a clone and when *Motor* carried out its first full road test before the Cortina was launched, observers mistook it for a Victor.

British Ford stylist John Fallis (who had also worked on the Corsair and had produced the competing MkII design to that of Roy Haynes) has been credited as largely responsible for the MkIII Cortina, while the team was headed by Ron Bradshaw, who had produced the Escort – which itself had something of the 'Coke-bottle' style.

Looking to the front of the car, Ford of America imposed its will on both Cortina and Taunus. Instead of the bonnet edge running in a straight line across the front of the car, a central section protruded a little. This was known as the 'Knudsen nose' a style beloved of Semon 'Bunkie' Kundsen, whom Henry Ford II had poached from GM along with quite a few of his ideas. Roy Brown, who designed the original Cortina, said of Knudsen that he was a frustrated car designer who would fail to see the whole and obsess about small details such as the position of the ashtray. So it was that Knudsen immediately clashed with his new bosses when he redesigned the 1970 Thunderbird to resemble a big-nosed Pontiac; he

lasted 19 months. Although the European 'Knudsen nose' was fairly subtle, it was marginally more pronounced on the Taunus than the Cortina, perhaps because it was already present on the big German Fords. Ford of Britain said the new grille shape was 'no longer flat but sculpted, to give it a classic look'.

This new look was setting up problems even before the public gave its verdict on the new Cortina. "It was a fit-and-finish nightmare," Le Quément recalls. "There were an enormous amount of visits by Engineering and the manufacturing people, muttering about the feasibility of stamping problems. It clearly wasn't done with a search for reducing the manufacturing cost. You had to apply lots of little finishers to hide some of the flaws on the vehicle, like around the tail lamps, and chrome strips across the back to hide some of the shut lines."

The interior was similarly exuberant, and common to both Cortina and Taunus. The square and sensible dashboard of previous Cortinas was replaced by swept-away panels for driver and passenger containing deeply recessed instruments and a deceptively small glovebox. Not even the sacred round Aeroflow vents were retained, ventilation coming instead through horizontal slots. On up-market versions a very contemporary (and unconvincing) stick-on wood trim was added to the front of the glovebox, around the instruments and along the door trims. GXL and GT models carried four extra gauges in a panel ahead of the gearlever, pointed towards the driver but nonetheless difficult to read at a glance.

Cortina body styles were as before – two-door or four-door plus a five-door estate. Although the Cortina grew no longer overall, its wheelbase did, being extended 3.5in to 101.5in. It was also 2.1in wider and 2.1in lower, with the front track being increased by 3.5in and the back by 5in. The extra width plus the lower ride-height and wider track succeeded in giving people the impression that the 1971 Cortina was bigger than it was in reality. With a kerb weight of 20.6cwt, a 2000GXL was 2cwt heavier than a 1600E had been. The lightweight Cortina was long gone.

The increase was entirely logical as the bigger range – extending from the 1.3-litre to the 2-litre class – was expected to take over in addition the market the Corsair had filled. And again, the Vauxhall Victor had a wheelbase only ½in longer, although it was a whole 9in longer overall, which the public regarded as too much. The new Cortina's boot was billed as one of the largest in the class, with 12cu ft of space made more usable by a bootlid which opened level with the rear bumper and a spare wheel housed under the floor. It was ironic that just as British Leyland rushed the Morris Marina into production as a Cortina riposte, the target car had morphed into something else altogether.

No more struts

After it seemed as if all British Fords were destined to have a MacPherson strut front suspension, and many other car makers were eagerly adopting it, Ford surprised all commentators by giving the third Cortina a completely different design of front suspension, as well as radically altering the rear set-up, abandoning leaf springs in favour of an axle with coil springs and upper and lower trailing arms. The new car also ushered in rack-and-pinion steering.

Rather than using struts, the front suspension was now by coils and double wishbones, with an anti-roll bar on the GTs. There were arguments for and against both systems. The MacPherson strut was essentially simple, and therefore cheap, but demanded a relatively high bonnet line. As well as allowing a sleeker front, the twin-wishbone arrangement – given the American term SLA, for 'short and long arm' – brought with it the mounting of the suspension on a separate subframe. This was a more costly way of doing things, but one that favoured refinement, loads being transmitted into the body in two stages, first through the subframe, then through the bodyshell. The subframe could also be pre-assembled away from the car.

Harley Copp, Ford of Britain's engineering supremo for much of the 1960s is commonly held to have imposed SLA on the Cortina as he did trailing-wishbone rear suspension on the Zephyr MkIV, but ride-and-handling development engineer David Garrett remembers it as a diktat from accountant Jack Hooven which took a great deal of trouble to get right. "They had a scrub radius [a suspension/wheel angle which affects the contact patch of the tyres] of 80mm which was huge and if you got a situation where one wheel was on a good surface and one wheel was on a bad surface you literally couldn't hold the steering wheel. It would break your wrist if you tried to when you were braking – we had enormous problems when you put the brakes on."

However, without going into great technical detail, the pros and cons of MacPherson versus SLA suspension were more complex than cost versus refinement. Fans of the former would argue that struts reduced load stresses by the wide spacing of the attachment points but those advocating SLA – as Geoff Howard of *Autocar* did in his technical review – argued the wheel geometry was more versatile

and longitudinal wheel location is more positive, allowing sophisticated use of voided bushes that were rigid for control but soft for absorption.

However, as Howard wrote in his 1970 technical review praising the new Cortina suspension: 'Pro-MacPherson engineers at Ford have apparently come up with a few answers meantime, and the next new Ford will most likely be back on struts.' In the event the 1972 Granada also had wishbone front suspension and the Cortina stayed with it for the rest of its career, but the next Escort and new Fiesta stuck with struts.

"There were certainly problems with the MacPherson strut, it was by no means perfect," says Rod Mansfield. "But in my view it was a retrograde step going to SLA, particularly the way it was done. It was all huge great stampings – an accountant's suspension rather than a designer's suspension."

An international engine

A new family of engines was introduced with the 1971 Cortina, single-overhead-cam (ohc) four-cylinder units of 1,593cc and 1,993cc, the camshaft being driven by a cogged rubber belt. It was a very contemporary engine, even if General Motors had once again stolen a march on Ford by ushering in Britain's first mass-produced belt-driven engine in the 1967 Vauxhall

ABOVE In a complete break from MacPherson struts, the SLA front suspension sat in its own subframe. Rack-and-pinion steering was another innovation, as was a collapsible steering column.

ABOVE A cutaway display unit of the 'Pinto engine' shows its belt-driven overhead camshaft. Replacing the V4 engines, for cost reasons it had to be an in-line design.

Victor and other car makers were going to overhead-cam designs as the third Cortina was being readied.

Ford had been more cautious on belt-driven overhead camshafts. Correspondence between Detroit and Dagenham in 1960 shows that a Cologne-designed 1,500cc belt-driven overhead-cam engine had been subjected to tests in England and found to be very efficient, but there was considerable doubt about the durability of the belt; seven years later Vauxhall still had to reassure its customers about belt sturdiness.

The new engine was designed in Germany and tested in Britain over four years. In late 1969 a total of 350 ohc engines were durability-tested across Europe in company Capris, racking up mileages of up to 40,000 miles. Cologne 'Pinto' production started in April 1970 and versions of the unit went on to power Fords into the 1980s. Early problems included high oil consumption and premature wear, as a spraybar under the rocker cover, to spray oil onto camshaft lobes, would easily block, until redesigned. Belts, too, were found to last only 25,000 miles or so before replacement.

The new ohc unit was crossflow, but it dispensed with the bowl-in-piston design of the previous pushrod crossflow unit.

At launch the new engines were only offered with the upper trim levels, a 1600 'Kent' developing 68bhp being retained in standard cars while the 1600GT received an 88bhp ohc unit. The fastest new Cortina was the ohc 2000, with 98bhp and a claimed maximum speed of 103mph, which got pretty near to that of the now-obsolete Lotus-Cortina.

Manufactured in both Cologne and Dagenham (which had once again expanded its engine-making facilities), the new engine also marked a useful rationalisation between Europe and America – at least for a time. At launch it was simply referred to as an ohc engine but over time it became known as the 'Pinto' unit because it not only powered the Cortina from 1970 but also the American sub-compact Ford Pinto launched the same year (see panel). The Pinto used both the 'Kent' 1600 and the ohc 2000 engine in its early years – an international economy of scale only dreamt about a decade previously. In 1970 Ford of Britain said the ohc engine contract was 'expected to be the biggest single dollar order ever received by the British motor industry'.

Back in the Cortina, the 1300 and 1600 'Kent' engines were not left untouched, being billed as improved 'performance plus' versions. Changes included revised camshaft timing, and new inlet manifolds, carburettors and piston bowl profiles. The 1300 gave 57bhp (net), losing one horsepower to its predecessor, while the 68bhp 1600 was 3bhp down on the Cortina MkII, and with peak power developed at 5,200rpm rather than 5,000rpm.

The 2000 used a new German-built four-speed gearbox, while the others had carry-over items. All engines bar the 1300 could be specified with a Borg-Warner automatic transmission. As before, the clutch was cable rather than hydraulically operated, for lower pedal pressures.

Too much choice?

Given that the 1971 Cortina was replacing not one but two ranges, the combination of engines, trims and options appeared mind-boggling to everybody but Ford. *Car* magazine called it 'almost too complicated to describe because of the almost limitless variations'.

As far as the UK market was concerned, there were 35 basic versions broken down as a series of two-door and four-door saloons and estates – with the new estate coming on stream very quickly from launch. Then you threw in up to three engine choices for most trim levels. Emboldened by the success of the Capri, Ford of Britain swept away the de Luxe, Super and Executive badges and replaced them with a standard car just called Cortina, then L, XL, GT and GXL 'packs'. Optional accessories only added to the complexity.

Whichever one you chose, though, all cars had more equipment. To put the 1971 Cortinas in context, a base Cortina 1200 of October 1962 had drum brakes all round and a heater was extra. Eight years later a UK-specification Cortina 1300 'base' had the front disc dual-circuit brakes of the whole range, plus a heater, but it still had a rubber floor covering, crossply tyres and a dynamo. A brake servo was optional and for some countries you could still get a bench seat with a long cranked gearlever.

On the subject of seats, there was a lot of noise about the new Bri-Nylon fabric developed over three years by Ford in conjunction with a number of British companies. It was claimed to match the 'softness of touch and richness of home furnishings' and to 'breathe', resist stretching and wipe clean.

A bumpy launch

According to Martin Rawbone's Ford history, the MkIII development was pushed along an an unrealistic pace against management infighting. The company was only able to hand-build half-a-dozen models for the long-lead press to sample at Boreham before the August holiday shutdown, and there was worse to come at the European driving event held at the Lommel test track in Belgium the next month.

Ernie Unger, product problem-control manager at the time, had a team working flat out in a series of marquees on Frog Island (thus named because French prisoners were kept there during the Napoleonic wars), one of a series of islands in a hinterland around Dagenham PTA, to assemble acceptable launch cars. "We were literally having to hand-finish them," he recalls. "The first problem was the fit of the doors. The bodyshell structure had been designed over here and the doors had been designed over in Germany (or vice versa) and when it came to bolt the two together, if you found a door which fitted a door opening you were exceptionally fortunate."

"We started the launch and the cars were coming in twos and threes. We had both Taunus and Cortina and some markets were taking both and others just taking Taunus, so we'd tuck the Cortinas to one side," Harry Calton remembers. "There was horrendous oil consumption on the 'Pinto' engine. The oil was running down the valve seals: on some cars we were getting 30 miles to the pint. There were creaks, groans

and water leaks and interior door handles were snapping off like carrots. We were replacing them two or three times."

Fully shown to the public at the October 1970 London Motor Show, the new Cortina was billed as 'More car between the wheels'. The British press, just like the British public, had to quickly revise their ideas of what they thought a Cortina should be. "I thought it just looked terrible," Ray Hutton says of the moment he came across an unbadged pre-launch Cortina. "By that time we'd got used to the idea that the Cortina was a certain size and a certain configuration and then suddenly there's this thing that didn't seem to have any of the chunky sporty character we'd got used to. It looked like a kind of transatlantic mess to us, a car trying to look bigger than it was. We all thought it the kind of thing that Vauxhall had been doing and a bit unworthy of Ford, almost as if America had taken over again."

When *Motor* – starting at the top of the range – published its first full test of a 2000 GXL towards the end of October, it found the car to be more stylish than its predecessors, but noted that most people disliked the flashy interior décor of the GXL, especially the stick-on wood. The test gave a

ABOVE Laid bare at the 1970 London Motor Show, with the end of the Corsair line the new Cortina had to occupy a market slot ranging from economy runaround to junior executive car.

ABOVE The new Cortinas may have won four gold medals from the Institute of British Carriage and Automobile Manufacturers at the show, but real-life quality was far from prize-winning.

qualified welcome to the Cortina, tempered by the fact that one model couldn't fully represent a range of 35 cars which went from £914 to £1,338 in price. 'As Ford of Europe's first major enterprise, the new Cortina (read Taunus in Germany) is perhaps 1970's most significant new car and it is hard to see anything but success for it,' commented the magazine.

It was not all good news. While the testers appreciated the sporting nature of the car, with its good performance, sweet gearchange, roll-free cornering and light, positive steering, the efforts at improving refinement did not seem to have brought a breakthrough. 'Despite the new suspension, we were disappointed with the ride, which is rather harsh and thumpy at low speeds, too bouncy when driving over fast or indifferent roads … its lack of refinement may disappoint anyone seeking a much cheaper alternative to, say, a Rover or Triumph,' observed the weekly. However, the old bugbear of wind noise seemed to have been solved, at least on the test car. Understeer was the dominant roadholding characteristic, while a power slide could be easily provoked, with the tail breaking away in a gradual way with no hidden vices. Better

location of the axle was also in evidence, providing 'much improved adhesion over bumpy roads'.

There were complaints of engine resonance (*Autocar* also found a severe driveline vibration), an automatic choke which didn't work on *Motor*'s car, and some confusion as to whether a rear anti-roll bar should have been fitted in addition to the front bar fitted to all 1600s and 2000s. The test car didn't have one but the magazine was told this was to be added from 1971; in fact, a rear anti-roll bar was only added to the facelifted range introduced for 1974. Meanwhile, the magazine surmised that the 2000GXL's tendency to bounce at high speed and rock from side to side would only have been heightened by adding the anti-roll bar and thereby increasing roll stiffness.

On the plus side, there was praise for the new seats and their range of adjustment, and the amount of legroom and headroom in the rear, while despite the pronounced kick-up in the waistline, visibility from the rear was deemed very good, with occupants 'not conscious of the Coke-bottle shape'.

While press road tests cars were carefully prepared at

ABOVE The estate was claimed to offer the same rear comfort as the saloon, with a backrest the same height. For load space the longer wheelbase came into its own.

LEFT The GXL was to all intents and purposes a direct replacement for the 1600E, and could be picked out by its vinyl roof, sports wheels and quad headlamps.

ABOVE The all-new dash curved away from driver and passenger for more legroom and kneeroom. At the time it was all considered rather garish. The GXL's stick-on wood and badly placed switches made the interior less appealing than that of some BLMC cars, said *Motor* magazine.

Aveley to give the best possible performance and may have appeared of reasonable quality, it became suspiciously hard to get hold of one. Meanwhile, poorly built cars were filtering through to customers to such an extent that a 'Dealer Reassurance' programme had to be run to convince suppliers the problems would be tackled.

Eric Jackson, who ran a Ford dealership in Harrogate and had become well known for his Ford endurance runs in the 1960s, remembers facing up to management. "The dealers complained about the quality of the vehicles. We'd

never had this with Ford products before. By and large they were body problems, such as ill-fitting doors, and the dealers were getting a lot of hammer. We had this meeting in London and [managing director] Bill Batty stood up and said 'The problems have now been solved. You will find that on any vehicle you will have had as from this morning.' Well, I had had one delivered the previous day under the Reassurance programme and I could actually get my hand between the door and the rear wheel arch. I stood up and I heard him say 'Oh shit.' And I told him there and then that the car I'd had

LEFT No 'wood' for the Cortina L, but at least everything is colour keyed for 'complete harmony'.

delivered had bad door-gapping. He didn't say another word. He had the most awful temper."

UK Cortina sales at the end of 1970 stood at 123,256 units. This was higher than in 1969 but then this was a crossover year between the popular MkII and the MkIII, with both on sale until beyond October 1970. In that month, in fact, Ford readjusted the price of the MkII 1300 de Luxe two-door to £862 tax and delivery paid, making it £39 cheaper than the nearest MkIII.

The launch troubles were not over. In the wake of a new government which attempted to legislate against unofficial disputes, 1971 was a record year for motor-industry strikes and Ford suffered an 11-week dispute over a new pay deal in the early part of the year, depleting stocks to the lowest level in its history, and causing the loss of an estimated 150,000 vehicles. It is, however, worth noting that Ford of Germany was also not immune to strikes.

In spite of this context, the new Cortina was clearly what the public and the fleet owners wanted. In October 1971 it was Britain's best-selling car. In a reference to the strikes, Bill Batty told *Ford News* that had they been able to fulfil all the

Cortina orders on the books the figure would have broken all records. Then again, monthly British car sales figures of this period can be viewed as who could manage to push most cars out when not being shut down by strikes: the Mini had actually just beaten the Cortina for overall market share (8.9 per cent to 8.7 per cent) the previous month. In a direct comparison for the whole year, British buyers still bought more Austin/Morris 1100/1300s than Cortinas.

The picture was reversed for 1972, in what was to be the 1100's last full year of sales, but there was now a more direct competitor from the same stable, the Morris Marina (see page 232). The Cortina remained the standard car for the fleet user, in 1972 accounting for 30 per cent of all Ford of Britain's business sales. 'There's no denying that the Mark Three has been selling like crazy', *Car* magazine wrote in July 1972. 'But then you would expect it to be. After all, the non-delivery situation created a pent-up demand for the car and the salesmen, hungry after months of thin commissions, are trying even harder to avenge the famine.'

That same issue devoted a cover and a number of inside pages to 'exploding the Cortina myth'. Looking back

ABOVE This GT is finished in Maize – one of ten new paint colours with glamorous names such as Tawny, a brown metallic for the GXL, and Garnet, a 'luxurious' red.

RIGHT Like its competitors, the GT gave you black high-backed seats but its extra instruments below the dash were not easy to see.

LEFT "Which one is this?"
A journalist sets forth in a
Taunus at the Euro-launch
of both Taunus and Cortina
at the Lommel test track
in Belgium. As it closely
resembled the larger
20M models, the Taunus
blended well into the
German Ford range.

on what it regarded as the honest simplicity of the MkI, it bemoaned the quality and design of the third Cortina, taking each claimed innovation and shooting it down, along with a road test comparing it to a Granada V4, which it much preferred. Buyers would only put up with this kind of Cortina for so long, it warned: 'The rebound could occur when, in the distant future, Ford announces the Mark Four Cortina. By then the pushy, flashy, heavy and unsatisfactory Mark Three may well have sunk the good ship Cortina.'

Ford versus Leyland

But what about the main competition? The contrast between British Leyland and Ford was always striking. Ford would routinely replace its best-seller every four years, with significant detail improvements year-on-year, while Leyland would keep churning out the same car, albeit one which might have been technically bolder from the start. Between 1962 and 1970 there were three Cortinas, the last virtually all-new. In that time the biggest change for the Austin/Morris 1100 was a larger engine.

Yet due in no small part to its sprawling offering, from Minis to Jaguars (even including the antique Morris Minor, which only bowed out in 1971), Leyland always beat Ford on overall numbers. Despite (or perhaps because of) a smaller range of vehicles, Ford finally won on overall UK sales in July

1974, by which time the Cortina was firmly embedded at the top of the sales charts. It was a matter of huge pride for new chairman Sir Terence Beckett. "It was very important. Mind you, poor old British Leyland was floundering, so we really were picking up their failures. We got leadership in light cars, medium, large cars, vans, medium vans and trucks. We got the leadership on the lot."

Housekeeping and real improvements

Some paring down of the confusing UK Cortina range was inevitable and in early 1972 the 2-litre engine was confined to the more expensive XL, GT or GXL versions, while from April 1973 the estate was no longer offered with the hardly up-to-the-job 1,300cc engine option.

On past form, another Cortina might have been expected for 1975 but instead the MkIII Cortina was given extensive revisions in autumn 1973, most of which put right many of the wrongs of the earlier model through both trim and mechanical changes to improve refinement and roadholding; many of these upgrades were applied to the Taunus at the same time. 'More than just one car it is really a range of 18 different models which effectively plug the whole market in family saloons from 1300 to 2000 cc,' commented Geoff Howard in *Autocar*.

The most visual change was that while the Cortina and

Cortina L models retained circular headlamps set in a restyled grille, the XL, GT and new 2000E received oblong units fitted with tungsten-halogen bulbs in place of the former twin headlamps. The major piece of engine rationalisation was the wholesale adoption of a 72bhp version of the 1600 'Pinto' unit in place of the 1600 'Kent' – with a single-choke Ford carburettor fitted instead of the previous GT's twin-choke Weber. The 1.3-litre 'Kent' engine continued but shared a revised closer-ratio gearbox with the 1600. The Cortina 1600GT, meanwhile, was dropped in favour of a 2.0-litre GT.

Underneath, a lot of work was carried out to remedy the criticisms levelled at the ride of the first cars. Front and rear anti-roll bars were standardised and the 2000GT given a stiffer front spring rate than the other 2-litre cars. Sound-insulation was improved and the bushes for the front subframe enlarged and changed from rubber to polyurethane. *Autocar* found the cars had much less roll, better-balanced handling with less understeer, and a substantial improvement in ride brought about by the 16 per cent reduction in bump rate. The propshaft was now a two-piece item to reduce the vibration which had bedevilled early cars.

Inside there was equally good news. Ford had completely discarded the old car's dashboard with its difficult-to-read instruments for a neat rectangular panel with the instruments in a line under a non-reflective plastic panel. This was in fact an early introduction of the Cortina/Taunus MkIV dashboard, as that car was already under development. The testers eulogised over the clarity of the new unit, which went on to win a design award, and concluded that the Cortina now truly merited its place at the top of the sales tree. They were equally pleased to see that the thin air vents had also been scrapped – 'Ford admit that the ventilation system introduced on the MkIII Cortinas did not come up to expectations' – and that the dashboard air vents had reverted to eyeball-style 'Aeroflow' items. The only quibble was that rationalisation with the Taunus had moved the indicator stalk to the left of the column on the right-hand-drive Cortina, which was considered a little un-British.

Never mind that, though – real wood was back in a Cortina. The biggest news for 1974 was the revival of the 'E' Cortina, as the 2000 GXL gave way to the 2000E. Ford in its own advertising acknowledged the gap that this top-of-line variant was filling: 'Remember the 1600E Cortina? The one with the wood and thick carpets? We stopped building it three years ago. But even today owners write us love letters about it.'

True to the beloved original, the new 2000E was a parts-bin special, with a host of extras thrown in for the price. A vinyl roof was standard, along with sports wheels. In contrast

BELOW The rather pleasing lines of the Taunus coupé supplemented a conventional two-door Taunus in Germany. A Cortina coupé was ruled out on cost grounds and there was also a clearer tradition for a saloon-derived coupé in Germany, after this style had been offered on previous generations of the 12M.

Taunus and Cortina III and IV: the differences

'Same car only different' best sums up the 1971 Taunus/Cortina range. Many of the outer panels were unique and the engine range differed quite markedly, but you could at least get some spare parts common to both at whatever Ford dealer you went to in Europe.

No 'Kent' engines were used in the 1970s Taunus ranges, the 1300 and the 1600 both being ohc 'Pinto' units; in place of the 2,000cc 'Pinto' engine used in the top Cortinas, the Taunus used the existing 2-litre and 2.3-litre V6 units. Body styles were the same as for the Cortina apart from the existence of a coupé; there was also a commercial version of the estate, with no rear seats.

The new Taunus soon proved to be Ford of Germany's best seller, accounting for one-third of the 775,717 cars and light commercials it produced in 1971. In a remnant of the old 'two fishing lines' approach, Ford dealers could choose which model they wanted for their market. Whereas the French had quite liked the MkII Cortina, France became very much Taunus territory after 1970, although the Cortina was still offered, while Scandinavia took both but leaned more to the Cortina.

While the British press was well aware of the Taunus as a kissing cousin (*Custom Car* remarked amusingly on the slightly different-shaped Cortinas it saw on holiday in Berlin), it was not listed in the UK, although right-hand-drive versions of the bigger 17M and 20M were exhibited at Earls Court in 1970.

September 1973 saw the Taunus sharing the Cortina's dashboard and suspension changes. On the arrival of the rationalised MkIV Cortina and its Cologne sister, the Taunus engine choices were unchanged. With the German car there remained more variance on body/engine combinations. Although UK-market Cortina MkIV two-doors were very much on the poverty side of the range, Taunus buyers were offered the choice of the S trim with the two-door bodyshell and two V6 engines. Finally, rather than being a trim level only the Taunus 1600S had more power than the standard engine: output was up from 68bhp to 72bhp, thanks to a twin-choke Weber rather than a single-choke Ford carburettor.

RIGHT Engineers appearing in the Ford Film Unit film *Prototype* toy with a grille for a full-sized Taunus mock-up. Note the ruthless hubcap rationalisation behind them.

The Ford Pinto

After having made very little of a dent in Volkswagen Beetle sales with imported Cortinas, Ford-US finally rushed its own subcompact into production for the 1971 model year.

Developed in a record 25 months on an all-new platform, the Pinto had utterly conventional engineering, smart Euro styling (at first a two-door, then a hatchback) and at 13ft 7in was longer than a Beetle but shorter than a Maverick.

Very much a project of Ford vice-president Lee Iacocca, the Pinto had to be as cheap to run as a Beetle (owners were encouraged to send away for their own maintenance kits), but more importantly very cheap to build. In a parallel with the first Cortina, weight and price became a mantra: the Pinto had to be a 2,000lb car selling for no more than $2,000.

With no small engines of its own, Dearborn looked to Dagenham for the 1.6-litre 'Kent' and Cologne for the new ohc 2-litre shortly to power the new Cortina/Taunus range. At its launch in September 1970 the Pinto 1.6 came with a four-speed manual gearbox, the 2-litre with an automatic only. The 'Kent' engine was dropped for the 1973 model year, and the ohc unit locally sourced.

The Pinto was initially a big hit, with 400,000 sold in the first year, but it famously tarnished the reputation of its maker. In May 1972 a Pinto unexpectedly stalled on a Californian freeway and burst into flames when hit from behind by another car. The driver, Lily Gray, died from her injuries and her 13-year-old passenger, Richard Grimshaw, was seriously burned and needed many operations.

A landmark trial followed in 1977 and Harley Copp, who had returned to Dearborn in 1968 and headed the Pinto crash test programme, testified against Ford that management had been well aware that the short Pinto had little 'crush space', that its fuel tank could be punctured by bolts on the rear differential in an impact,

and that the filler pipe could rupture, yet it had chosen not to implement a $10-per-car fix. Copp later became a safety consultant.

American magazine *Mother Jones* published an article in the year of the Grimshaw trial in which it claimed 500 deaths had resulted from Pinto fires and that Ford had lobbied against new safety standards for eight years. Ford eventually paid $3.5m in damages over the case, and recalled half a million Pintos for modification in 1978; production eventually ceased in 1980.

The furore was such that the Pinto became embedded in the American psyche as a lethal car and a symbol of corporate callousness. However, there was a counter-argument, propounded by law professor Gary T. Schwartz, that the whole Pinto débâcle was based on a number of misconceptions. These included a misunderstanding of cost-benefit analysis, and the fact that the cost-per-life figure in an infamous Ford memo was a sum devised by the National Highway Traffic Safety Administration itself and the Ford memo was intended for use in discussion with the NHSTA over future standards. Schwartz and others also pointed out that behind-axle fuel tanks were common to a number of other small cars and that annual overall Pinto fatality rates were similar to those of its competitors. Schwartz didn't, however, excuse the Pinto's inferior performance in rear-end impacts.

'We resisted making any changes, and that hurt us badly,' says Lee Iacocca in his 1984 autobiography. 'The auto industry has often been arrogant, but it's not that callous. The guys who built the Pinto had kids in college who were driving that car. Believe me, nobody sits down and thinks "I'm deliberately going to make this car unsafe."'

LEFT Originally a two-door, the Pinto gained a hatchback in 1971 to become the Pinto Runabout. It was pitched as a second car for the youngster of the house.

ABOVE Export Cortinas wait for shipment, possibly on 'Frog Island'. The side reflectors indicate they may be Canadian-specification cars.

to the unloved plastic style of the 1970 Cortinas, real wood returned, with matt-finished teak door cappings and dashboard plus deep-pile carpeting and even carpet on the lower half of the doors. The deep new seats were finished in a new cloth trim called 'Savannah', which was claimed to be stain-resistant and crumple-free.

At the poor person's end of the range Cortina L was treated to a strangely named attempt to make the specification a little less grim as the Cortina L Décor, this new variant being given carpeting, a lockable glovebox and more sound-insulation. As to the new bread-and-butter Cortina, represented perhaps most accurately by the 1600XL, the *Autocar* test concluded that drivers would be 'well pleased by it, while those who knew the model before will also have been struck by the really worthwhile improvements that have been made'.

Six-cylinder Cortinas for some

This was clearly a Cortina that was engineered for a V6 engine; the Taunus even had two six-cylinder variants from launch. But although the Ford of Britain press team

The death of de Luxe

The Cortina MkIII ushered in an era when most car makers denoted model increments by an alphabet soup of meaningless initials. The old de Luxe was the new L, the Super the new XL, Ford explained in 1970. The GXL was, if you liked, the new 1600E. And somehow we got to know that a GL trumped an XL, but a GXL was rather better than both. It just sounded better.

The plain Cortina was a functional tool for tight-fisted business buyers, with little retail appeal other than furnishing an alluringly priced entry into the range. From 1970 to 1973 the Cortina saloon and Cortina L were both identified by single round headlamps. Inside the Cortina had a rubber floor covering with nylon flocking on the transmission tunnel while the Cortina L added carpets, a colour-keyed interior and fully reclining front seats in 'superior grade vinyl'. Both could be specified with either the 1300 and 1600 'Kent' engines or the 2000 'Pinto' unit. A dynamo was fitted to the 1300 and an alternator was standard from the 1600 upwards. Cortinas from the L upwards gained a foot-operated windscreen wash/wipe. A bench front seat, under-dash handbrake and wand-like gear lever were options only on the Cortina and Cortina L.

The XL went beyond an L by having bright metal trim around the wheelarches, full-width metal trims replacing the hubcaps, a trim panel between the tail lights, and rubber bumper inserts. A quilted-effect vinyl covered the seats and simulated wood appeared on the dashboard and door trims. Interior upgrades included a clock, a vanity sunvisor mirror and a document pocket on the driver's door. The GT went all-black inside, with high-backed seats, and included a centre console with fuel, temperature and oil gauges and an ammeter. There was a sports steering wheel and a gearshift gaiter. Outside there were twin halogen headlamps, Rostyle sports steel wheels, a black radiator grille and a coachline.

The range-topping GXL combined the XL and GT specifications with a standard vinyl roof, a special radiator grille, Rostyle wheels (to late 1972, when they were replaced by all-steel Minilite lookalikes), cut-pile carpet and a heated rear window. Fabric seats were optional on all Cortinas until the arrival of the 2000E, which had them as standard.

The estates mirrored the base, L and XL trims, only differing in the XL having a carpeted load bay rather than a rubber mat and the rear seat not having a centre armrest whatever the trim level. Even in 1971 all the lower three UK Cortina trims rode on crossply tyres whatever engine you chose, unless you paid

extra for radials. Braking was also similarly low-specced, with servo assistance only standard on the GT and GXL saloons.

There were thirteen paint finishes and five colour-keyed interior trims in 1970–73 but it wasn't a free-for-all on choice. You couldn't have a 2000GT engine in anything other than a GT saloon, but you could have the 1600GT unit in a GXL saloon. As described, the 1300 was wisely withdrawn from estate duty. Some options came with conditions; if you wanted a heated rear window in a 1300 you had to pay extra to replace the dynamo with an alternator. An automatic gearbox was available on all engines bar the 1300.

To stay in the game Ford was always obliged to ratchet equipment upwards, and the 1974 model-year facelift saw radial-ply tyres standard on all Cortinas bar the base model and a heated rear window standard from the XL upwards – this also going over to the new rectangular headlamps. By the middle of the decade and the hard times selling new cars, Cortina optional became Cortina standard, with the base car for the 1976 model year having carpets, cloth seats, a cigarette lighter, a brake servo, hazard warning lights and a heated rear window. The sales rep's stalwart XL even had a real wood centre dashboard panel. The craze for special editions had yet to start, however, and the only factory-produced Cortina MkIII special was the summer 1976 Olympic 2000E, available in gold, silver or bronze and sporting extra driving lamps.

LEFT **This 1971 Cortina XL boasts one of the five colour-keyed interior trims – a match for Fern green or Evergreen metallic paint. (Author's collection)**

distracted journalists with their own Cortina V6 at Lommel, there was no intention of introducing it into the Dagenham product mix.

For countries with big distances, a big engine was definitely desirable, however. As far as South Africa was concerned, that was far from the only issue surrounding the MkIII. "It was inconceivable for this car to be presented to the public – it was that bad," declared product planning manager Jim Hossack, speaking in the early 1970s. "We wrote to Britain asking what sort of mess they had sent us. It needed a great deal of work to sort out the problems." Neither were the Port Elizabeth engineers impressed with the suitability of the suspension – especially of the estate – and the interior dustproofing for dirt roads. But at least

ABOVE **Growly-voiced singer Eartha Kitt christens a new Cortina at dealer Grays of Guildford; note the ski-resort theme.**

BELOW **Costing £650 extra in 1971 when first seen as a full soft-top, the later Crayford Sunshine Cortina retained the side structure and windows of the two-door saloon in an effort to improve the wobbliness of previous Cortina ragtops. It was popular, with 400 built. (Giles Chapman Library)**

The Morris Marina

With the 1968 formation of the British Leyland Motor Corporation, Lord Stokes looked at the rag-bag of models he had inherited and saw nothing to counter the Cortina. "They were terrified of it, Stokes particularly," says Cortina MkII stylist Roy Haynes, who was entrusted with styling ADO28, as a Cortina competitor for BL.

The Marina, as it was eventually named, had to be quick, cheap and conventional and take on the Cortina, Escort and the Vauxhall Viva. "The Marina was regarded as a sort of late BMC copy of an earlier Cortina," Ray Hutton recalls. "It was as if they'd said 'Ford is doing much better than we are and their cars are much cheaper'.. The thing about the Cortina was that not only was it an intermediate size but it was also an example of how to make a car that had been pared to a price that probably nobody did again until the Japanese came along. Everything was at the minimum but quite well put together."

Swiftly under way in 1968, the specification of the Marina was down to Austin-Morris director of engineering Harry Webster, who had come across from Triumph. Naturally he looked around the corporate parts bin. The front suspension was of similar design to that of the Morris Minor, the gearbox from the new rear-driven Triumph Toledo, and the engines the trusty 1.3-litre A-Series and 1.8-litre B-Series – with twin carburettors for the performance 1.8TC version.

The bodyshell took a leaf out of the Cortina's book. Haynes recalls a conversation with Joe Edwards, director of engineering at BL subsidiary Pressed Steel Fisher, about the Marina bodyshell. "He asked me about the Cortina, to give him some sneak ideas. The body in white of the MkII weighed 500lb and was made for £100. He said the nearest we get to that is the Hillman Hunter, so we'll make the Marina 500lb for £100, which they achieved." In production, Marinas did weigh a little less than the equivalent Cortina, which of course was by then a bigger car.

Roy Haynes's design was approved in August 1968, his brief having been to produce an attractively styled car; it was certainly an adequately smart offering by the standards of the time. The Marina was notable in having its two-door version as a coupé style, and Haynes managed to do this at little extra cost by retaining the saloon's front doors.

Haynes has always portrayed his Leyland period as one of constant arguments with Webster and Stokes, such as over the use of the Triumph gearbox when the MGB's gearbox was already designed to handle the power of the 1.8-litre B-Series engine. His ideas for a series of cars built on a common platform having been spurned, he resigned from Leyland in 1971.

It was hoped that the Marina would be ready for the 1970 London Motor Show, where it would have faced the new Cortina, but despite its frantic timing, the launch had to wait until April 1971. The 1969 Maxi should have held the fort – and undoubtedly did nibble at some Cortina sales to family buyers – but it started off with too high a price and a terrible gearchange. It never achieved the sales figures BL had hoped for it, not least as fleet managers generally fought shy of front-wheel-drive Austins and Morrises.

After a well-documented embarrassment, where both the motoring weeklies were so appalled by the handling of the 1.8 Marinas that they obliged BL to modify the front suspension before the car went on sale, the Marina range – including an estate version from 1972 – settled down to a UK sales career which peaked in 1973 with 115,000 annual sales.

Ford listened. "They were pretty switched on," Basil Green of Perana tuning fame recalls. "I was always impressed. If I went to a meeting on the design of a vehicle there would be at least five different engineers sitting at the same table. I'd be answering to the brakes, the suspension, to the engine power, to weight, to all different engineers that headed up different divisions. I had to know what I was talking about."

In the course of responding to the technical deficiencies of the MkIII, Ford came up with variants more suited to the market. As well as a unique-to-South Africa pick-up, or 'bakkie', introduced in 1971, there was a Cortina Big Six, a 3.0-litre V6 Cortina not only subjected to plenty of local shakedown testing but to secret pre-production tests in Australia, running flat-out for 24 hours a day. Basil Green also undertook some of the development work.

Although Ford cars were shipped from Dagenham to South Africa in 'Knocked Down' form, there had to be a strong element of local content in the finished article to avoid high taxes. Starting with smaller items such as trim, wheels, glass and batteries as local production, entire body pressings and major mechanical components such as the rear axle ended up domestically sourced. With the Big Six at the top of the tree – a MkIII Perana was advertised but the

At face value, the Cortina outsold the Marina comfortably, like for like, but there was another way of looking at this, as *Motor* did in October 1973, albeit omitting to mention the Escort. 'Talking of league tables, the Cortina is still no 1 for the same nine-month period [Jan–Sept] with sales of 156,681 cars. To compare these figures with the Marina in 2nd place (91,651) is, we believe, and as British Leyland have said (perhaps not loudly enough), not really accurate. After all, the Marina, the 1100/1300 and the Allegro are all aimed at much the same market – hence the significance of the 1500 and 1750 versions of the Allegro. Thus adding the figures for these three models giving the 164,026 total sales for the relevant BLMC sector of the market may be more realistic. What it does mean is that Ford can concentrate their efforts on only one basic design, where BLMC have to spread theirs around more.'

It was partly because of dividing its effort between the Allegro and the Marina that Leyland had no money for any radical change and that the Marina consequently lasted far longer than planned. Overhead-cam O-Series engines arrived in 1978 and the embarrassingly hyped 1980 Morris Ital facelift took the design to the end of its career in 1984 after two generations of Cortina had passed by and the Sierra was already on the market.

The Marina was too little, too late to compete with the Cortina, but it isn't fair to write it off. By the admittedly not over-high standards of the day it was a perfectly acceptable car; furthermore, it was only ever intended to be a quick-to-the-market stop-gap, so its shortcomings need to be understood in that context.

RIGHT **The Morris Marina at least trumped the Cortina with a unique coupé body style cleverly retaining the front doors of the saloon and available across the range. (LAT)**

idea was dropped in favour of a V8 Granada Perana – the Cortina became a South African institution.

"It was a number-one seller," says Green. "The span from 1300 upwards was a tremendous range – it could be a daughter's car, a son's car and a father's car when you had four cars in a family. It was tremendously well respected and durable." Indeed, it became the stuff of South African slang, for a certain kind of man: 'One litre brandy, two litre Coke, three litre Cortina.'

Ford of Australia departed even further from British specification. It had taken the 1600 and 2000 Cortinas from launch (and been highly critical about their reliability and durability) but had nothing to respond to the six-cylinder versions of the Viva-derived Holden Torana that General Motors had introduced in 1969. During 1972 intensive development went on to rustle up a Cortina competitor in the 'light six' class, the Cortina Six.

However, rather than the Essex V6, the engineers at Broadmeadows near Melbourne chose to squeeze the 3.3-litre and 4.1-litre in-line 'sixes' from the Australian Ford Falcon into the Cortina, without changing its wheelbase. The Falcon, based on the American original, had become Ford of Australia's top-seller once it had been suitably beefed up for the wide open spaces.

The advantage of local content again played a part in the choice of engine and the sheer lazy, durable power that the simple straight-six provided seemed ideal. The range put British Cortinas into the shade, with quoted power outputs of 130bhp, 155bhp or even 170bhp on the GT model. But it was lazy power. "The biggest 'six' ever fitted to a Cortina was a 250 cubic inch (4.1-litre), good for a pretty feeble 150 horsepower or so, but packing very good torque at very low revs," recalls Steve Cropley, Australian editor-in-chief of *Autocar* magazine, who was working for *Wheels* in the 1970s. "Grunt was these cars' saving grace. They didn't have much else except a Blue Oval badge – trusted at the time – and lots of metal for the money."

The Falcon 'sixes' certainly had a much more laid-back character than the Essex/Cologne V6, and a three-speed manual sufficed as the standard transmission (with a column gearchange), with a four-speeder and an automatic available higher up the range. The low-revving engines, turning over at under 3,000rpm at 70mph, meant high-speed cruising was effortless; a 4.1-litre Cortina Six tested by *Wheels* in January 1973 achieved 112mph.

Shoehorning a 'six' into an engine bay which wasn't designed for it meant the firewall had to be reshaped for the back of the engine and transmission, the new radiator

ABOVE Super Speed's very fast Cortina conversion announced its presence with a bonnet stripe and a Ford Zodiac 'gunsight'. (LAT)

RIGHT A Specialised Mouldings bonnet was an option on the Cortina Savage, matched to the colour of the car, and not averse to flying off at speed. Note how 'Uren' is substituted for the Ford lettering. (LAT)

moved 3in forward and the sump revised to clear the front crossmember. All this meant that most of the extra length and weight of the six sat behind where the last cylinder of the four-cylinder engine would have been. Different springs and dampers also had to be specified but there was no power-assisted steering. A number of minor Falcon trim and mechanical parts also became common to all Australian Cortinas, as did the modified bulkhead.

After racking up 1,500 miles in a pair of the new Cortina Six models in late 1972, *Wheels* was impressed. Though the six-cylinder engines weighed about 110lb more than the 2-litre Cortina 'four', the additional weight wasn't found to have any noticeable adverse effects on steering effort or handling. On the contrary, wrote the magazine, the car felt as if it had been designed around the 'six', rather than the 'six' designed into it. This generosity of spirit didn't last long. In 1972 the magazine withheld its 'Car of the Year' award, but the Cortina certainly wasn't a contender. Familiarity with the Six revealed 'dubious roadholding and handling on rough surfaces', it said, and misgivings were raised about 'quality control and long-term durability when things began falling off or going wrong'.

There were occasions when the extra weight and power simply overwhelmed the Six, such as on a poorly surfaced bend known to the writers: 'Even the finest European aristocrats can't completely ignore the dip but are nudged only a little off line. The Cortina Six came close to setting a new mark by twitching out a good two feet when encountering the deviation. Through most pronounced and unsettling on uneven corners, the condition also arises on straights where the surface is sharply irregular or corrugated. Here the Cortina skitters disconcertingly from the intended path, especially when travelling at middling to high speeds with the power on.'

"These were fast and long-legged cars without much finesse," comments Steve Cropley. "They lacked the ability to rev, and had far too much weight over the front wheels, so that they attacked practically every corner with tyre scrub and moaning understeer. Oh, and pretty poor steering, too. Power steering wasn't standard. Other properties included plenty of body roll and big nosedive under braking."

In 1973 to 1974 Ford of Australia allegedly proposed a three-door coupé version of the Cortina to compete with the upcoming Holden Torana hatchback, using the Pinto tailgate and longer two-door Cortina doors, but the idea was rejected on cost grounds.

British go-faster conversions

With a new range of more powerful 'Pinto' engines in Britain, plus faster Capris, there was less of a market for tuned MkIII Cortinas, but by 1972 several familiar names – and some new ones – were offering Cortina upgrades or engine swaps.

Broadspeed, Janspeed and Piper Engine Developments worked with the new 98bhp 'Pinto' 2-litre engine, while John Young's Super Speed and Jeff Uren's Race Proved focused on a V6 conversion. In February 1972 *Motor Sport* was able to report on four faster Cortinas.

The only 2-litre sampled was the Broadspeed, which had a gas-flowed head, stronger valves, a reworked Weber carburettor and a completely new exhaust system. This

TOP Unique from the front doors backwards, the South African Cortina 'bakkie' had a locally designed tailbox which retained some of the original styling. There were also a few 3-litre Perana bakkies. (©VMP/RM)

ABOVE Laid bare at the Port Elizabeth plant, the box-frame chassis had leaf-sprung suspension for tough roads. (Giles Chapman Library)

The turbo Cortina project

Having in 1971 investigated boosting power of the Essex V6 to at least 160bhp, with Kugelfischer fuel injection, Ford AVO engineers, headed by Erich Fuchs, debated either supercharging or turbocharging the engine. Hitherto primarily used in diesel engines, the turbo won because of its relative ease of installation and because Ford had some first-hand experience: German engineers had worked with Swiss tuner Michael May on a 'blown' V6 Capri. Rod Mansfield also recalls a May-equipped Taunus 20M on the British AVO fleet in the late 1960s.

PWC 906K, a 3-litre Cortina GXL that had possibly been a press car, became the test bed, and received a well-developed conversion using a Garrett AiResearch T-04B turbocharger, with a lower compression ratio of 7.6:1 (compared to 9.1:1) and modified pistons to allow running on 97-octane fuel. The standard inlet manifold was retained, as was the carburettor, repositioned and adjusted to cope with higher fuel pressures. Engine output was measured at 210bhp.

The turbo Cortina GXL racked up many European miles, taking in summer congestion in Milan, altitude tests in the Swiss Alps and plenty of high-speed motorway runs where it could reach 133mph. Motoring writer and former AVO employee Jeremy Walton commuted to work for a time in PWC 906K. "It was a much better-mannered drive than the later highly tuned Uren Savages and a lot 'real world' faster.

The conversion was exemplary. It picked up from 1,000rpm with a big slug of power and torque that slaughtered any overtaking opportunity between 1,750rpm and 5,000 rpm. I did run it to an indicated 135mph, but the rest of the Cortina body felt a bit too rock-and-roll at that speed – anywhere around 60–100mph was more natural."

In November 1973 Messrs Fuchs, Parker and Pritchard-Lovell (from Ford, Garrett and Weslake) detailed their research in a paper to the Institute of Mechanical Engineers in London. The overall conclusions were that turbocharging had produced power and torque improvements of 30 per cent and 26 per cent and that 'a unique combination of vehicle performance and driveability' had resulted, with exhaust and intake noise readily controlled. Mechanical reliability was said to have presented no problems, and specific fuel consumption was described as being 'no higher than that of the normally aspirated version of the engine' and being accompanied by low emission of oxides of nitrogen.

However, as far as Ford of Britain was concerned, the turbo Cortina went no further. The author has seen no evidence that it was being considered as a production model, even though a 180bhp turbocharged Consul GT was also built by AVO. "It was a promising conversion that could have been applied across the Ford 'Essex' V6 ranges of the period, but chassis abilities were so primitive then

[especially braking and adhesion] that a turbo V6 Ford was an engine more than a decade ahead of its time," Jeremy Walton observes.

Official turbo Fords did not arrive until the 1980s but in 1973 Broadspeed produced a short-lived turbo V6 Capri conversion called the 'Bullitt', the same engine later being adopted by TVR. Janspeed also offered a turbo package on the next-generation Cortina's 'Pinto' engines.

ABOVE LEFT Pictured at Ford AVO in South Ockendon, the outwardly standard 2.0 GXL hides its secrets under a Specialised Mouldings bonnet from a Uren Savage – with clips.

ABOVE A cast aluminium plenum chamber sits atop the 3-litre V6, feeding pressurised air into the carburettor. The lack of upper suspension mounts allows more space for the bigger engine and turbo trunking.

LEFT The facelift for 1974 also saw the introduction of the 2000E. New rectangular lights were common to all higher-specification Cortinas.

RIGHT The new interior and dashboard swept away the original messy item at a stroke. The easy-to-read instrument cluster won a Design Council award in 1974.

ABOVE The 2000E's interior featured real wood atop the doors and 'Savannah' cloth trim. Automatic transmission was a perfect luxury option.

sampling at the same time. 'Well, that is until the car broke away (which it often did in the wilds of Scotland) when the steering lightened exactly to the best point for judging the amount of corrective lock that would be needed', the testers nonchalantly wrote, adding that the brakes also lost much of their power on the trip.

The Super Speed Cortina was already a 122mph car but Jeff Uren's Savage conversions on the MkIII went even further. The early 'basic' offering was a two-door V6 GT, but the no-holds-barred conversion was a 2000 GXL equipped with a 3-litre V6 reworked by engine-builder Weslake and sporting Tecalmit mechanical fuel injection. It was quoted as giving 218bhp, had a heady price tag of £2,645 when £1,363 would buy a standard GXL, but boasted performance to frighten a Ferrari – or a Jaguar E-Type V12, which is what *Motor Sport* tested it against, achieving an identical 0–60mph time of 6.7 seconds. Once more, keeping all this power on the road was down to a comprehensive package of suspension and braking revisions. Both the Super Speed and Uren conversions appear to have been thorough, but the author has not been able to ascertain how many of either were built; it is doubtful there were many. Price was certainly a deterrent, while going into the fuel crisis of 1973–74 with a car that was hard-pushed to deliver 13mpg can't have helped, which also partly explains why Ford's intriguing Cortina Turbo (see previous page) was a non-starter.

added an extra 8bhp, and the suspension was lowered by an inch with shorter springs and Spax dampers. The whole package and was judged to improve handling and greatly increase the versatility of the car, the engine being both smooth and potent. Top speed in wet weather was 109mph compared to a measured 103mph for a standard 2-litre estate the magazine had tested.

For a more fundamental power shift nothing less than a 3-litre V6 would do. Super Speed's transplant mated the newly uprated (up 10bhp to 138bhp) Ford V6 to the 2000's gearbox. The conversion required a revised front crossmember, sump and engine mountings plus a new radiator, uprated suspension with wider wheels giving a 2in-wider track, and brakes with a changed front-to-rear balance and harder linings. *Motor Sport* found the car an impressive high-speed cruiser on a trip to Scotland – and rather more transatlantic in feel than many British cars, though of course a lot like the Uren conversion it was

Cortinas for hard times

Back in the real world of Cortinas, for the second half of its career – the longest of any series – the MkIII didn't change very much. There was the new 2000E estate in 1974 and the following year a new three-speed automatic transmission was introduced, produced by Ford itself at its French Bordeaux plant. To emphasise the importance it placed on this new transmission, Ford in France launched a dedicated automatic model bearing the name of the factory: the Taunus Bordeaux was a dressed-up Taunus L at a promotional price less than that of a manual.

A minor facelift in October 1975 saw a matt-black grille, and the Cortina continued its reign as Britain's best-selling car until displaced temporarily by the Escort MkII in 1976. With tough economic times and a continuing interest in fuel economy, the emphasis for all car makers shifted to smaller models. Ford was well placed to cope, with the Escort and then the new Fiesta. However, while the Cortina was still selling well, both Ford and

ABOVE The 2000E estate was the most luxurious Cortina load-carrier to date and featured a tailgate wash/wipe for the first time.

LEFT Ford of Australia's Falcon straight-six engine just fitted the Cortina engine bay. Rocker covers were painted orange on the 4.1-litre, blue on the 3.3-litre. Note the deeper radiator compared to that of a 2-litre Cortina. (Greg Wallace)

ABOVE Bonnet shut, an early Cortina Six could be distinguished by a small power bulge to clear the larger engine, an extra air intake below the bumper and twin headlamps. This is a restored 1973 TC XLE, which has a polished grille and clear indicator lenses. (Greg Wallace)

its competitors were now losing domestic share to Japanese imports, many of them Cortina clones. They were being beaten on price, levels of equipment and perceived quality.

Ford went on a determined 'Value-for-Money' campaign, juggling the standard specification of all models to offer more for the price and reintroducing the Popular badge on a stripped-out Escort. On Cortinas, a brake servo, heated rear window, hazard warning lights and a cigar lighter were made standard across the board and the estates were given tailgate wash/wipes.

The company had also been working on improving fuel economy across its range for three years (it said), with development work to re-calibrate carburettors and ignition curves across the whole range. The economy objective, set in 1975, was to improve the average fuel consumption of the model range by 15 per cent before 1980.

"Before the oil crisis, the emphasis was always more towards competitive performance and brisk acceleration,"

manager of Performance and Economy George Cayliss told *Ford News* in February 1976. "With rising fuel costs the need for improved economy is becoming more acute and we are now offering the customer the ability to make some considerable savings in running costs."

For the Cortina this meant the introduction in February 1976 of surely the least-appealing MkIII of all, an economy-tune 1300. Power was down from 57bhp to 49.5bhp, for an economy gain of up to 15 per cent. That was all very well, but it made for a miserable drive, Graham Robson later writing that the car 'felt as if it was tied to a tree'.

Dynamic director of sales Sam Toy boasted that in the first eight months of 1976 UK Cortina sales actually rose by 30 per cent to 94,768 units. This was in spite of the fact that from January 1976 any regular readers of the motoring press would have surmised that there would soon be a new Cortina, as a new Taunus had been launched at that month's Brussels Motor Show.

RIGHT **The Cortina MkIII's racing career in the UK was confined to 'celebrity races'– some more serious than others. Disc jockey Noel Edmonds ran a 2000 GT in the 1974 RAC/Castrol Anniversary Touring Car Championship event, fettled by Willment and with a limited-slip differential and blueprinted engine.**

BELOW RIGHT **This 1975 base model bears no bright trim at all and has the matt-black grille common to all late Cortina MkIIIs.**

It was an irony that perhaps the mostly fashionably styled Cortina had been allowed to linger on as its looks rapidly aged, but investment in new models from all car makers was slowed by the fuel crisis, plus in Ford's case the need to bring the Fiesta to market. Nonetheless the MkIII Cortina, aided by Ford's marketing and pricing skills, had kept to the tradition of being a top-seller and yet again had sold a million by October 1975, even if Ford did take longer to get there.

When looking back on its career in October 1976, with the introduction of the MkIV, *Autocar* observed that when the MkIII had been launched it had been the only time the Cortina had temporarily fallen from grace, beset by quality and delivery problems. But it also wondered if the early setback had been because 'for a year or so, it ran just a little too far ahead of what the market wanted. Perhaps that was why it survived for six years, rather than the four of its predecessors.'

Chapter 8:
Euro-Cortina: the MkIV and Cortina 80

Given that the 1971 Taunus Cortina had been virtually all-new and had suffered such a difficult start in life, its replacement was logically going to be a re-skin and refinement of existing components. Following the Escort, Granada and forthcoming Fiesta, complete design rationalisation was inevitable – all the other Ford of Europe cars were essentially the same for British and mainland European markets.

Work on the fourth Cortina started in 1972, with four internal objectives identified by the initials S-A-F-E: Safety, Aesthetics, Function and Equipment. Under the Aesthetics heading, a timeless look was required to take the new Cortina into the 1980s, so none of your high-fashion Coke-bottle-type styling, thank you. This became a bit of a struggle.

"Design and engineering responsibilities were split between Dunton and Merkenich," recalls Geoff Howard, who had left journalism to join the Ford of Britain press office in 1974. "In logistical terms it was a nightmare to get an integrated and fully co-ordinated new model launch. To compound the problems, the UK and Germany had independent marketing and sales organisations which had their own agendas."

This included testing new styling concepts in separate customer clinics. Many of those who attended British clinics were recent Cortina buyers who naturally tended to favour

LEFT A new shape for 1977 and a new badge: a Cortina Ghia in front of a suitably aristocratic setting. From the front, there was now no way to tell a Cortina from a Taunus.

ABOVE Possibly taken at Merkenich and labelled 'cube front', this photo appears to be of an early experiment to marry a flat front end to MkIII Cortina doors – more curved at the top edge and lacking the lower ridge of those of the Taunus TC.

BELOW By August 1973 the Taunus at least was near its final shape. This split styling clay tests two different frontal treatments. (LAT)

RIGHT Ford of Britain released this 'generations' shot with the new car. The 1977 Cortina might have become lower and wider, but it was no longer than the 1962 original.

shapes and styles most closely related to the car they had just bought. European exterior car design had now devolved to Merkenich and was headed by Uwe Bahnsen. "At the time the MkIV shape was being proposed, Ford had an American vice-president of design, a British VP of product development and a German in charge of exterior styling," Howard explains. "The Coke-bottle Cortina hips were a success in the UK and Sam Toy and the clinics supported an evolution from this. But the 'bean counters' won the battle for integration with Germany."

Patrick Le Quément, now relocated to Germany, was charged with coming up with a proposal to compete against a fellow designer. The starting point was that the car would retain the doors of the German Taunus TC because the styling of the waistline was thought neutral enough to blend into a new front and rear and thus save money.

"When I joined the programme there were two programme approaches. Firstly, a minimum investment with an all-new front end, keeping the rear-end sheet metal of the Taunus. So you would have a Taunus with a new front end and very light surgery such as new tail lamps etc. The second approach was to change the front end and the rear end. In all cases you kept the Taunus doors. So there were two designs in competition; my design, where there was no change to the rear, and then there was a second one by Klaus Kapitza whose brief was to design a vehicle with a new front and rear end."

Le Quément's frontal styling proposal took account of the likelihood of regulations demanding a raised bumper-height and large US-style 'Federal' bumpers, and so raised the headlamps; to allow for a bonnet line with no protrusions for pedestrian impact they were flush, protected behind rectangular glass panels. There was a connection here to the new Fiesta and this became a common look for other 1970s European cars.

Meanwhile, there was hesitation in England, where it was anticipated they would have to sell a different Cortina, preserving the Coke-bottle rear of the MkIII with a new front. David Burgess-Wise in *Ford at Dagenham, the Rise and*

ABOVE The new square style was intended to align the Taunus-Cortina with more prestigious marques such as Audi and Mercedes, especially in Ghia trim. Some bemoaned the high sill to the boot.

LEFT Goodbye 2000E, hello Ghia – but still with crushed-velour seat material and plenty of wood. The dashboard was already familiar to late-model Cortina MkIII users and praised for the clarity of its instruments.

ABOVE All-black body trim, twin halogen spotlamps, sports wheels and wide tyres mark out a Cortina S. It matched the Taunus almost exactly in looks, but German buyers could have two-door versions with 2.0-litre four-cylinder or 2.3-litre V6 engines.

RIGHT The S had the loudest trim of any Cortina. The very of-its-time Cadiz fabric could be specified in five deckchair-like hues.

Fall of Detroit in Europe tells of a mock-up with a MkIV front and a MkIII rear being made at Dunton (which retained the advanced exterior design studio and responsibility for trucks), just to humour managing director Bill Batty; apparently it was duly wheeled out, and then never seen again.

Harry Calton largely confirms this account, and recalls it as a proposal foisted on Dunton by US bosses. "We were taken to a product presentation of what was to be the new Taunus and the Cortina version. There was a version with the MkIII centre section and the future MkIV front and rear. It looked a right dog's breakfast. It was a genuine proposal, but the reaction was so adverse. But that was the mindset: 'Ford of Britain can sell anything that it can make.' And it was going to be less expensive to make. But in the end we got the best design."

If Britons had lost their curvy Cortina, the Germans might have been sadder to have lost the Taunus coupé in the transition. Le Quément recalls that one was prepared, but only put into production in the Argentinian market much later. "That was a kind of favourite. When a car wouldn't work in one location there was always an opportunity of trying it in Argentina or Brazil and that happened many times. Not necessarily because that market required it but they were desperate to have the cars, so the tooling, having been done, was shipped."

The new euro-Taunus Cortina design was neat and certainly more conservative than the 1970 Cortina, in a way resuming the evolution from the square MkII as if nothing had happened in between. The glass area was said to be 15 per cent bigger than before and the taller and deeper rear window claimed to offer a whole 40 per cent improvement. Much larger rear extractor vents meant that yet again a complete air change was supposedly achieved in 18 seconds at 70mph; in the 1965 Cortina that figure had been 40 seconds.

The carry-over from the 1970–75 Taunus was most obvious on the estate, which adopted the previous Taunus estate bodywork from the front doors backwards; compared to the MkIII Cortina, the squared-off Taunus rear doors made access slightly easier. A sill panel had now reappeared across the rear of the saloon instead of a bootlid opening to bumper level, helping structural rigidity and performance in crashes. Ford also claimed – somewhat dubiously – that customers had not appreciated objects toppling out of a fully packed MkIII boot when opened. The spare wheel was in a well below the boot floor, with the fuel tank alongside it, as before. At the front the bonnet line was 3in lower to enable the driver better to see the end of it and an integral spoiler

below the front bumper was claimed to reduce lift by 10 per cent front and rear, improving motorway stability.

Being a repackaging of existing components, the Cortina MkIV retained the 101.5in wheelbase of its predecessor and was about 3in longer overall but no wider in body or track. Weight was up by around only 40lb, it was claimed. The dashboard, released earlier on the 1974 model-year Cortina was virtually the same, and touches such as the curved plastic over the instruments, to avoid reflections, were appreciated.

Suspension was changed only in detail. One degree of negative camber was built into the front suspension to improve cornering and reduce parking effort. Power steering was not at first available, being introduced to Cortinas with the later 2.3-litre V6, before becoming an option on 2-litre cars.

At the rear, the live axle was still located by two trailing and two semi-trailing links but their attachment points to the axle were lowered by 15mm (a little over half an inch), and where they attached to the body the bushes were increased in diameter to isolate suspension vibrations. The standard-fit rear anti-roll bar was a third stiffer and the rear springs were

ABOVE In the '70s and '80s Ford would carry over rear sections of estate cars from one generation to the next. The MkIII Cortina estate style did not, however, survive.

ABOVE The base two-door Cortina was still available, but was a fringe model assembled in Cork, Ireland, and Genk, Belgium.

now variable-rate – thicker at the bottom than the top. In theory these offered most benefit to people travelling in lightly laden Cortinas; before, the rear springs had been biased towards full-load conditions. The GT specification was discarded in favour of 'S' models, which received gas-filled dampers and stiffer springs. There were servo-assisted dual-circuit 9.75in front discs on all cars, coupled to rear drums, and wheels were of either 4½in or 5½in width.

Engines for the October 1976 UK launch were the familiar 1300 'Kent' and 1600/2000 'Pinto' units. Owners (especially the fleet operators) could now choose between the grim 49.5bhp economy 1300 introduced earlier on the run-out Cortina MkIII and an economy 1600 with Sonic Idle carburettor, lower axle ratio and modified inlet manifold. Power was down from 72bhp to 59bhp in this format and

Ford claimed a rather unremarkable touring fuel economy of 37.4mpg, against the previously quoted 34.5mpg; presenting this as a 10 per cent improvement sounded better. More upmarket trim levels were only available in conjunction with the standard 72bhp 1600 and 98bhp 2000 engines.

Having established Value-for-Money branding, Ford of Britain could hardly remove equipment from the new model and the five new Cortina saloons and four estates all had carpeting, a cigar lighter, electric screenwash, reversing lights and a passenger door mirror. The five trim levels were standard, L, GL, S and Ghia, meaning the disappearance of the 2000E label. All good things come to those who wait, and what was once luxury equipment continued to trickle down the Cortina tree – and there were no more rubber mats and cross-ply tyres. As Ford of Britain's sporting activity was now

and many happy hours could still be spent with the options list. New goodies here included a tilt/slide steel sunroof first seen on the Granada, rear foglamps, rear seatbelts, alloy wheels for the Ghia, and high-pressure headlamp washers. "The vinyl roof became the thing of choice," Harry Calton recalls. "They were great from the manufacturing point of view. No extra finishing on the roof panel, stick the vinyl on, then a strip and a badge."

As previously advertised

Being distracted by the potential attractions of the 'hybrid' MkIII/IV design lost Ford of Britain time in launching the MkIV. Consequently Cologne had committed to tooling before Dagenham and months were lost while duplicate tooling was organised. This might not have been of great importance, given that Britain was having no trouble shifting the ageing Cortina MkIII. Meanwhile, the new Taunus had started rolling off the German production lines in November 1975 and was launched the following January at the Brussels Motor Show. Dagenham production started in late September 1976, with the full range available from the start. *Autocar* was able to test both a 2000 Ghia and a 1600GL alongside technical descriptions and an interesting back-to-back comparison of four generations of Cortina saloons to gauge progress.

The original MkI Cortina 'stood up in the comparison very much better than we had expected it would and in some respects even proved superior to its successors', it commented. This judgement mainly related to interior space and how the evolution of the seats from skimpy to comfortable had eroded interior room. Sitting in the back of all four cars one after the other, the magazine found that in the MkIV the headroom had been 'whittled away to zero' and that all three of the testers were in contact with the headlining. Happily though, performance, safety and handling had all improved in this 13-year period.

The 2-litre Ghia was found to be a 'very pleasing driver's car' with excellent equipment, reasonable performance and economy and good handling, steering and instrumentation, with the only low marks being for a bumpy ride over poor surfaces and a higher level of steering kickback than might have been expected. The aerodynamic attention to the body was found to have produced excellent stability on motorways and noise was judged to have been reduced. Given the increased weight, it came as no surprise that performance had decreased compared to the 2000E tested in 1973 (maximum speed was down from 102mph to 100mph), but the in-gear

entirely Escort-based, the S was the sportiest Cortina in the new range, and was available as a four-door saloon only.

It had stiffer suspension settings and sporting kit such as long-range driving lamps but no increase in power, retaining the standard 98bhp 2.0-litre engine with its twin-choke Weber carburettor. There were to be no RS Cortinas. However, in 1977, when Ford of Britain introduced the Series X options range for Escort and Fiesta, they also offered a pick-and-mix cosmetic package on the Cortina, consisting of a rear spoiler, alloy wheels, stiffer suspension, a short-throw gearshift and sports seats.

The number of engine/body combinations was reduced and the two-door Cortina became a marginal car, only available in standard or L trim. Seventeen different models were offered – one fewer than after the 1973 range re-jig –

Ford and Ghia

Although Ghia was once an illustrious Italian styling house, Ford's ownership only ever seemed to manifest itself as an upmarket trim level, taking over where the 'Executive' cars had left off.

Founded in 1915 by coachbuilder Giacinto Ghia, Carozzeria Ghia's most notable series of styling specials was produced for Chrysler throughout the 1950s. Its most commercial design was the Volkswagen Karmann-Ghia. After its guiding light Luigi Segre died suddenly in 1963, Ghia spent much of the decade in turmoil, passing between uninterested owners while names such as Pininfarina and Bertone scooped up further clients. By the late 1960s the influence of Italian car styling was at its peak and mass-market European, American and especially Japanese car makers were employing the big names to design or produce full production cars.

Seeking to introduce some Italian influence into its own designs, in 1969 Ford set up a small rented styling studio in Bruino near Turin, headed by Filippo Sapino, formerly of Pininfarina and Ghia. He reported to the head of design of Ford of Europe, Joe Oros, known as the 'father' of the Mustang, and whose influence was rather heavily felt. "At very little expense Joe Oros was able to acquire a design activity which enabled him to have what he hoped would be independent Italian input, but he was so directive that all the models, whether from Britain, Germany or Italy, looked alike," recalls Patrick Le Quément.

The next year Ford of America acquired an interest in Ghia in order to put the De Tomaso Pantera into production: this junior-league 'supercar' had a Ford V8 engine and was sold in Lincoln-Mercury dealerships until 1975 when it fell foul of the energy crisis. In December 1972 Ford acquired full stock ownership of Ghia, fully buying out Alejandro De Tomaso's share and combining the two Italian studios to form Ghia Operations, headed by Sapino. Whereas Bruino had been a Ford of Europe enterprise, this was a Ford International outpost with a heavy leaning towards the US.

The first manifestation of Ghia-Ford styling was the Ford Ghia Mark I, a reworked Granada with a Lincoln-type radiator grille shown at Geneva in 1973. This was followed by the European-sized Mustang II in September. However, while the skilled panelbeaters of Ghia had indeed produced the prototype Mustang II in the metal, in reality Ghia had nothing to do with the styling, which hailed from Detroit.

As far as Ford of Britain was concerned, in March 1974 it announced that the first Fords with Ghia interiors would be the MkII Capri and the Granada. 'The name will become to motor furnishing and appointment what Chanel and Rubenstein became to perfume and cosmetics,' it gushed. The German-styled Granada Ghia coupé followed in July. "Ghia had no influence whatsoever on the

LEFT In this 1973 shot, Ghia staff busy themselves with the Ghia MkI, a dressed-up Granada shown at the Geneva motor show. In the foreground can be seen the nose of a De Tomaso Pantera, which Ghia was then building.

LEFT AND BELOW
This undated studio photo shows a losing Ghia proposal for a facelift of the next-generation TC Taunus. Shown in French magazine *L'Auto Journal* in July 1975, it was surmised to be a new Taunus Ghia. (Author's collection)

Ghia trim," says Le Quément. "The name Ghia was looked on as something that could be translated into hard cash through the trim level." It was, however, a name which worked worldwide.

Although it was meant to provide healthy competition to the designers in Britain, Germany and America, Ghia designs tended to err towards pleasing management in Dearborn and looked little different from proposals from the main Ford studios. For a production car to emerge from Ghia was the exception, although in the very early days there had been a lot of input into the stillborn Ford GT70 and Ghia's Tom Tjaarda had produced the winning 1972 design for the original Ford Fiesta in competition with Dearborn.

"Ghia did some good work for Ford, none or very little of which ever got into production," Ray Hutton recalls. "Every motor show I would go and see Filippo Sapino. There'd be a fabulous show car of some kind and I'd say 'What's going to happen to this?' and he'd say 'Nothing' – and nothing ever did."

In 2001 Ford cut 95 per cent of the 48-strong staff, making Ghia a 'virtual' design studio with no coachbuilding function. Filippo Sapino retired and the building's lease expired in 2002. The name would appear on the occasional concept car and the last UK Ghia-badged Ford was the 2008 Galaxy. By 2011 Ghia was a dormant company, existing in name only. Top-range Fords were badged 'Titanium' across Europe.

"Rather than Ghia giving Ford a premium image I think it debased Ghia," comments Ray Hutton. "It was a way of signifying the poshest car but didn't mean anything to people really, apart from some people in the car business."

ABOVE The 1996 Ka-based Saetta was one of Ghia's later designs; it previewed elements of the Ka and vaguely translated through to the StreetKa roadster of 2003.

acceleration times were slightly better, with peak power developed at 5,200rpm rather than 5,500rpm: 'What is more important is that the Cortina remains one of the quickest cars in its class,' commented the magazine. As for the 1600 GL, this was judged to be free of the Ghia's bounciness and to be a quick and well-equipped car with appeal to the private buyer.

Regarding the new looks, passers-by apparently mistook the Ghia for something more expensive when the badges

---

MkIV UK equipment, autumn 1976

Standard Cortina:

Hazard warning flashers
Heated rear screen
Brake servo, front discs
165-section radial tyres
Two-speed wipers
Electric windscreen washers
Temperature gauge
Cigar lighter
Dipping interior mirror
Driver's door mirror
Two-spoke steering wheel
Carpet
Chrome bumpers
Reversing lights

For Cortina L, in addition:

Glovebox lock and lamp
Trinket tray
Vanity mirror
Cloth upholstery instead of PVC
Reclining seats
Bumper rubber inserts
Side stripe
Halogen headlamps
Tailgate wash/wipe for estate

For Cortina GL, in addition:

Intermittent windscreen wipers
Clock
Trip mileage recorder
Map pockets
Four-spoke steering wheel

Wood instrument panel surround
Rear centre armrest
Side mouldings instead of stripes
Sports wheels
Pushbutton radio

For S, in addition:

185/70 tyres
Rev-counter
Centre console
Sports-style seats
Head restraints
Rear centre armrest deleted
Halogen driving lamps
Overriders
Gas-filled dampers
Stiffer springs
Side stripe instead of moulding
Black bumpers

For Ghia, in addition:

Remote-control door mirror
Wood-veneer dashboard
Luxury cloth seats
Cut-pile carpet
Extra sound deadening
Rear centre armrest
Bumper inserts
Wide side mouldings
Vinyl roof
Driving lamps not fitted
Stiffer springs not fitted

---

were taped up, and the 1600 also collected admiring glances. However, there were some people who were still very attached to their Coke-bottle Cortinas. 'Why then the Europeanisation of what was, I suppose, an Anglo-American design. It must surely have been the sleekest Ford of all time', wrote an unhappy *Motor* reader in 1976. 'I can assure Ford that my MkIII is staying in the garage. I would not sell it or part with it for any ridiculous sum of money.'

In Ford's market research prospective buyers had listed the most important features of any new Cortina as durability, reliability and quality, so it was no surprise that the MkIV was worthily launched as 'A car that's built to last' and with emphasis on the (albeit modest) engineering changes over the last model, plus efforts to make the car less rust-prone, not least with fewer dirt traps.

It needed to be a good investment too, as prices of all goods in Britain were subject to rapid inflation in the mid-1970s. In September 1973 a Cortina 1600 XL four-door cost £1,350 tax-paid. In October 1976 a 1600 GL was £2,548. It was cold comfort that prices were broadly close to the outgoing model.

But thanks to the sheer power and conservatism of the fleet market, plus expert specification juggling and pricing, the new Cortina continued its stranglehold on the British sales charts, backed up by the Escort, Fiesta and Granada. The second-generation Capri, meanwhile, was viewed by fleet buyers as a kind of exotic Cortina for talented employees.

"The MkIV was quite tidy, quite a nicely resolved ordinary car," Ray Hutton recalls. "It was regarded as a bread-and-butter car. It was alright without being exceptional but the pricing was quite good. There was a general feeling that it was there as the solid background car which other people tried to match. It became a sort of model for everything."

But there were now more would-be Cortinas. The Morris Marina hadn't proven a great challenge, but was by no means a lost cause, and by 1976 there were a couple of British newcomers in the shape of the front-wheel-drive five-door Chrysler Alpine (joining the elderly Hunter) and the very competent Vauxhall Cavalier – essentially the Opel Ascona with a new nose. This rear-wheel-drive Victor replacement was slightly smaller than the Cortina but was well received by private and company buyers. Available with 1600 and 1900 engines, the Cavalier range lacked an estate but offered smart two-door and three-door coupés. General Motors also sold the Ascona range in UK Opel dealerships, but this was a more significant rival to the Taunus in the wider European market.

More for the private buyer, in 1978 the Renault 16 was replaced by the Cortina-like 18 saloon. The Citroën GS wowed individuals but frightened the fleets, while the Fiat 131's anonymous style hardly made it an alluring alternative to the Cortina. Ford was much more concerned by the steady progress of the Japanese manufacturers, who provided a selection of boxy rear-driven Cortina clones, well built, well equipped and well priced. These included the Datsun Violet, the Toyota Carina, the Mazda 626 and the Mitsubishi Sigma.

Although the new Cortina had been well received, far from being content during the first full year of sales Ford management spent much of 1977 in a fury over the shortage of cars stemming from industrial disputes. In 1976 there had been only four working days where there hadn't been a dispute somewhere in Ford of Britain, according to a company report.

In April 1977 major customers obligingly wrung their hands for the staff journal *Ford News,* in a bid to shame errant employees. The manager of Bristol Street Motors in Birmingham was waiting to fill orders for about 600 Cortinas, the fleet manager at GKN was waiting for 300, and Mr Norman Bardell of a division of British Steel had been pleading to Ford dealers for just 40 cars. "We finally had to settle for Vauxhall. That's the damage this supply situation is doing to your reputation," he remonstrated.

European dealers turned to the Taunus and faced with buyers going for foreign imports, Terence Beckett warned that Britain might have to consider importing Cortinas (or rather re-badged Taunus models) if productivity did not improve. Nonetheless, UK Cortina sales for 1977 of around 120,000 were at least 14,000 up on the worst year of 1975. This was a better result than that of the drowning British Leyland, which lost 250,000 cars alone in a strike between February and March 1977.

An official V6 and a swansong for Cortina tuners

With the German and British cars now so closely aligned there was little reason why a Taunus V6 couldn't transmute into a right-hand-drive Cortina, which is just what happened in autumn 1977. The 2,296cc V6 was of course the 'Cologne' engine, a design which had been in service in Germany since the 1960s. In this guise it was good for 108bhp and a claimed 106mph top speed. The V6 was not a great deal heavier than a 2000 'Pinto' engine, so running-gear changes were limited to standard-fit power steering, the stiffer front springs of the 'S' and lower-profile tyres. A three-speed automatic transmission

was a logical option. The V6 Cortina was imported from Cologne, the first time a German-built Cortina was sold in Britain, and was available in either S or Ghia trim and from 1978 as an estate. It was the most expensive Cortina to date, at £4,445 for a Ghia saloon in 1977, but it gave the company-car driver one more rung to aim for, even if a 2.3-litre Cortina would remain a rarefied item. "You never saw them on my fleet," recalls Peter Eldridge, a former fleet manager with 250

BELOW An Italian-spec Taunus Ghia starred briefly in the 1977 James Bond film *The Spy Who loved Me* before being sent off the road by 007's Lotus Esprit in Sardinia, appearing to land in a house. (LAT)

RIGHT Something new for a British Cortina, the 2.3-litre V6 was a snug fit. To the left the big washer bottle is for the windscreen and the new headlamp washers.

BELOW Produced between 1975 and 1981, the MkI Vauxhall Cavalier's UK sales were about a fifth of the Cortina's but it was an accomplished competitor which would give Ford a run for its money in its successive generations. (Vauxhall)

Fords at one stage in his care. "If you were getting to that level you were against things like 3-Series BMWs."

The market for Cortina performance conversions was now a shadow of the thriving cottage industry it had once been, but Super Speed was still in the game, and in early 1977 would slot a 3-litre 'Essex' V6 into a low-mileage Cortina saloon or estate for £1,432 including VAT. The engine was 90lb heavier than a 2-litre Pinto and slightly bulkier, so some reworking of the engine bay was required in addition to improved cooling, altered suspension, harder brake pads and a short-throw gearshift from the Escort RS1800. A close-ratio gearbox and a limited-slip differential (which Super Speed did not normally recommend because it increased rear tyre wear) were optional. These were fitted to a car tested by *Autocar* in March 1977; the magazine enjoyed power-sliding around and achieving a mean maximum speed of 117mph. 'At a price near that of a Granada, the Super Speed Cortina offers

a worthwhile performance option', it concluded. However, the car's prospects were surely curtailed by the advent of the official 2.3-litre Cortina, which was not that much slower and was priced about the same as a standard converted Super Speed car without options.

Jeff Uren had branched out into other businesses and relocated to Devon but a Cortina Savage conversion was still available, and was tested by John Miles of *Autocar* in August 1979. The conversion cost £1,760 on top of the price of a 2-litre or 2.3-litre and again involved transplanting the 3-litre 'Essex' V6, optionally tuned to give 170bhp or 190bhp, plus the usual upgrades of stiffer springs and beefier brakes. Miles had fond memories of earlier Savages, but the 170bhp test car – loaned by a private individual – did not impress. 'Firing this one up destroyed that memory at a stroke. Running at the cammy and tappety-sounding tickover the deep-throated exhaust resonated badly – almost painfully – through a body shell that

appeared to be acting as a sounding box,' Miles wrote. Liking the performance well enough, and the instant response (advising turbo buyers to take note), he remarked that if you omitted the exhaust, the low gearing and the high-tuned engine you would get close to the 'excellent' Super Speed Cortina. Otherwise the Savage was 'a very expensive way to go faster'.

Neither conversion impressed Miles as much as British tuner Janspeed's turbocharged 2-litre Cortina Ghia, sampled in November 1978. After turbocharging Datsuns and Colts, Janspeed turned to aftermarket turbo conversions for 'Pinto'-engined Cortinas and Capris plus the 3-litre V6. The 'Pinto' turbo kits comprised a cast-iron exhaust manifold onto which a Rotomaster turbocharger unit was mounted, with a crossover pipe linking the turbocharger with the standard inlet manifold. The standard carburettor was replaced by a single SU, claimed to give excellent part-throttle economy. A decompression plate was included to lower the compression ratio and an oil

ABOVE In 1977 the white-striped Ford Gran Torino featuring in the US *Starsky & Hutch* TV series inspired Ford of Britain to turn a two-door 1300 into a scaled-down lookalike. "It was a real dog, all noise and no go," says Geoff Howard. "But it looked the part."

As good as it looks.

Cortina Ghia in four or six cylinder models with: Vinyl Roof; Tinted-band, laminated windscreen; Tinted side and rear glass; Cord and cashmere knit fabric upholstery; Thick cut-pile carpeting; Four-spoke 'soft-feel' steering wheel; Front centre console with electric clock; Heated rear-window demister; Intermittent windscreen wipers; Tachometer, oil gauge and trip meter; Directional power-boosted ventilation; Remote-control exterior rear-view mirror on driver's side; Quartz halogen headlights; Steel belt radial ply tyres.

FORD CORTINA GHIA *makes beautiful sense.* **Ford**

cooler supplied with all the necessary pipework. At £494 fitted (including VAT), the conversion was considerably cheaper than an engine transplant.

Boost was claimed to be sufficient for a 30 per cent gain in power and torque, and put to the test the Janspeed turbo whisked the Ghia to 60mph from rest in 8.3 seconds, compared to 11 seconds for the standard car, and 50–70mph in top gear was achieved in 6.6 seconds compared to 11.3 seconds. The development car suffered some fuel-vaporisation problems and was accordingly due to be fitted with a smaller carburettor, but was otherwise found to be smooth, flexible, free of turbo lag, and 'indecently quick'. 'In percentage terms the improvement in performance is staggering,' Miles enthused. 'Niggles apart, the conversion is so nearly right. It gave no trouble over 539 hard miles and must be almost impossible to beat in terms of value for money.'

The Janspeed kit was also marketed for fitment by (brave) home mechanics, and was claimed to take an unappealing 30–40 hours to fit if you had access to brazing equipment. At the end of the sales leaflet came a slightly ominous warning that the 'Pinto' engine was 'not entirely suitable' for conventional tuning resulting in increased revs, and that while a turbocharger was preferable in that respect, purchasers would be well advised to check that their engine were in first-class condition before going ahead.

ABOVE Known as the TE series, all Australian MkIV Cortinas featured heavy-duty bumpers and the Six a fairly subtle raised centre to the bonnet. The 4.1-litre straight-six was the largest engine ever offered in a production Cortina. (Author's collection)

RIGHT Given that nothing else distinguished it externally, buyers of Janspeed's turbo conversion might have done without the sidewinder stripes. Koni dampers and harder brake pads were the only running-gear upgrades. (LAT)

Foreign six-cylinders

Other Cortina territories remained wedded to the idea of beefy six-cylinder models. Australia stayed with a mixture of four-cylinder 'Pinto'-engined cars plus the 3.3-litre and 4.1-litre six-cylinder Falcon engines, which gained improvements such as a crossflow cylinder head. The MkIV was known as the TE series and the later Cortina 80 as the TF series, but the real sales success was the Falcon, now somewhat of an Australian institution.

Ford of South Africa also continued with its Big Sixes and in 1980 introduced the very sporting 3-litre Cortina XR6, to take over from the 3.0S. This was a rather more specialised model with a 3-litre 'Essex' V6 producing 140bhp and a unique five-link rear suspension to cope with South African conditions. A racing presence had been maintained with previous Cortinas, and the 1981 XR6 Interceptor was a homologation special intended for production-car racing; it produced 160bhp on triple Weber carburettors, and had a modified camshaft, cylinder head and exhaust system. Only 250 Interceptors were made (compared to over 9,000 XR6s); an even more limited dealer-edition was the 1983 Cortina X-Ocet with a Holley carburettor.

The last Cortina convertible

If you were after an open-air Cortina, Crayford would still oblige, although it was now majoring on estate and hatchback conversions to cars such as the Mercedes S-Class and Leyland Princess. Thus the 1976 London Motor Show saw a conversion on the new MkIV rushed to the stand in time for press day. At a hefty £4,200, it was a more attractive drop-top than the company's offering on the MkIII, retaining just the central pillars of the two-door saloon as part of a roll-bar. As well as this T-bar arrangement, the usual extra bracing was inserted into the sills, under the rear seat and across the scuttle. The rear quarter window was incorporated into the hood frame and folded down with it to form a nearly flat rear deck when covered by a tonneau. The Cortina Convertible Coupé by Crayford, to give it its full name, was claimed to provide exactly the same front and rear legroom as the saloon.

By 1979 the convertible was available solely through the Bristol Street Motors dealer chain as the 1.6-litre, 2.0-litre and 2.3-litre SL. In August 1979 UK all-inclusive prices ranged from £6,989 to £7,970, making the cost of the conversion at least £2,000 more than the four-door Ghia saloon equivalent. However, mainstream manufacturers had left the soft-top market by the late 1970s, erroneously fearing that US

Corcel: the Brazilian relation

Some relation? The 1978 Brazilian Ford Corcel, launched in October 1977, bore a strong resemblance to the MkIV Cortina. This was no accident, because it was a rushed facelift of an earlier styling proposal, and was carried out in Dunton by Patrick Le Quément, back as a design executive in the truck studio since 1976.

"I was given the assignment of making a facelift of a design which had not yet come out," he recalls. "The basic package was not very good. The proportions were wrong. The original design had been done by the US international studio but bombed in a clinic – it was a real disaster. We did this crash programme. ... Working day and night, we did this car in I think two months."

The style was adopted after some changes dictated by pre-ordered tooling for the earlier design, but there the resemblance to a Cortina ended. The underpinnings of the Corcel II were in fact those of the front-wheel-drive Renault 12. In 1967 Ford of Brasil had bought out WIllys Overland of Brazil, which was making the Renault Dauphine and was about to replace this with its own substantially rebodied version of the new Renault 12. Ford took over the project and at the end of 1968 the Ford Corcel was announced as a four-door saloon, later joined by coupé and estate versions; a restyle for 1973 gave the car a certain resemblance to the Ford Maverick. After the re-jig for 1978 the Corcel continued until 1986, and the spin-off Del Rey until 1991 – or 1997 in pick-up Pampa form.

ABOVE The Brazilian Ford Corcel II had British, rather than Latin-American, styling roots.

regulations would outlaw convertibles, and if you wanted a British four-seater convertible that was remotely affordable, a Cortina conversion was the only option.

Facelift plus

As might have been expected, autumn 1979 saw a facelift for the MkIV Cortina and the sister Taunus. The revised British car was known internally as the Cortina 80 but has since been dubbed the MkV.

It was rather more than the usual nip-and-tuck. Instead of a cost-effective revision of the radiator grille and some new seats, Ford of Britain confessed to having invested £50m in a new 'top-seller for the eighties'. Despite this expenditure, when press cars were loaned to British writers during August 1979, *Autocar* remarked that very few owners noticed anything different about the new cars. However, although superficially similar, just about every exterior body panel had been modified in some way to incorporate more window glass than before and new wraparound front and rear light clusters, while additionally the door openings were extended by an inch to allow better access.

Once more the work was largely down to Patrick Le

Quément. "It was a light but rather expensive facelift," he recalls. "We spent quite a bit of money on the greenhouse surgery, which had the merit of making the whole greenhouse look a lot lighter. At the end of the day it was a car that, on the one hand we were lightening but then we heavy-handedly applied the corporate trademark in Europe, supposedly a louvred grille and rather fake and heavy and Mercedes-style tail lamps, copied from the S Class." Ford claimed that the grille's 'aerofoil' slats formed a boundary layer of air which built up to divert surplus air up and over the bonnet rather than through the radiator.

The 1in of extra glass depth was claimed to have improved forward upper vision by 34 per cent and rear vision from the deeper rear screen by 41 per cent. As to the other changes, they were '[a] lot more than the eye can see' – as Ford put it at the time – but they were all on the worthy rather than exciting side, somehow reflecting the mood of continuing domestic economic woe.

The Fiesta had won a Design Council award for its cost-of-ownership features in 1978 and the Cortina was next for attention, at the time of the MkV facelift. Major service intervals were set at 12,000 miles with an oil change and safety check

every 6,000 miles. Service times were lowered by items such as a self-adjusting clutch, rear brake inspection apertures and front brakes which could be inspected with the wheels in place. A new multi-stage corrosion treatment was trumpeted, not before time as part of the Cortina's heritage had been an ability to rust just as well as its contemporaries, according to a pan-European analysis of 4,500 competitor cars.

One of the key features was a new Ford-designed carburettor for the 1300 and 1600 'economy' Cortinas, the 1600 Ghia retaining its twin-choke Weber. The Motorcraft Variable Venturi carburettor, made by Ford in Belfast, was said to have taken five years to design, and in the Cortina was claimed to give economy gains of up to 7.5 per cent while meeting future emissions controls. Such was the complexity of the new design that *Autocar* devoted a full page to its description and apologised for not going further.

Without going into similar detail, the basic premise was that by using a sliding intake valve and tapered needle in the orifice controlling the flow of fuel, the design was claimed to provide high (therefore efficient) gas velocities carrying fuel into the carburettor at all speeds. Carbon monoxide emissions were claimed to be reduced by 30 per cent in tests. The 1976

Sonic Idle system from the previous economy 1600 further helped efficiency by atomising fuel droplets. There was also a fully automatic cold-start system. 'We congratulate Ford on the VV,' the magazine concluded. 'It shows once again how, even if they aren't always first with innovations, Ford do so carefully learn, research, and apply.'

Although other manufacturers offered electric fans, all Cortina engines still had an engine-driven fan with its speed governed by a viscous coupling. This was claimed to engage progressively according to the rising temperature of the air passing through the radiator and to provide a faster warm-up by allowing the fan to idle when the engine was cold.

Ford claimed the engines gained 2bhp at peak power with the fan disengaged and the first press power listings were quoted in this way. Overall power outputs were indeed up, by varying degrees. The economy 49.5bhp tune having been dropped, the 'Kent' 1300 (now the only available engine with the two-door base Cortina) was up from 57bhp to 61bhp; for the 1600 there was a hike from 72bhp to 75bhp, with the new 1.6-litre Ghia, thanks to a revised camshaft profile and twin-choke carburettor, now producing 92.5bhp. Peak power for the 2-litre rose from 98bhp to 102bhp while output

ABOVE For 1980, the estate's rear styling was unchanged from the previous car, missing out on the saloon's increased glass area. A 'business wagon' option brought changes to the suspension, wheels and axle, to allow a higher payload.

ABOVE The 1980 Cortina range offered five different engines and more trims and colours. An S-pack and Ghia saloon are nearest, L and GL four-doors in the middle and an L three-door and estate at the back in the middle.

of the 2.3-litre V6 rose from 108bhp to 116bhp, courtesy of larger valves and a higher compression ratio, making it the most powerful UK-market Cortina ever offered.

There was a little tinkering with the suspension, perhaps in reaction to criticism of the earlier car's ride, front spring rates being reduced by 9 per cent while the diameter of the anti-roll bar was slightly increased. The variable-rate rear springs were now 5 per cent stiffer in initial movement and 9 per cent stiffer at full load for 'more consistent ride characteristics' and gas-filled monotube dampers were standard on the rear for all models.

UK trim levels were largely as before, but the S model disappeared in both Britain and Germany, to be replaced by the same specification as an optional 'S' pack, which could be applied to all but a few models, starting with the 1.6L and including the estate. As before, it brought a firmer ride and included alloy wheels, overriders, long-range driving lamps, a four-spoke steering wheel and a 'sports' gear knob.

A 'business wagon' estate car derivative with heavy-duty suspension, reinforced rear axle and larger rear brake drums for an increased payload was introduced as a 1300 and a 1600, and by 1979 Ghia trim was available on 1600, 2000 and 2.3-litre Cortinas, having only initially been offered on the 2-litre car.

An extra pair of air vents was fitted in the centre of the dashboard in a space vacated by the radio, which moved to a below-dash console. Interior trim changes aimed at making the Cortina feel lighter were a change from black to dark brown for the carpets, steering wheel and dashboard cappings, while newly designed seats incorporated 'see-through' head restraints on GL and Ghia versions, with a removable pad for the Ghia.

All these earnest improvements were treated equally earnestly by *Autocar* magazine in tests of the 1600L and 2.3 Ghia in September 1979. After having fully tested the 1600L it found a thoughtfully improved car with one or two surprises. The main finding was that the fuel economy measures seemed

Confessions of a fleet manager

LEFT Mind if I smoke? This fleet obviously belonged to Rothmans cigarettes, but most company Cortinas were incognito.

Ever since the first Cortina, Ford had finessed the range of engines, body types, trims and options to appeal to corporate buyers. In the 1970s this market was at its peak. It wasn't necessarily that there was no competition to the Cortina (the Cavalier was a good entrant, and even the Marina had its adherents), but the fleet manager was largely a conservative creature, wanting a big range and low fixed running costs. After the standard three-year/60,000-mile cycle, a Cortina would always find a willing used buyer and be quickly replaced by a local dealer for at least 10 per cent off the list price.

"Loyalty was habit, a 'Buy British' kind of attitude which left a choice between Leyland, Ford and Vauxhall," says Ray Hutton. "By the mid-1970s everybody was looking at Leyland as a lame duck. So Ford took over and never looked back."

At the time Peter Eldridge was fleet manager of a division of Grand Metropolitan, a British building-services company which had over 250 Ford vehicles in its fleet, operated via an in-house workshop in Hammersmith, West London. He ran three Cortinas himself.

"The reason the Cortina was so strong was because Ford were very clever," he says. "They created various derivations and specifications levels. The company I worked for had a 12-year Cortina policy effectively. You had a 1300L as your first car, a 1600L as your second (over a three-year period), then you got to 2-litre GL and in the twelfth year it might be a 2-litre Ghia. It was a great way of keeping staff!"

Equally, it was a good way to upset people. "That was particularly prevalent with the distinction in terms of perceived status between the L and the GL. We had two levels of manager; the junior managers had the L spec, the senior managers the GL. They were very keen to mark that difference."

There may have been a fair few sales representatives who wore out their Cortinas carrying samples, but plenty were just driveway status symbols. In 1970s Britain, rather than pay employees to run their own cars for work, businesses would buy cars and award them according to grade for both work and pleasure. It was a way of paying people more without subjecting them to more income tax, a ploy eventually curbed by the Inland Revenue.

"The majority were perks," says Eldridge. "One of the things people were doing in those days – particularly if fuel was included – was moving out of the main towns to nicer more rural areas, enjoying the benefit of lower house prices and charging the business. One of the guys I worked with did 147 miles a day to and from work!"

With Grand Metropolitan able to carry out its own servicing – as many firms did – it was able to build up a picture of items which gave trouble and Eldridge remembers the Cortina as pretty trouble free, with the 'Pinto' engines snapping the occasional timing belt but having sturdy clutches and gearboxes. "The things that stood out were exhausts – with back boxes and rear silencers falling off – and the VV carb. That was the most awful thing on God's planet. It had a sticking point with cold-start problems."

RIGHT Crayford continued to find a small but loyal bunch of clients for a four-seat convertible Cortina; latterly Carbodies carried out the conversion. (Giles Chapman Library)

BELOW The difference is the name on the brochure. Taunus and Cortina 80 were once again indistinguishable, although the German range still offered a wider choice of engine/body combinations. (Eric Foléa)

to have worked on the 1600 sampled; the overall test figure of 29.3mpg bettered the 1976 MkIV's 27.4mpg and compared to 23.7mpg achieved by a 1973 1600XL. There was no obvious improvement found on the 2.3 Ghia.

The operation of the new cold-start mechanism for the VV carburettor was met with some doubt, testers noting that the engine also took rather more turns on the starter motor to get going than expected. 'One could not help forming the impression that the mixture has been reduced to the limit that will burn in the interests of economy,' commented the magazine. While the testers didn't experience stalling, the VV carburettor did not meet with much enthusiasm in the real world. "Certainly, the VV carb was not a marvellous piece of engineering and made many a strong man cry," Harry Calton observes.

As to the suspension changes, their effect must have been very subtle indeed. 'Frankly we must confess that if we had not been told of the alterations we would not have noticed them,' the *Autocar* test commented. 'Although adequate and acceptable, the ride is not a good feature of the car,' it said, finding a tendency shared with the 2.3 Ghia to hop about when cornering on poorly surfaced roads, as with the previous model.

For the test, the nearest competitors were now judged to be very closely matched to the Cortina: the Datsun 180B, Renault 18 GTS, Toyota Carina, Vauxhall Cavalier 1600L and – yes – the old Morris Marina, now with a new 1,700cc engine. The Renault was considered the strongest contender, but the Cortina still had the fleet market cornered because of the sheer breadth of models Ford offered. This was underlined by 1979 being the best-ever year for UK Cortina sales, with 193,784 versions of the MkIV/Cortina 80 finding buyers – 11.3 per cent of the British market.

FORD TAUNUS

The Carbodies convertible

For 1980 the Crayford Cortina was superseded by a version repanelled with the front and rear wings from the new Cortina 80, but retaining the MkIV doors. However, Bristol Street Motors wanted to sell the convertible as a new showroom model warranted by Ford rather than a conversion based on a technically used car. This meant that Crayford had to put one Cortina 80 conversion through the costly and difficult process of UK Type Approval for the first time, via a contractor. However, it was looking to move out of the car conversion business to concentrate on its Argocat amphibian vehicle. Enter London-taxi manufacturer and one-time builder of Ford convertibles Carbodies, keen to broaden its business beyond cabs.

According to Bill Munro's Carbodies history, Crayford's David McMullan and Jeffrey Smith had offered the company the rights to the Cortina in 1978 but had been rejected. Another approach to boss Grant Lockhart in 1980 succeeded, as on reflection the project seemed a good fit, not least given the company's new wish to be less dependent on the taxi market.

Unfortunately the transition was an unhappy one. The Carbodies engineers described the project they had been handed as a 'complete shambles' – with no drawings and no jigs to hold the bodyshells together while they were cut, plus a poorly finished prototype. As well as the usual reinforcements, the Carbodies conversion retained fixed rear side windows.

There was a further difficulty in that the only two-door Cortina 80s on the market were 1300s or 1600s and made in Belgium, and so Ford had to reprogramme its ordering system to enable buyers to have larger-engined variants; thankfully the company was said to be supportive of the project.

Launched at the 1980 Birmingham Motor Show the Carbodies Cortina Drophead Coupé was available as a 1600, 2000 and a 2.3-litre, with either manual or automatic transmission and in six colours. Mechanically warranted by Ford and bodily by Carbodies, it was to be sold by three UK dealers; alas it was by now prohibitively expensive – a top specification car was in excess of £10,000 when a Cortina 2.3 Ghia estate was priced at £7,152. Consequently in the end 30 Carbodies Cortinas are said to have been built, against the 50 Crayford MkIV-based cars which found buyers.

It was the end of the Cortina-class convertible, although Crayford kept in the game by converting a handful of Fiestas into the Fiesta Fly. Ford of Europe finally re-entered the convertible market with its first factory soft-top, the smart Karmann-designed Escort, in 1984.

The P 100 pick-up

The Cortina shape did not entirely disappear from British roads in 1982, as June that year saw the introduction of the P100 pick-up, which carried its front end. This was an import of the South African-built 'bakkie' – itself made with a proportion of components that had already come from Dagenham.

Since the MkIII-derived model, the South African Cortina pick-ups had sold over 130,000 domestically until the advent of the Cortina 80 shape, and been quite an export success. The cab had been facelifted with successive generations of Cortina while retaining the unique heavy-duty box-section rear chassis with its leaf springs and 15-gallon fuel tank just behind the cab. Its workaday interior included a bench seat with a cut-out for the floor-mounted gear lever.

The South African P100 was available with 1600 and 3-litre engines in short and long wheelbases and as 'Leisure' versions with hardtops. The choice for the UK was restricted, however, to the 1.6-litre long-wheelbase version, with no diesel option, sold as the P100 or P100L. It lasted until 1988, when the Sierra-based cab was introduced and in this form it ran for another five years, with a facelifted version also produced in Turkey.

ABOVE 'Built like a truck, drives like a car,' said Ford. The P100L offered cloth-trimmed seats, a mat for the pick-up bed, a loadspace cover, and a set of stripes. (Author's collection)

ABOVE AND ABOVE RIGHT
The revival of two-tone paint for the Cortina Carousel (left) and Crusader (right) limited editions went down surprisingly well. The Crusader has pinstriping and could be ordered in single colours.

Final British sales

After such a thorough sorting, the last years of UK Cortina production were essentially marked by frequent small specification changes. For the 1982 model year radios became standard on all UK Cortinas other than the base model, with a radio-cassette on the Ghia and cloth seats across the range. Catering for a particular market, a run of 482 unique base-specification Cortinas were built for registered disabled buyers, these cars having the 1600 engine with automatic transmission, in a two-door shell equipped with twin door mirrors; the price was 20 per cent less than a similarly equipped car. By now the Cortina was regarded as a very worthy conventional package that sold largely on its trustworthiness to the fleet market. This can only have been heightened in late 1981 when the new front-drive Opel Ascona and Vauxhall Cavalier appeared as a full range of hatchbacks and saloons. The Sierra was still under development and the Probe 3 concept car shown at September's Frankfurt Motor Show had signalled that a radical Cortina replacement was on the way.

Ford of Britain responded in the time-trusted way of any car maker with a model seen as old hat, by launching a

---

Carousel specification over base Cortina

- Forest Green/Crystal Green metallic paint with green trim, Graphite Grey/Strato Silver with grey trim, or Roman Bronze/Tuscan Beige with tan trim.
- Bodyside mouldings, bright bumpers, door handles and drip rails.
- Remote-control driver and passenger door mirrors.
- Four-spoke steering wheel.
- Simulated wood dashboard; centre console with radio; intermittent wash/wipe.
- Same seats as L, and L-type door panels trimmed in 'York' fabric; head restraints and seat valances.
- Vanity mirror on passenger sunvisor; grab handles for rear passengers; loadbay carpet on estate.
- Saloon option pack of sunroof, tinted glass and electric aerial available at £185; same pack for estate, with tailgate wash/wipe but no sunroof, costs £116.

Retirement abroad

While Dagenham rapidly cleared the decks for the Sierra in 1982, Cortina assembly in other parts of the world ended at a slower pace, South African, Australian and New Zealand assembly finishing between 1983 and 1984.

Argentina had been a loyal Taunus territory, and from 1974 to 1980 built its own version of the 1970 Taunus TC, using the American 'Lima' version of the 'Pinto' engine found in some Mustangs, in 2.0-litre and 2.3-litre form. Bypassing the MkIV design entirely, it moved to the final Taunus/Cortina shape while retaining the old Taunus coupé which Europe had discontinued in 1976. This was facelifted with the Cortina 80 front and received some restyling at the rear. These were overtly performance-orientated cars, with up to 132bhp.

The last Argentine Taunus was made in September 1984 but the following year the Taunus saloon started production at Ford Otosan in Turkey. There was already a Cortina relationship as Turkey's first mass-produced 'national' car had been the Otosan Anadol A1, a glassfibre saloon designed by Reliant and Ogle and using Cortina engines.

At first the Turkish Taunus was sold in its original 'Cortina 80' guise, being lightly facelifted with deeper bumpers and an optional four-headlamp grille in 1987. However, in 1990 it received a major reworking with new front and rear lighting, contemporary body-coloured bumpers and integral spoilers. There was a new dashboard, electric windows, and even air conditioning, and the car stayed in production until 1994.

ABOVE The Argentina-only Taunus GT SP5 was produced in 1983, and was available with four paint schemes. SP5 signifies a five-speed gearbox. (Alejandro Luis Angrigiani)

BELOW The Turkish Taunus of 1985–94 featured sheet metal and cosmetic restyling unique to the market, plus a new interior. (Alejandro Luis Angrigiani)

RIGHT South Africa remained wedded to racy 3-litre Cortinas such as the 1980 XR6, which was distinguished by unique body-colour bumpers. It was followed by a Sierra XR6 but Ford pulled out of South Africa in 1988 in response to growing pressure to boycott the apartheid régime, only returning in 1994.

BELOW In 1980, although the just-obsolete Escort RS1800 was still a force in rallying, Ford took a 1.3-litre Cortina and endowed it with a 250bhp 3-litre V6 and substantial modifications including a rally Escort axle and rear disc brakes. Handed over to a privateer, it enjoyed a reasonable but short career, its debut on the March 1981 Gwynedd Welsh Rally, where it broke a propshaft, being pictured here. (LAT)

special-edition base Cortina loaded with items normally seen as extras. The Cortina Carousel of June 1981 (in company with the Granada Consort and Capri Calypso) came as a saloon or estate with the 1300 and 1600 engines and offered two-tone metallic paint and sports wheels, a simulated wood-trimmed instrument panel and upgraded interior trimmings, plus options such as a sunroof and tailgate wash/wipe on the estate. In August 1981 a 1.6-litre Carousel saloon cost £4,780 when a base 1600 saloon came out at £4,597.

According to David Burgess-Wise this first run of Carousels numbered 6,000. The model reappeared in the final production months of 1982 alongside the peculiarly British Cortina Crusader. This was another special edition, concocted in a deal with the *Daily Express* and featuring the newspaper's knight emblem on the bootlid. Offering more goodies than the Carousel, such as wood door cappings and plush seats, and available with the 2.0-litre engine, the Crusader was a pseudo-Ghia and a huge hit with private and fleet buyers alike. With 30,000 built in the end, it was hardly a limited edition, though; indeed, both the Carousel and the Crusader were part of the final range catalogue.

After 20 years and 4.3 million cars, the last Cortina was driven off the Dagenham line on 22 July 1982. The MkIV/Cortina 80 had kept up the tradition of surpassing a million produced – 1,131,850 cars were made in nearly seven years – and in its last six months it notched up 135,745 UK sales. The Taunus also ended production that summer and interestingly had clocked up a higher production of over 1.5m units, making it the most popular Taunus ever. As well as being a good product, that may also be explained by the extent of the European market it then occupied; while the Cortina was confined to Britain, Ireland and Portugal, the remainder of Europe was Taunus territory, alongside markets such as Argentina.

The historic occasion duly marked, the Dagenham production lines were cleared to make way for a £120m investment in robotised facilities for the new Sierra, which made its public debut at the Paris Motor Show in September 1982. However, Ford would not find the Cortina quite so easy to shake off as it might have imagined.

LEFT The last Cortina, a single-tone Crusader, was produced at Dagenham on 22 July 1982, and driven off the line by Chairman Sam Toy. Registered that December, it was kept by Ford of Britain for its museum.

Hyundai makes its own Cortina

From its beginnings with the MkII Cortina, Hyundai continued to assemble each new generation, following the UK 1600 Cortina specification until 1981 when local taxes on engines of over 1,500cc saw a 1,400cc Mitsubishi engine swap – much to Ford's consternation. In fact, the Koreans had become so fond of the Cortina that the prospect of its demise caused quite some anxiety. The company president refused to take on the Sierra because he didn't like the styling, so Hyundai set about designing its own Cortina-like saloon to join the Pony hatchback. Giugiaro's Ital Design had styled the Pony, so Hyundai returned to the Italian stylist for a full-sized body buck which was then only lightly modified to become the 1983 Stellar. It's been said that the Stellar sat on the last Cortina's floorpan but that's not quite true. Hyundai merely followed its style and layout very closely, with coil-and-wishbone front suspension and a live rear axle located by four links. Engines were by Mitsubishi. Introduced to Britain in 1984 and priced to undercut the Sierra, the Stellar was used to spearhead an expansion in British sales, possibly picking up private buyers who just wanted another Cortina.

ABOVE The Cortina-clone Hyundai Stellar lasted from 1984 to 1991 in the UK, changing little during this time. (Hyundai)

Chapter 9:
Post-Cortina

ABOVE **Probe 3 was strictly for show, and its faired-in wheels, moving front air dam and smooth floorpan gave a drag factor of 0.22 compared to the real-life Sierra's Cd of 0.34.**

The Cortina is dead – long live the Sierra! Not so fast. With hindsight, a car that had become part of the fabric of British society was not going to go quietly. By 1982, like the Mini, most adults in Britain had owned, ridden in, or known somebody who had a Cortina or three.

Such was the appeal of the 'limited edition' Crusader that only a little dust gathered on the last Cortinas in British showrooms. All the same, records show that 11,598 cars

were to be sold in 1983, and a further 139 in 1984, with Cortinas continuing to be registered until 1987, when nine very stale cars finally found buyers.

Sierra – the shock of the new

The origins of the 1982 Sierra, or Project Toni, dated back to 1977. Its radical 'Aeroback' looks came from a desire for a definitive break with the Cortina/Taunus and especially

RIGHT **This staged shot of the Dunton styling studio in Essex in 1980 shows the Sierra 'aeroback' shape already fixed and the estate being prepared.**

to give Ford of Germany a chance at unseating Opel and Volkswagen from their domestic market dominance.

Ford of Europe vice-president of design Uwe Bahnsen was very keen on aerodynamics and momentum was building for Ford to have its own wind-tunnel. Although not often mentioned in connection with the Sierra (largely because of the politics surrounding its shaky start, according to former Ford designer Patrick Le Quément), the driving force behind the Sierra shape was Ray Everts, the American head of exterior design at Ford of Europe. He was backed – initially – by Bob Lutz, then president of Ford of Europe.

"There were an awful lot of models done," says Le Quément. "There must have been between 20 and 30. The Sierra was looked upon as being radical and Bob Lutz gave it his support, but there were a lot of people who were really not convinced, including Henry Ford."

"One of the greatest challenges around the appearance of the new Sierra arose about a year before its launch," says Geoff Howard, at that point manager of technical product information at Ford of Europe. "When we saw the final clay models of its unprecedented shape, we knew immediately that we would have an image problem when it was publicly revealed. I remembered reading about a similar issue faced by General Motors with the Chevrolet Corvette, and how Bill Mitchell had developed a special show car, the Mako Shark, to lead public taste towards the design trend in advance. I talked it over with Uwe Bahnsen and he adopted my suggestion of repeating the same strategy with our own 'taster', the Probe design study."

Thus the Probe 3 took a bow at the 1981 Frankfurt Motor Show. On the surface it was linked to a German government programme for improving fuel efficiency, but in reality was a primer for the Sierra. Ford let it be known that some of Probe's less extreme ideas might find themselves translated

ABOVE The front of the Sierra Ghia showcased the new aero look, with flush headlights and no obvious radiator grille. Early basic Sierras were lumbered with an ugly black grille, which was soon dropped.

ABOVE The performance-orientated XR4i was nicknamed the 'Belgian biplane' for its double spoiler, inherited from Probe 3.

into the next Cortina/Taunus. Although common practice now, a concept car which became reality was highly unusual in 1981, but even the name Sierra was floated around and the mainstream press became just as intrigued as the specialist magazines at the potential demise of the legendary Cortina, whose sales continued to steam along regardless.

The production Sierra was shaped in the Daimler-Benz wind-tunnel in Stuttgart. One example of its aerodynamic soundness was the boot 'bustle' which extended beyond the bottom of the rear window and created less turbulence than a rear panel that dropped vertically from the same point. Three months and 1,000 different wind-tunnel tests were expended to arrive at an undisputed drag coefficient of 0.34, which was

24 per cent better than the Cortina – perhaps only to have been expected when you're starting with a boxy saloon.

The claimed drag coefficient had to be real. Ford had been severely stung when German magazine *Stern* had shown the figures claimed for the 1981 Escort to be exaggerated (in fairness, not helped by inconsistent panel gaps on an early car), so the entire Sierra range was put through the tunnel and an average drawn. There was also real competition from Audi, which had also shown a concept car at the 1981 Frankfurt show under the federal fuel-economy programme. It was fully functioning, unlike the Probe. Launched, as would be the Sierra, in 1982, the production Audi 100 had a drag coefficient of 0.30, claimed to be the world's lowest – even

though it was a conventional booted saloon. Flush glazing and five years in the wind-tunnel had helped here, and the Cd factor was proudly stencilled into the rear side window.

In British showrooms from 15 October 1982, Ford boasted that the Sierra had taken £660m to bring to market, with engineers in England, Germany and America staying in touch via a satellite link. The name of course meant nothing, but it was truly pan-European; Cortina was too British and Taunus didn't have a high value even in Germany. Ford wanted to bury the Cortina, and the Sierra was modernity in itself – 'Man and machine in perfect harmony' ran the UK advertising line. The copy in *Ford News* was more brisk, with little sentimentality for the outgoing legend: 'After 20

years of Cortina, Cortina and yet more Cortina, the Sierra is revolutionary.'

While it retained rear-wheel drive and familiar engines, the Sierra was far from a re-skinned Cortina, having semi-trailing-arm independent rear suspension and a return to MacPherson struts at the front, with an anti-roll bar mounted behind the axle line. The estates had self-levelling rear suspension. Engines were an evolution of the overhead-cam 'Pinto' units – with a new 1300 variant joining the 1600 and 2000 – plus the 'Cologne' 2.3-litre V6. A Peugeot-sourced 2.3-litre diesel was a new departure.

The question of why the Sierra didn't have front-wheel drive was immediately raised by commentators. The space-

ABOVE As much attention was lavished on the interior of the Sierra as the exterior, with storage space galore. There were two types of instrument panel and centre console; this is the more basic.

AUTOCAR

4 FEBRUARY 1987 70p

FORD'S NEW SAPPHIRE

CORTINA COMES BACK

9 770005 092010

ABOVE The conventionally booted Sierra Sapphire drew immediate comparisons with the last Cortina of nearly five years before. (Author's collection)

saving benefits had been accepted in the small and medium sectors and the Ford Fiesta and Escort were comfortably established fwd designs, so why not this one? Ford must also have winced when the 1981 Vauxhall Cavalier/Opel Ascona emerged as a front-driver.

With the help of Geoff Howard, the company argued that space was not so much of an issue in larger cars. Rear-wheel drive, it stated, was more able to handle the power from larger engines (traction control was still years away), weight distribution was more even, and rear-wheel-drive cars handled more predictably in most conditions. 'Rear-wheel drive is better on balance,' apologetically said the first

brochure, stressing that it was cheaper to maintain and that even the tyres lasted longer. Some comfort was taken from BMW and Mercedes resolutely sticking with rear-wheel drive.

It wasn't that bad ...

In car history the early 'failure' of the Sierra has become somewhat overblown. It was not a disaster of Edsel proportions. But the Sierra did have its problems. The first was timing. In its first full year of UK sales the Vauxhall Cavalier had already sold over 80,000 units before the Sierra was launched, many of them the booted saloon versions the Sierra range would at first lack. This growth in Cavalier sales continued after the launch of the Sierra and by 1984 it was Britain's second-best-selling car (with the Escort above and Fiesta below). By 1984 the Sierra was in fifth place and Ford was simply not used to this.

"Sierra got off to a fairly shaky start because of Manufacturing wanting to start with the basic models and then move up to more complex ones," Harry Calton says. "They started off with some very dull colours and base specs. It did get off to a slow start."

There were other problems, albeit exaggerated. The Sierra gained a reputation for poor stability on motorways in crosswinds and acquired the nickname 'raspberry ripple' because the bodyshell was said to distort under minor impacts, with the polycarbonate bumpers disguising this damage. But most of all it seemed that while Europe was quite happy with the Sierra, the British market – and for this read the all-powerful fleet buyers – had simply taken against its looks. The car was dubbed the 'jellymould' Ford.

Peter Eldrige, the former fleet manager for Grand Metropolitan, remembers attending the first preview of the Sierra versus Cortina in London's Docklands, with a group of corporate customers. "Ford spent a vast amount of money on a football-stadium seating plan with the cars down in the basement coming up through a cloud of smoke. One of the guys I was there with was looking at the Cortina Crusader on the left-hand side. He turned to me and said: 'Do you know if I didn't know the time differences here, I'd probably pick the Cortina.'"

By early 1984 Detroit was well and truly spooked by relatively slow Sierra sales, although these fears had been amplified by an issue only known within the company, and later found to be erroneous. Late one evening that year Patrick Le Quément was summoned to a meeting in the deserted directors' dining room at the top of Ford's Cologne

HQ. The cast included Bob Lutz and Uwe Bahnsen. Lutz was by then US-based as vice-president in charge of Ford Truck Operations, but had been summoned back to Europe.

"It haunts me still because the situation was so complex and political," Le Quément says. "Uwe Bahnsen was accused of having led the company down the wrong path, not knowing how the trend was going. This car was clearly not working in Britain. OK, it was working in Germany, in Italy and in France but the big market with the real volume was not working. Murray Reichenstein [head of product planning] was taking an aggressive stance – and also, to my surprise, Bob Lutz, as it was he who had promoted the Sierra and convinced Mr Ford."

However, at the time of that meeting the US Ford Taurus and its sister Mercury, the Sable, were still in development, and destined to have a more radical 'aero' look than even the Sierra. Having left Germany in 1981, Ray Everts headed the styling of the Taurus project and had included a lot of Sierra

ideas. As this inquest took place in Cologne, the Taurus and Sable had just been through a customer clinic in California and emerged with disastrous results. Ray Everts was the fall guy. However, after a second clinic took place with very little modification the results were extremely good. It turned out there had been a major mistake in that the people that had been invited to the first test were clearly not those who would have bought a Taurus, which turned out in the end to be a major sales success.

Uwe Bahnsen left Ford in 1986 and Le Quément, initially sent to the States with a view that he was to succeed him, was head-hunted by Volkswagen in 1985 after spending three months in the wilderness at Dearborn with the promised job not materialising. He left Volkswagen for Renault in 1987 and remained until 2009.

"It's a lesson of history," he concludes on the Sierra. "Don't try too many 'firsts'. We made the mistake of going from the classic, rather well-designed Cortina to a pretty radical shape and on top of that we didn't do a three-box design, we did a hatchback. That was the ultimate mistake. Had we launched the fastback in Europe and the notchback in Britain it would have been much better."

Sapphire: the new Cortina?

Without being able to restyle the Sierra, Ford was swift to act on detail changes. By 1985 all versions had the body-coloured Ghia front end, and side mouldings which helped lighten the styling. The slow-selling three-doors were dropped and the controversial three-door XR4i replaced by the five-door XR4x4. Two thin strips running down the roof pillars behind the third side window were fitted to all hatchbacks to counter the crosswind stability problems.

A major facelift came in 1987, with new frontal styling for all versions and the addition of a conventional 'three-box' saloon, the Sierra Sapphire. Inevitably viewed as a kind of lost-generation Cortina, it had been long predicted and apparently pushed by demand from the German as well as British market. It followed a trend of manufacturers adding a booted derivative to a hatchback as a separate model line, just as Ford had created the Orion from the Escort a year earlier. *Autocar* mused that had the 1987 Sierra range been introduced in 1982, the jump from the Cortina would not have seemed so shocking.

The Sierra range continued to be developed and improved, including formidable high-performance versions such as the

Cosworth. Like the Cortina it was sold abroad, including a brief stint in America as the Merkur. The hatchback's styling was perhaps just a little too ahead of the market and by the late 1980s didn't look nearly so out of place. The Sierra went on to sell a respectable 1.5m in 11 years.

The Cortina's legacy

It was the Escort, rather than the Cortina, which went on to be Ford of Britain's best domestic seller, with 4.1m sold between 1967 and 2000. However, commentators felt that during the 1980s Ford had lost sight of making its bread-and-butter cars as engaging to drive as the Cortina had once been – performance versions aside.

The 1990 Escort was a crucial low point in Ford design and engineering, panned by the critics as average in most areas and poor in refinement. "The MkIV Escort was deplorable," Ray Hutton recalls. "At the launch, I asked the engineers what their competitors and parameters were and with which cars Escort was best in class. 'We're not really best in class with any of

RIGHT MkIII Cortinas on display at the 2010 British Classic Motor Show, joining the other Cortina clubs. (Author)

RIGHT The film *Carry on Cabby* lodged Glamcabs and its drivers in the public mind – recreations have been a regular 'tableau' at the Goodwood Revival nostalgia-fest, as here in 2010. (Author)

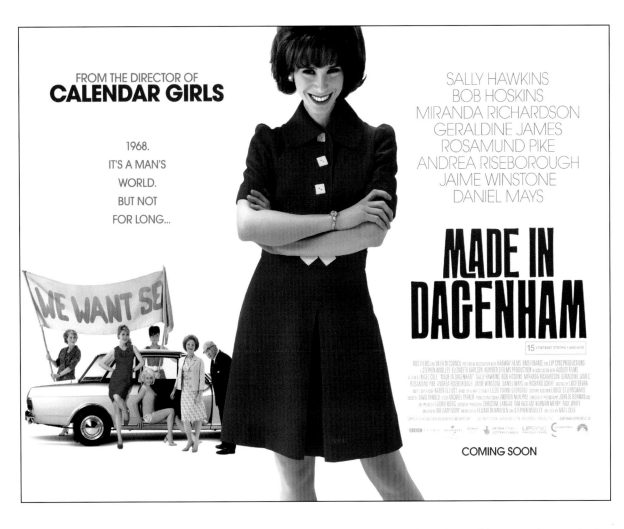

FROM THE DIRECTOR OF
CALENDAR GIRLS

1968.
IT'S A MAN'S
WORLD.
BUT NOT
FOR LONG...

WE WANT SE

SALLY HAWKINS
BOB HOSKINS
MIRANDA RICHARDSON
GERALDINE JAMES
ROSAMUND PIKE
ANDREA RISEBOROUGH
JAIME WINSTONE
DANIEL MAYS

MADE IN DAGENHAM

COMING SOON

LEFT The MkII Cortina had plenty of exposure in the 2011 British film *Made in Dagenham*, which told the story of the landmark Ford women's pay strike of 1968. (Paramount Pictures)

them', they said. Their objective was to be good enough, to do the minimum to keep their place in the market."

A quantum leap was needed and the 1993 Ford Mondeo marked a great revival of the sharp-handling quality Ford and this achievement was surpassed by the 1997 Focus, which was to replace the Escort. Ford had remembered that family cars could be engaging to drive, and honour was restored.

But the boom days of Dagenham were long gone. Faced with overcapacity in the European market – as were Ford's competitors – car manufacturing ceased on 20 February 2002. By 2011 Ford employed 15,000 workers in the UK and was the main engine producer in Europe, but the only vehicle built in the country was the Transit van, in Southampton. In 1953 Dagenham alone had employed 40,000 people.

With such a high turnover, the Cortina had been the ultimate throwaway car. Engines went on, but rust claimed them one by one; the MacPherson strut mountings were a favourite spot for welded repairs. In spite of the vast volume

pumped out of Dagenham, 20 years after production ended the chances of seeing a Cortina on the road are today slim. Of the 2.8m sold in the UK, a total of 3,624 of all types were still on the road in 2010, according to data from the Department for Transport. This shows licensed cars by make and model and year of first registration in Great Britain. In theory these 3,624 Cortinas were cars which were still on the road – if they were not, owners were required to notify the authorities, although this may not have happened in all cases.

The biggest number of survivors falls under the plain 'Cortina' heading, with 1,307 cars listed. Reflecting its early classic status, the 1600E is next in terms of numbers, with 245 runners, 129 of which are 1970 registrations, this also being the year with the largest number of Cortinas still on the road, at 323 cars. For the mid-1970s there is a big statistical dip, with numbers in the thirties or forties, and then 1982 represents the next biggest total after 1970, with 284 cars, 87 of them Cortina Crusaders.

The Private Life of the Ford Cortina

In January 1982 the BBC screened a documentary featuring the Cortina. Made under the multi-purpose Arena series banner (a previous edition had centred entirely on the Sinatra song 'My Way'), it pulled in a significant audience of 5.2m and has become an oft-repeated minor classic to TV people.

Directed by Nigel Finch, the associate producer was Anthony Wall and executive producer Alan Yentob. Finch passed away in 1995, Wall became Arena series editor and a prolific documentary-maker and Yentob creative director of the BBC. Speaking to the author in 2011, *The Private Life of the Ford Cortina* was still one of their favourites.

"We were taking something familiar but looking at it from a different point of view," Yentob recalls. "One thing we did want to do about it was to change people's concept of what it was. It was rather snootily disregarded by many people – even many people in the programme. We were trying to say that you can have an object which can transcend itself. It was a very affectionate portrait of the car and its position in the world."

Shot over a large part of 1981, it was a random arrangement of musings on the Cortina and its place in British life. The narrator, who would pop up here and there, was stand-up comedian Alexei Sayle, who had just had a hit with 'Ullo John! gotta new motor?' – often performed against a background of Cortinas.

Decades before 'reality TV', people spoke unselfconsciously to the viewer while Finch gently asked questions off-camera. There were John and Sheila Isherwood, the owners who wrote a love letter to Ford about their MkIII Cortina passing 100,000 miles, and their home movies of the beloved car. Then there were customisers and a parade of 1600E club members and their cars, lights blazing to a background of choral music. One committee member earnestly

Given that only 3,301 were built, the MkI Lotus-Cortina has fared well, with 137 registered, the best year of roadgoing survivors being 1965. As the data counts cars by date of first registration not year of manufacture, there are inevitably some anomalies, principally for cars brought into the country and registered later. This would have to explain why one sole MkI GT was registered in 2010.

But the Cortina had long moved from 'Dagenham dustbin' to national treasure. What few Lotus-Cortinas which hadn't been written off were in the vanguard of the 1970s classic car movement and are now ever-appreciating assets. The 1600E

had a following from the moment it ceased production and each new generation of Cortina has gained its own clubs. Like the Mini and the Volkswagen Beetle, a Cortina was part of the childhood of many Britons, and this has fed into enthusiasm for the cars as a classic purchase.

In any period television programme or film a Cortina has become required street furniture for the particular decade in which it is set, but alongside a revival of interest in 1970s music and style the once-controversial MkIII has started to develop a particular cachet. In 2001 coffee brand Nescafé aimed at a younger clientele with the 'Hairy Old Cortina' ad, explained why a concours Cortina must be as clean on the bottom as it is on top.

It was a very playful programme, even though there were establishment figures such as Sir Terence Beckett (Sayle told the viewers he used to go for his lunch at Mr Mancini's Cortina sandwich bar and named the car after it) and beloved English poet Sir John Betjeman, who recited his poem 'Executive', partly reproduced here:

I am a young executive. No cuffs than mine are cleaner;
I have a Slimline brief-case and I use the firm's Cortina.
In every roadside hostelry from here to Burgess Hill
The maîtres d'hôtel all know me well, and let me sign the bill.

Finch then asked Betjeman, famous for his love of steam engines, if he had ever been in a Cortina. The great man answered after a pause. "I expect so. I know the sound of the words. Sounds marvellous doesn't it? A bit foreign, a bit South American and not quite human."

The programme did, however, gently infer that this very, very, familiar car had become just a little bit of a joke by 1982. Paul Welton and his band the Weltones sang their Cortina song and then Welton told us that all Cortina owners in North London were called Terry. "All got perms, gold bracelets. Girlfriends tend to be called Sharon or Sylv. They work behind bars if they're called Sharon. Sylvs don't work at all."

The programme-makers were already editing when they found out what Ford had known all along – that the Cortina was doomed. "Ford was fantastically cooperative," Wall says. "They gave us all this footage, no problem at all. It was definitely a case of 'This is bloody good publicity, even though we are getting rid of it.' They didn't tell us, but they knew. We found out in a newspaper. At first it was a source of extreme disconsolation, but it forced Nigel to find an ending to the film, which turned out to be a blessing in disguise."

So before the end titles where a MkI Cortina goes to the crusher, Sayle sits at the Cortina sandwich bar, broken up by the news of the Cortina's end. "You know what they're gonna call the new car? The Sierra, the bloody Sierra! What's that all about, what does that say to me as an English person?"

LEFT Alexei Sayle sings the ballad of salesman Roger Spotty, who loved his car too much. "He did things to his Cortina that no stable man would. He's got a vinyl roof even though he's not allowed one." (Copyright © BBC Photo Library)

RIGHT The BBC's time-travelling police series *Life on Mars* gave this MkIII Cortina prime billing. The car was bought by a fan on eBay in 2007 for £10,000. (©Kudos Film & Television Limited)

featuring 'Charles the funky coffee drinker' who had the idea of giving his beloved MkIII Ford Cortina an Afro hairstyle to match his own. Instead of a vinyl roof the Cortina cruises the streets with an enormous Afro haircut. A MkIII also provided a backdrop to models posing for a Levi's jeans campaign run in South Africa in 2009/2010.

But the Coke-bottle Cortina shot even further to fame – and pushed values up – with the 2006 BBC series *Life on Mars*, where a detective appears to have time-travelled to the politically incorrect 1970s. A brown vinyl-roofed MkIII dominated the look of the show. The Cortina was cool. Again.

Appendix 1

Cortina total production figures

MkI (1962–1966): 1,013,391

Standard saloon: 34,514

De Luxe saloon: 704,871

Super saloon: 77,753

1500GT: 76,947

Lotus-Cortina: 3,301 (As noted in Chapter 3, this Ford figure varies
from other estimates by 14 more or 7 less)

De luxe estate: 108,219

Super estate: 7,786

Corsair (1963–1970): 330,735

Corsair 1500 standard: 1,288 (335 two-door, 953 four-door)

Corsair 1500 de Luxe: 136,446 (33,352 two-door, 103,094 four-door)

Corsair 1500GT: 21,857 (6,610 two-door, 15,247 four-door)

Corsair V4 de Luxe two-door: 6,450

Corsair V4 de Luxe four-door: 118,065

Corsair V4 GT two-door: 1,534

Corsair V4 GT four-door: 12,589

Corsair 2000E: 31,566

Corsair V4 estate car: 940

MkII (1966–1970): 1,024,869

Standard saloon: 19,238 (14,324 two-door, 4,914 four-door)

De Luxe saloon: 598,999 (251,537 two-door, 347,462 four-door)

Super saloon: 135,093 (18,950 two-door, 116,143 four-door)

GT: 117,130 (62,592 two-door: 54,538 four-door)

1600E: 60,087 (two-door 2,563, four-door 57,524)

Lotus-Cortina: 4,032

Estate: 90,290

MkIII (1970–1976): 1,126,559

Saloon two-door: 143,420

Saloon four-door: 824,068

Estate: 154,216

Pick-up (Bakkie): 4,855

MkIV and Cortina 80 (1976–1982): 1,131,850

Total Cortina production: 4,279,079

Total Cortinas built at Dagenham: 3,155,161

Figures courtesy Ford of Britain and David Burgess-Wise/Graham Robson

Countries assembling Cortinas

As well as fully built cars Dagenham was also an important supplier of 'Knocked Down' KD kits for Cortina assembly. CKD 'Completely Knocked Down' kits went to South Africa, Australia and New Zealand for full assembly and assembly was also carried out in Belgium, Ghana, Ireland, Malaysia, Malta, the Netherlands, the Philippines, Singapore, South Korea, Taiwan, Trinidad and Tobago and Turkey.

Total Knocked Down kits supplied from Dagenham: 788,012

Appendix 2

Cortina evolution in figures *(from Autocar magazine)*

Model	Date tested	Price	Mean maximum speed	0–60mph	Fuel consumption (overall)
MkI 1500 Super	25/1/63	£688	81mph	19.0secs	27.2mpg
MkII 1600E	2/12/67	£982	98mph	13.1secs	25.1mpg
MkIII 1600XL	27/9/73	£1,350	93mph	15.1secs	23.7mpg
MkIV 1600GL	2/10/76	£2,548	93mph	13.7secs	27.4mpg

Model	Date tested	Length	Width	Weight
MkI 1500 Super	25/1/63	14ft 3in	5ft 5in	1,842lb
MkII 1600E	2/12/67	14ft 2in	5ft 5in	2,064lb
MkIII 1600XL	27/9/73	13ft 11.7in	5ft 7in	2,240lb
MkIV 1600GL	2/10/76	14ft 2.3in	5ft 7in	2,325lb

Appendix 3

Cortina-based kit cars

Compiled by Steve Hole, author of the A to Z of Kit Cars, the definitive encyclopaedia of the UK's kit-car industry since 1949 (Haynes).

The Cortina was a popular donor option for its day because it gave manufacturers the option of a rear-wheel-drive configuration and readily obtainable parts that didn't cost the earth. Even though it was eventually usurped by the Sierra as a donor car, in 2011 there were still some kits using components of Cortina origin.

The sheer variety of Cortina-based kit cars was immense, from original designs to replicas of every flavour. Cortinas have been used to underpin Lancia Stratos lookalikes and Corvette Stingray and Ferrari 250LM clones. There have been Jaguar D-type and E-type replicas, numerous hot rods plus many Cobra replicas and roadsters imitating the Lotus Seven. Some, it is worth pointing out, have been more successful than others.

Top primarily Cortina-based kits and approximate number manufactured, where known

Robin Hood (various types) – 4,000 approx.
Started with Lotus Seven clones on Triumph Dolomite base and made a good number of them, before moving to Cortina underpinnings. Changed to Sierra parts in circa 1990, and made even more of them.

Spartan – 4,000
Big-selling kit over 14 years or so but hard to fathom accurately how many were Cortina-based, as many would have been built around Triumph components for which car originally designed. Due to sheer numbers made, deserves a mention all the same.

Pilgrim Bulldog – 2,000
Humble little roadster first seen in 1986. Again, hard to know how many were Cortina-based as lion's share used Marina components.

Pilgrim Sumo – 3,000
As with its brother the Bulldog, only a percentage Cortina-based, this time before moving to Sierra parts. Pilgrim has some detractors, but has earned a prominent place in the kit car industry's roll of honour with a couple of

milestone models, including the Sumo, the first affordable 'man-in-the-street' Cobra replica of 1987.

JBA Falcon – 2,000 approx.
Very popular kit; again most probably Sierra-based but perhaps 45 per cent use Cortina parts.

Challenger E-Type
Began life Cortina-based before making somewhat logical switch to Jaguar XJ6 parts, as with JPR Wildcat. Both are the two most respected E-type clones ever offered in pure kit form.

Jago
Best known among kit car folk for Sandero utility (Escort-based in the main), Geoff Jago was arguably responsible for putting the street rod on the map in the UK in the mid-sixties; latterly he offered Cortina-based rod kits.

LEFT AND ABOVE
These shapely sportscars owe a lot to the Cortina: the red car is a Kougar Monza while the other is a JPR Wildcat. (Steve Hole)

Appendix 4

The Cortina in song

The Cortina has held a strong fascination for songwriters and there have been dozens of tunes with either a Cortina in the lyrics or the title. It has even been celebrated in song by New Zealand rapper MC Dubstar as recently as 2004 when he shot to fame with – you guessed it – *Cortina*. The best-known British Cortina homage was probably Tom Robinson's 1978 anthem *Grey Cortina*. Why grey? "In the early to mid-1970s the 1600E was the boy-racer's car of choice in the area of North London around Finsbury Park where I happened to live and work," Robinson told the author in 2011. "Since the Silver Fox finish was also the colour of choice among the flashiest and fastest of these lads, it seemed to me that the colour probably gave those particular cars a competitive edge – hence bothering to specify 'Wish I had a GREY Cortina.'"

LEFT **Bristol's first punk band, The Cortinas, burned brightly but briefly between 1976 and 1977. (Bristolarchiverecords.com)**

Wish I had a grey Cortina
Whiplash aerial, racing trim
Cortina owner – no one meaner
Wish that I could be like him

Twin exhaust and rusty bumper
Chewing gum at traffic light
Stop at red but leave on amber
Grey Cortina outta sight

Wish I had a grey Cortina
Whiplash aerial, racing trim
Cortina owner – no one meaner
Wish that I could be like him

Furlined seats and lettered windscreen
Elbow on the windowsill
Eight track blazing Brucie Springsteen
Bomber jacket, dressed to kill

Wish I had a grey Cortina
Whiplash aerial, racing trim
Cortina owner – no one meaner
Wish that I could be like him

Never cop a parking ticket
Never seem to show its age
Speed police too slow to nick it
Grey Cortina got it made

Wish I had a grey Cortina
Whiplash aerial, racing trim
Cortina owner – no one meaner
Wish that I could be like him

The Cortina song list

British Cortina fan Simon Jones (www.worldofcortina.co.uk) has painstakingly assembled a list of songs where Cortinas either feature in the title or lyrics. The list is reproduced by kind permission here, with no comment on artistic merit. ...

1. *Ullo John! Gotta new motor?* Alexei Sayle
2. *Cortina!* Automatic Slim
3. *Cortina Cowboys* Blue Steam
4. *My old Cortina* Charlie McGettigan
5. *Janie Jones* (Cortina mention) The Clash
6. *Cardboard Cortina* Dave Morrison
7. *Gold Cortina* The Dirty Strangers
8. *1st Ford Cortina* Dominic Collins
9. *Cortina* (MC) Dubstar
10. *Funky Ford Cortina* Dustin The Turkey
11. *Made In England* (Cortina mention) Elton John
12. *New Cortina Is More Cortina* Ford (Ivor Raymonde & Tony Clark)
13. *Cortina* (Safari) Ford (Music)
14. *White 64 Cortina* Greg Champion
15. *My Old Cortina* Gruppo Sportivo
16. *Ford Cortina* Collapsible Deckchairs
17. *Billericay Dickie* (Cortina mention) Ian Dury
18. *Saturday's Kids* (Cortina mention) The Jam
19. *Mk2 Cortina* The Lambrettas
20. *Blue Cortina* Loopy
21. *My Baby Drives a Ford Cortina* Mel Alexander
22. *Early Cortina* Michael Chapman
23. *1967 Ford Cortina* My Twin Sister Lulu
24. *Blue Cortina* Paul Mulligan
25. *Gina* Salford Jets
26. *The T-C Theme* Samantha Jones
27. *Red Cortina* Saw Doctors
28. *Red Cortina* The Rowdy Neighbours
29. *King Of The Cortina Cars* Dave Kay
30. *Apathy* Subhumans
31. *Grey Cortina* Tom Robinson Band
32. *Wild boys in Cortinas* Urban Disturbance
33. *Ford Cortina* Vivid Ultramarine
34. *Red Cortina* God Morgen Norge
35. *69-Modell, Grå Ford Cortina* Billa and The Kid
36. *Cortina Girls* Uncle Barney's Atomic Wobblers
37. *My Cortina* Big In Lights
38. *Gold Cortina* The Galta Gang
39. *Silver Cortina* Ex Nasa
40. *Construction of a Ford Cortina* Bronx Zoo

Index

Index *(continued)*